Preparation of Consolidated Accounts

Preparation of Consolidated Accounts

Neil D. Stein FCA, ATII

First published in 1988 by Financial Training Publications

© Neil D. Stein

ISBN: 1 85185 102 X

Typeset by LKM Typesetting Limited, London EC1

Printed for the Publishers, Financial Training Publications Ltd, Croner House, 173 Kingston Road, New Malden, Surrey KT3 3SS by Whitstable Litho Printers Ltd., Whitstable, Kent

Contents

Preface

The objective of this book is to provide a clear exposition of the principles and practice of consolidated accounts.

It is primarily intended as a book for students preparing for the examinations of one of the professional accountancy bodies, the Institute of Chartered Secretaries and Administrators or the Chartered Institute of Bankers, but practitioners too may find it of value.

The introductory chapter 1 explains the extent of study necessary to prepare for the main accounting examinations. It is obviously essential for you to familiarise yourself with the precise requirements of your syllabus.

Chapters 2 to 7 deal with the consolidated balance sheet, chapter 8 with the consolidated profit and loss account and chapter 9 with associated companies. All the examinations covered require the study of these chapters (except that Chartered Institute of Bankers students may omit chapter 8). Chapter 10 picks up the regulatory background: the requirements of the Companies Act 1985, SSAP 14 Group Accounts, and the EEC Seventh Directive.

Chapters 11 to 13 deal with three more advanced subjects: disposal of subsidiaries, the merger method of consolidation and accounting for overseas subsidiaries. You will obviously only study these if your syllabus requires it.

Features of the book are the many illustrations throughout the text, and the practice questions in chapter 14 which comprise almost half the book. At the end of each chapter you are directed to the relevant practice questions and it is absolutely vital, if you are to develop the speed and fluency needed in examinations, for you to attempt them – without looking first at the answers! It is helpful to rework questions at intervals, and there are also two sections of revision questions.

I should like to acknowledge the contribution made to this book by its predecessor, The Preparation of Group Accounts by Mervyn Frankel. Finally, I wish to thank the Chartered Association of Certified Accountants, the Chartered Institute of Management Accountants and the Chartered Institute of Bankers for permission to reproduce questions from their examinations.

Neil D. Stein

1 Introduction

1.1 Examination requirements

The preparation of consolidated accounts is one of the central features of all the more advanced accounting examinations. The main purpose of this book is to provide the depth of knowledge necessary for the examinations of the bodies listed below. Before you begin your work on consolidated accounts, study the syllabus details below to see how far you are likely to have to go. If the body whose examinations you are taking does not appear, you need to consult the syllabus and/or your tutors to define the extent of your work.

Chartered Association of Certified Accountants

2.9 Advanced Accounting Practice

A revised syllabus applies from the December 1988 examinations.

For examinations up to and including June 1988, the syllabus included the following topics:

> The legal and institutional requirements for disclosure in the accounts of holding companies and subsidiaries; the consolidated profit and loss account and balance sheet; the acquisition method and the merger method; associated companies and the criteria for group status; foreign subsidiaries and currency translations.

That syllabus implied study of the whole of this book. See below for the important reduction in the coverage required for examinations from December 1988 onwards.

For examinations as from December 1988, it is clearly stated in the syllabus that questions involving disposals of shares in subsidiaries and foreign currency translation will not be set. Bear in mind, however, that questions for this examination are still likely to be very demanding. Although you may omit chapters 11 and 13, you need to study the remaining chapters really thoroughly!

2.8 Regulatory Framework of Accounting

This paper, in its new form, requires a knowledge of legislation and SSAPs dealing with group accounts. Chapter 10 of the book is obviously the most relevant one.

3.1   Advanced Financial Accounting

The topic of group accounts is not specifically mentioned in the current syllabus, but questions appear regularly on both computational and non-computational aspects. Questions should be expected to deal with the most advanced aspects of the subject, and in particular the consolidation of foreign subsidiaries, the merger method of consolidation and disposal of shares in subsidiaries. The introduction of the new syllabus from December 1988 will make little difference in the area of group accounts.

Institute of Chartered Accountants in England and Wales

Financial Accounting 1 current syllabus (up to and including November 1988 sitting)

The syllabus requires study of: 'Accounting for groups of companies and for associated companies (excluding overseas companies)'. Students preparing for this examination may thus safely omit chapter 13.

Financial Accounting 2 current syllabus (up to and including December 1989 sitting)

Group accounts are not specifically mentioned, but 'Accounting for overseas operations' appears. It may therefore be expected that questions in this paper will pick up the subject of groups with overseas subsidiaries which is excluded from Financial Accounting 1.

Financial Accounting 1 new syllabus (examinable in November 1988 and subsequent sittings)

The new syllabus gives more detail of the scope of the paper than the previous one:

    (a)   Definition of subsidiary and related/associated companies.
    (b)   Basic consolidation techniques including:

        (i)   treatment of intra-group transactions and balances,
        (ii)   treatment of goodwill,
        (iii)   treatment of minority interests,
        (iv)   acquisitions of subsidiaries during the year,
        (v)   treatment of dividends out of pre-acquisition profits,
        (vi)   different group structures.

    (c)   Accounting for related/associated companies.

Significant topics that are excluded from Financial Accounting 1 but which all appear in the new Financial Accounting 2 syllabus are:

    (a)   Disposals of subsidiaries.
    (b)   Non-consolidation of subsidiaries.
    (c)   Accounting for mergers.
    (d)   Overseas subsidiaries and associated companies.

Chapters 11, 12 and 13 may be omitted.

Financial Accounting 2 new syllabus (examinable in December 1989 and subsequent sittings)

The new syllabus includes all the items listed above as included in Financial Accounting 1, plus all the items listed above as excluded from that paper. Study of the whole of this book is therefore needed.

Institute of Chartered Accountants of Scotland

Financial Accounting

The syllabus states:

Consolidated accounts

Preparation and presentation of consolidated accounts and associated companies. Relevant SSAPs.

Some information about the precise scope of this rather broad syllabus requirement would be appreciated. In the absence of this it would seem prudent to study the whole of this book.

Institute of Chartered Accountants in Ireland

Financial Accounting 3

Consolidated financial statements

Preparation and presentation of financial statements for groups of companies together with associated companies.

Knowledge level 3, the highest, is specified. It would appear wise to study the whole of this book.

Final Admitting Examination

Questions set in the multi-discipline papers could clearly cover any aspect of group accounts.

Chartered Institute of Management Accountants

Advanced Financial Accounting

The syllabus includes:

Consolidated accounts involving one or more subsidiaries and associated companies; inter-company transactions, problems of transfer pricing; acquisition and merger methods.

Foreign currency translation; accounting for foreign branches and overseas subsidiaries.

Disposal of subsidiaries is not specifically mentioned, but candidates should study the whole of this book to be on the safe side.

Association of International Accountants

Financial Accounting 3

This is the only examination of the AIA requiring a knowledge of group accounts. The syllabus is not very detailed, but it is clear that merger accounting and foreign currency transactions are included. Candidates should therefore study the whole of this book.

Society of Company and Commercial Accountants

Paper 9 Financial Accounting 2 new syllabus (examinable from November 1987)

This paper includes introductory aspects of group accounts:

Group accounts: background; consolidated balance sheet; consolidated profit and loss account. Excluding associated companies, exclusion from consolidation, merger accounting, foreign subsidiaries.

The list of relevant SSAPs does not include SSAP1 or SSAP14. Students for this examination should therefore be able to restrict their studies to chapters 2 to 8 and chapter 10.

Paper 13 Financial Accounting 3 new syllabus (examinable from November 1987)

The syllabus as regards group accounts is:

Syllabus for paper 9 together with: associated companies; exclusion from consolidation; merger accounting; foreign subsidiaries; source and application of funds statements.

It should therefore be necessary to study the whole book for this examination.

Paper 9 Financial Accounting and paper 14 Company Accounts old syllabus (examinable up to and including November 1988)

Neither of these syllabuses gives details of the extent of coverage of group accounts. It is, however, reasonable to suppose the requirement to be broadly as indicated above for the corresponding papers in the new syllabuses.

Institute of Chartered Secretaries and Administrators

Paper 15 Financial Accounting

Consolidated accounts. Definitions of holding, subsidiary and related (associate) companies. Comparison of acquisition and merger methods. Use of acquisition or merger methods as appropriate to financial statements. Consolidating requiring calculations of premium or discount on acquisition; minority interests; elimination of inter-company profits and dividends. Equity accounting and the treatment of related companies.

Under 'Accounting policies' in the syllabus it is stated that questions on students' 'conceptual understanding' of foreign currency transactions may be set. So chapters 2 to 9 and 12 are the most relevant. Note the inclusion of the merger method of consolidation. A brief study of the introduction to chapter 13 on foreign subsidiaries could be useful.

Association of Accounting Technicians

Paper 9 Financial Accounting

The syllabus includes:

> Simple consolidation statements for groups of companies, to include preparation of a consolidated balance sheet and profit and loss account, minority interests, pre and post-acquisition profits, the reconciliation of current accounts for cash and goods in transit, and the elimination of profit margins on intra-group stocks.

Study of chapters 2 to 9 should suffice for this examination.

Chartered Institute of Bankers

Stage 2 Accountancy

The syllabus includes:

> Group accounts: presentation and principles of consolidation, subsidiary and associated companies. (Students must be able to compute the balance of profit for inclusion in the balance sheet but will be asked neither to prepare a consolidated profit and loss account nor to present the consolidated balance sheet in a form suitable for publication, though they may choose to do so).

Note that SSAP 1 and SSAP 14 are both included in the list of examinable SSAPs. Study of chapters 2 to 7 and 9 will suffice for this examination.

1.2   Studying consolidated accounts

To build up fluency at handling questions on consolidated accounts requires a great deal of practice. It is also a very 'progressive' subject — it starts at a very easy level and develops through stages to become fairly complicated. It is *vital* to master each chapter really thoroughly before proceeding to the next.

The technique explained in the text is that of using ledger accounts for workings. This is the recommended standard approach.

1.3   Acquisition accounting and merger accounting

The basic techniques of consolidation explained in chapters 2 to 9 are based on the use of *acquisition accounting* in which the profits or losses of companies entering a group are brought into the group accounts only from the date of acquisition, and assets acquired are stated at cost to the acquiring group. The alternative is the use of *merger accounting*, in which the financial statements of the combining companies are aggregated and presented as if they had always been together. The circumstances in which merger accounting may be used in the UK are defined in SSAP 23 and the method is explained in chapter 12. Basic questions on consolidated accounts will always require the use of the acquisition method. Only use the merger method when the question requires it.

2 Consolidated balance sheet 1: Definitions and basic techniques

2.1 What are group accounts?

When one company invests in another, the investment appears as an asset in its balance sheet, and dividends received are credited to profit and loss account. As long as the investment remains a small percentage of the total share capital of the company in which the shares are held, no one would want to quarrel with this treatment. Suppose, however, that the holding represents all or most of the total share capital. Now the investing company can be said to be in a position to *control* the other company, and for all practical purposes to be entitled to the whole or most of its profit, regardless of dividends actually declared. Also, the increase in value of its assets over the years, reflecting retained profits, accrues ultimately to the investing company. *Group accounts* is the name given to the accounting techniques which seek to reflect the true position, as regards both profits and assets, when one company controls another.

2.2 Definitions

These definitions are intended for introductory purposes only. More precise definitions will be provided in chapter 10.

(a) Holding company (or parent company). A company owning a controlling interest (e.g., more than 50% of equity) in another.

(b) Subsidiary company. A company which is controlled by a holding company.

(c) Group of companies. A holding company plus its subsidiaries.

(d) Group accounts. The term 'group accounts' is a general one meaning any accounting presentation which conveys information about the state of affairs and profit or loss of a group of companies to the members of its holding company.

The normal form of group accounts is *consolidated accounts* (see (e) below). Other possibilities permitted by the Companies Act 1985 are briefly considered in chapter 10.

(e)   Consolidated accounts. Consolidated accounts consist of a *consolidated balance sheet*, in which all assets and liabilities of group companies are aggregated, and a *consolidated profit and loss account* aggregating the profits and losses of all group companies. Group accounts are presented as consolidated accounts in the vast majority of cases.

(f)   Minority interest. If a company in a group is not wholly owned by other group companies, the 'outside' shareholders are referred to as the 'minority interest'.

2.3   Basic illustrations

2.3.1   Illustration 2.1

H Ltd was incorporated on 1 January 19X1. On 1 January 19X3 it acquired 100% of the ordinary shares in S Ltd which was incorporated on that day. Five years later, on 31 December 19X7, the balance sheets of the two companies were as follows:

	H Ltd £	S Ltd £
Fixed assets	10,000	5,000
Investment in S Ltd: 5,000 £1 shares	5,000	
Net current assets	5,000	3,000
	20,000	8,000
Share capital: ordinary shares of £1 each	10,000	5,000
Profit and loss account	10,000	3,000
	20,000	8,000

Prepare a consolidated balance sheet for H Ltd and its subsidiary.

Discussion

Preparing a consolidated balance sheet really means 'adding together' the two balance sheets. In doing so the £5,000 investment in S Ltd appearing in the H Ltd balance sheet is cancelled by the £5,000 share capital in the balance sheet of S Ltd.

Try to produce your own answer using common sense, then check with the solution below.

H Ltd and its subsidiary
Consolidated balance sheet as at 31 December 19X7

	£
Fixed assets	15,000
Net current assets	8,000
	23,000
Share capital	10,000
Profit and loss account	13,000
	23,000

The effect of the consolidation has really been to extend the balance sheet of the holding company. The investment in the subsidiary has been replaced by the underlying net assets of the subsidiary. The £3,000 increase in value of the assets since acquisition is represented by the £3,000 post-acquisition reserves of S, which are combined with those of H in the consolidated balance sheet.

It was possible to work out the answer to that illustration without workings but it will be helpful to use it to explain the basic workings that can be adopted as standard for more advanced questions. These workings may be set up in the form of memorandum ledger accounts, but it is important to realise that they do not form part of the accounting records of either the holding company or the subsidiary.

At this stage two accounts are needed — a *cost of control account* in which the cost of the shares in the subsidiary is set against the *share capital and reserves* of the subsidiary *at the date of acquisition*, and a *profit and loss account*. The profit and loss account balances of all group companies are entered into this account, then any parts which cannot be treated as distributable profit are transferred out. (Illustration 2.2 will show such a transfer.)

For illustration 2.1 these ledger accounts would appear as follows:

Cost of control

	£		£
Cost of shares in S	5,000	100% share capital S	5,000

Profit and loss account

	£		£
Balance to consolidated		H	10,000
balance sheet (CBS)	13,000	S	3,000

As H's shares in S were acquired on the formation of S, the whole of the retained profits of S are combined with the retained profits of H as they all arose after acquisition. Illustration 2.2 shows what happens if the investment is acquired after the subsidiary has been trading for some time.

2.3.2   Illustration 2.2

The situation is as in illustration 2.1 except that H acquired the shares in S for £6,000 at a time when the profit and loss account balance of S was £1,000. The balance sheets of the companies on this basis as at 31 December 19X7 are shown below. The net current assets of H have been reduced by £1,000 to reflect the increased cost of the investment.

Balance sheets

	H Ltd £	S Ltd £
Tangible fixed assets	10,000	5,000
Investment in S Ltd: 5,000 £1 shares	6,000	
Net current assets	4,000	3,000
	20,000	8,000
Share capital: ordinary shares of £1 each	10,000	5,000
Profit and loss account	10,000	3,000
	20,000	8,000

Discussion

Initially the process is the same as in illustration 2.1. All figures are entered either direct to the consolidated balance sheet or to the working accounts. However, instead of combining the whole of the £3,000 profit and loss account balance of S, it has to be split:

The £2,000 of post-acquisition retained profit may be combined with the H balance, but the £1,000 which arose before acquisition cannot. The logic of this is that the £1,000 of pre-acquisition retained profit will have been reflected in increased assets at the time of acquisition. H therefore obtained £6,000 worth of assets in buying the shares.

The working accounts will show:

Cost of control

	£		£
Cost of shares in S	6,000	100% share capital S	5,000
		Profit and loss account: 100% pre-acquisition profit S	1,000

Profit and loss account

	£		£
Cost of control: group share (100%) of pre-acquisition profit	1,000	H	10,000
Balance to CBS	12,000	S	3,000
	13,000		13,000

The whole £3,000 of profit is entered into the profit and loss account working, then the pre-acquisition portion is transferred out. As a result, the £2,000 of post-acquisition remains to be combined with the £10,000 balance of H.

The consolidated balance sheet will be:

H Ltd and its subsidiary
Consolidated balance sheet as at 31 December 19X7

	£
Fixed assets	15,000
Net current assets	7,000
	22,000
Share capital	10,000
Profit and loss account	12,000
	22,000

In the next illustration the amount paid by the holding company is different from the total of the subsidiary's share capital and reserves at the date of purchase. Such a difference means that the holding company has either paid *more* than the share capital and reserves of the subsidiary, giving rise to a debit balance on the cost of control account, or paid *less* than the share capital and reserves of the subsidiary, giving rise to a credit balance. If the holding company has paid *more* the debit balance represents the premium paid in order to gain control of the company, or goodwill.

SSAP 22 recommends that goodwill should be written off against reserves as it arises, though amortisation over its useful economic life is also acceptable under SSAP 22. For examination purposes you should transfer any debit balance on the cost of control working into the profit and loss account working to write off the goodwill immediately unless instructed to the contrary in the question.

If the holding company has paid *less*, the credit balance represents the 'discount' obtained on the purchase — the holding company has effectively obtained the net assets of the subsidiary for less than their face value. This is shown in the consolidated balance sheet as a reserve arising on consolidation. It is not, of course, distributable — only individual companies can make distributions in any case.

Here then is an illustration showing the writing off of goodwill.

2.3.3   Illustration 2.3

Facts as illustration 2.2, except that H paid £7,500 for the shares in S.

Balance sheets

	H Ltd £	S Ltd £
Tangible fixed assets	10,000	5,000
Investment in S: 5,000 £1 shares	7,500	
Net current assets	2,500	3,000
	20,000	8,000
Share capital: ordinary shares of £1 each	10,000	5,000
Profit and loss account	10,000	3,000
	20,000	8,000

Cost of control

	£		£
Cost of shares in S	7,500	100% share capital S	5,000
		100% pre-acquisition profit S	1,000
		Balance: goodwill written off	
		to P & L	1,500
	7,500		7,500

Profit and loss account

	£		£
Cost of control: 100%		H	10,000
pre-acquisition profit	1,000	S	3,000
Cost of control: goodwill written off	1,500		
Balance to CBS	10,500		
	13,000		13,000

H Ltd and its subsidiary
Consolidated balance sheet as at 31 December 19X7

	£
Fixed assets	15,000
Net current assets	5,500
	20,500
Share capital	10,000
Profit and loss account	10,500
	20,500

There is one last point to add to complete this introduction. What if the holding company does not buy 100% of the shares in the subsidiary? As long as it owns more than 50%, the company is a subsidiary. If the holding company owns, say, 80% of the ordinary share capital, the holders of the remaining 20% are referred to as the 'minority', or 'minority interest'. Total assets and liabilities are shown exactly as before, but a new item representing the 'minority interest' must be introduced into the share capital *and reserves* of the subsidiary. The minority interest can be calculated by taking the appropriate percentage of the net assets at the balance sheet date, but net assets will actually equal share capital plus reserves and it is convenient to calculate the minority interest by dividing up the share capital and reserves. Illustration 2.4 shows the technique.

2.3.4   Illustration 2.4

Facts as before, but H paid £7,500 for 80% of the share capital of S.

Balance sheets

	H Ltd £	S Ltd £
Fixed assets	10,000	5,000
Investment in S: 4,000 £1 shares	7,500	
Net current assets	2,500	3,000
	20,000	8,000
Share capital: ordinary shares of £1 each	10,000	5,000
Profit and loss account	10,000	3,000
	20,000	8,000

Discussion

The procedure is much as before, but there is a third working account entitled minority interest, in which the value of the 20% of S owned by the minority shareholders is computed.

In the cost of control account, only 80% of S's share capital and reserves is entered because, of course, the other 20% is in the minority interest account.

The stages in constructing the answer are numbered in the answer which follows:

Stage 1   Enter the basic information from the balance sheets to the working accounts.
Stage 2   Transfer from profit and loss to minority interest the 20% interest of the minority in the £3,000 P & L balance of S.
Stage 3   Transfer the pre-acquisition profit from P & L to cost of control.
Stage 4   Balance the cost of control account and write off debit balance to P & L (if a credit balance, show in consolidated balance sheet as reserve on consolidation).

Cost of control

	£		£
Cost of shares in S (1)	7,500	80% share capital S (1)	4,000
		80% pre-acquisition profit S (3)	800
		Profit and loss: goodwill written off (4)	2,700
	7,500		7,500

Minority interest

	£		£
Balance to CBS	1,600	20% share capital S (1)	1,000
		20% P & L S (2)	600

Profit and loss account

	£		£
Minority interest: 20% × £3,000 (2)	600	H (1)	10,000
Cost of control: 80% × £1,000		S (1)	3,000
pre-acquisition (3)	800		
Cost of control: goodwill written			
off (4)	2,700		
Balance to CBS	8,900		
	13,000		13,000

H Ltd and its subsidiary
Consolidated balance sheet as at 31 December 19X7

	£
Fixed assets	15,000
Net current assets	5,500
	20,500
Share capital	10,000
Profit and loss account	8,900
	18,900
Minority interest	1,600
	20,500

Notes

1 Minority interest £1,600 is 20% of net assets £8,000 (though this will not automatically apply in more complex questions when there are preference shares).

2 Minority interest must be shown separately from share capital and reserves in the balance sheet. The subtotal of £18,900 represents the interest of the holding company's shareholders in the group, while the minority interest of £1,600 is the outside interest. As an alternative, the minority interest may be shown as a deduction from the total assets.

3 In the profit and loss account working, note that the minority interest is calculated on the *closing* balance of the reserves of the subsidiary. The division of the subsidiary's reserves may be represented diagrammatically like this:

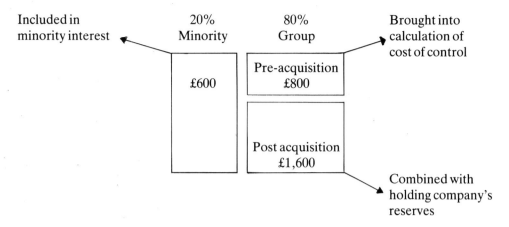

For the minority, the concepts of 'pre-acquisition' and 'post-acquisition' have no meaning.

The make-up of the final profit and loss account balance of £8,900 is:

	£
H Ltd	10,000
S Ltd	1,600
	11,600
Less: goodwill written off	2,700
	8,900

2.4   Sundry matters

2.4.1   Preference shares

If the subsidiary has issued preference shares as well as ordinary, this presents no problem. The ordinary shares and reserves continue to be split according to the percentage of ordinary shares held by the group. The cost of the preference shares is debited to cost of control, and the nominal value of the preference shares is split between cost of control and minority interest according to the percentage held inside and outside the group.

2.4.2   Additional reserve accounts

There may be other reserve accounts in the balance sheet of the subsidiary, such as share premium account, capital redemption reserve, revaluation reserve etc. The existence of these presents no additional difficulty. They are split in exactly the same way as the profit and loss account balance in the illustrations — the minority interest gets its share, and any pre-acquisition balances are transferred to cost of control.

2.4.3 Debit balances on profit and loss account

If there is a debit balance on profit and loss account this is simply treated in the same way as a credit balance, except of course that the entries are reversed (debit to minority interest instead of credit etc.).

2.5 Summary

The process of preparing a consolidated balance sheet normally requires three working accounts:

(a)   Cost of control, to calculate goodwill or capital reserve arising on acquisition.

(b)   Minority interest, to calculate the proportion of share capital and reserves attributable to the outside shareholders.

(c)   Profit and loss, to calculate the balance attributable to the group by taking out first the minority's share of the closing balance and second the group's share of the pre-acquisition profit.

It may be necessary to use more working accounts if, for example, there are other reserve accounts to be divided up.

The fundamental problem studied in this chapter is that of allocating the reserves of the subsidiary. The minority interest is entitled to its percentage of the *total reserves*. The remainder, attributable to the group, is then divided so that only post-acquisition reserves are combined with those of the holding company. Reserves existing at the date of acquisition of the shares must be regarded as forming part of the calculation of the value acquired and entered into the cost of control working.

Study this chapter really carefully, then work through the relevant practice questions (questions 1 to 3).

3   Consolidated balance sheet 2: Cancelling

3.1   Introduction

In the previous chapter the asset figures in the consolidated balance sheet were prepared by simple cross-casting. This is all that may be necessary if there are no inter-company transactions. However, both in practice and in examination questions there is considerable inter-company (or intra-group) trading, and other links such as payment of dividends and the like. All of these give rise to the need for *cancelling* of inter-company balances in the course of preparing the consolidated balance sheet. Most of these adjustments are common sense, and each of the main types of cancellation is considered below, roughly in order of complexity, except for dividends, which are covered in detail in chapter 4.

3.2   Inter-company balances

Trading between companies implies that there will be a current amount showing as a debtor in one company and as a creditor in another. You don't need to be told what has to happen — obviously both debtors and creditors are reduced to eliminate the internal balances. The only snag that can arise here is the existence of cash or goods in transit, causing differences between the balances. No great problem: simply put the difference into the consolidated balance sheet as cash or stock in transit, exactly as you do in autonomous branch accounts.

3.3   Stock at balance sheet date acquired from another company

This only causes a problem if the selling company has added a mark-up to its own cost. In that case there is an unrealised profit as far as the group is concerned, and it has to be eliminated. Stock in the balance sheet and profit and loss account are both reduced by the full amount of the unrealised profit. That means a debit to the profit and loss account working used in the illustrations in chapter 2 balanced by a credit to reduce the stock in the consolidated balance sheet.

Note that this adjustment could also apply to goods in transit if there was a mark-up on the goods.

There is actually another possibility here. It could be argued that if the sale was made by a subsidiary in which there was a minority interest, the profit attributable to the minority has been realised and we should adjust only for the group's share of the unrealised profit. Most of the books suggest that the main purpose of group accounts is to show the position from the point of view of the group and that it is perfectly acceptable to eliminate the whole of the profit as originally stated. As that is the simplest solution it can be gratefully adopted as standard for examination use, unless the question requires otherwise.

3.4   Debentures in subsidiary held by holding company (or vice versa)

Clearly the holding of debentures does not contribute to control, so there is no problem in that area. Normally, the nominal value of the debentures in one company is cancelled against the cost of the holding in the other. Any difference is debited or credited to capital reserves in the consolidated balance sheet.

3.5   Bank balances

We move now to an adjustment not arising out of inter-company transactions, but still potentially needing cancellation. What should be done if one company has a balance of cash at bank and another has an overdraft? Cancel? No. Unless there is a legal right of set-off, the figures are shown separately. A legal right of set-off would only exist if this had been formally arranged between the companies and the bank — in other words you must be specifically told this in an examination question if you are to offset.

3.6   Bills of exchange

Bills of exchange are fairly rare in practice, but do come up in examination questions from time to time. If a bill payable by one company is due to another group company, then in principle the bill payable in one balance sheet should be cancelled against the bill receivable in the other. But what if the company with the bill receivable has discounted it with a bank? The solution is not too complicated. The fact that the bill has been discounted does not affect the company which has the bill payable. It still has to meet the bill on maturity but it will pay the bank, not the other company. In effect it has become an external liability, not an internal one subject to cancellation. It therefore remains as a liability. Here is an illustration.

3.6.1   Illustration

Huge Ltd has a 75% subsidiary, Tiny Ltd. At 31 December 19X4 Huge Ltd had bills receivable in its balance sheet of £10,000, of which £8,000 were due from Tiny. Huge also had discounted another bill for £5,000 due from Tiny.

What figures will appear in the consolidated balance sheet to be prepared at 31 December 19X4?

Discussion

The following extracts from the balance sheets of the two companies may be constructed from the information given.

	Huge £	Tiny £
Bills receivable (including £8,000 from Tiny)	10,000	
Bills payable		13,000

The £8,000 of Huge's bills receivable due from Tiny will cancel against £8,000 of Tiny's £13,000 of bills payable. The figures for the consolidated balance sheet will therefore be:

Bills receivable	£2,000
Bills payable	£5,000

Note that the £3,000 net credit balance (£5,000 minus £2,000) remains the same as that derived from the original figures (£13,000 minus £10,000). There is one final adjustment to make. The balance sheet of Huge will have a note drawing attention to the contingent liability in respect of the discounted bill — the liability to the bank if the bill is not met on maturity. Since the £5,000 is recognised as an actual liability in the consolidated balance sheet, no such note is required to the consolidated balance sheet.

3.7   Fixed assets transferred between group companies

If fixed assets are transferred between group companies at their written-down value in the selling company's records there is no difficulty. No adjustment is needed on consolidation.

But suppose the selling company has taken a profit on the sale. This profit will be included in its profit and loss account and must be eliminated. At the same time the value of the asset, which is in the purchasing company's accounts at the agreed price including the profit, must be reduced. As with the adjustment in 3.3 above for unrealised profit on stock, it is customary to adjust for the whole profit (or loss) arising and not to use the group's proportion only.

3.7.1   Illustration

Small Ltd is a wholly owned subsidiary of Large Ltd. During the year ended 31 December 19X4, Small transferred an item of plant to Large at an agreed price of £16,000. The plant had originally cost £25,000 and accumulated depreciation up to 31 December 19X3 amounted to £10,000. Both companies depreciate plant at the rate of 20% per annum on cost, making full provision in the year of purchase and no provision in the year of sale. First the £1,000 profit on sale must be eliminated, and cost and accumulated depreciation must be adjusted from £16,000 and nil back to £25,000 and £10,000. The correction must be:

	Dr £	Cr £
Profit and loss account working	1,000	
Plant cost	9,000	
Plant depreciation		10,000

Next the current year's depreciation must be adjusted from 20% of £16,000 to 20% of £25,000:

	Dr £	Cr £
Profit and loss account working	1,800	
Depreciation		1,800

The overall effect of the adjustments has the following effect on the balance sheet:

	Position as recorded by Large	Adjustments	Position as corrected for consolidated balance sheet
	£	£	£
Plant cost	16,000	+9,000	25,000
Accumulated depreciation	(3,200)	(+10,000)	
		(+1,800)	(15,000)
Net book value	12,800	(2,800)	10,000

The reduction of £2,800 in the asset value in the consolidated balance sheet is balanced by a reduction of £2,800 in profit: £1,000 to eliminate the profit and £1,800 to increase the depreciation.

3.8   Stock held by one company sold to another as a fixed asset

This situation can arise, for example, when one company in the group manufactures plant which is sold to another group company for use in its factory. You can see what has to happen — in preparing the consolidated balance sheet the profit made by the selling company must be eliminated and the depreciation charge reduced. The adjustment is similar to that for fixed asset transfers between group companies.

3.8.1   Illustration

Dwarf Ltd is a manufacturer of plant and during the year ended 31 December 19X5 sold plant to its holding company Giant Ltd for £10,000. The profit element in the plant was £3,000. Giant provides for depreciation at 20% per annum on the straight-line basis, making a full year's provision in the year of acquisition. On consolidation the corrections to eliminate profit will be:

	Dr	Cr
	£	£
Profit and loss account working	3,000	
Plant		3,000

To adjust depreciation from £2,000 to £1,400:

	Dr	Cr
Depreciation	600	
Profit and loss account working		600

3.9   Dividends

In principle, dividends paid by one group company to another are cancelled out. There are a number of special situations involving dividends, so the whole question is covered in chapter 4.

3.10   Summary

In the course of preparing a consolidated balance sheet a number of cancellations may be necessary, most of them to eliminate the balances resulting from inter-company dealing of one kind or another.

When you have completed a thorough study of this chapter, have a go at practice questions 4 to 8.

4 Consolidated balance sheet 3: Dividends

4.1 Basic treatment of intra-group dividends

Understanding the treatment of dividends is a major key to confidence in tackling examination questions in which dividends have deliberately been wrongly treated so that you can have the pleasure of correcting the error. In principle, dividends cancel. If a subsidiary has a proposed dividend it will appear in its profit and loss account and as a creditor in its balance sheet. The holding company should have taken credit for the dividend in its profit and loss account, and have a debtor in its balance sheet for the dividend receivable. If the subsidiary is wholly owned, the profit and loss account items cancel each other out and the creditor in the subsidiary's balance sheet cancels with the debtor in the holding company. If the subsidiary is not wholly owned, there will be a difference between the creditor and the debtor because of the dividend due to the minority. This appears as a creditor in the consolidated balance sheet alongside the holding company's proposed dividend to its shareholders. Don't show it as part of the minority interest — this is the capital stake of the minority interest and the proposed dividend they are to receive is a revenue item.

4.1.1 Illustration

Lion Ltd owns 75% of Cub Ltd, having acquired the shares some years ago for £80,000 at a time when the reserves of Cub amounted to £20,000. The balance sheets of the two companies at 30 June 19X6 were as follows:

	Lion Ltd £000	Cub Ltd £000
Sundry assets	200	110
Investment in Cub Ltd	80	
Creditors:		
Trade	(30)	(18)
Proposed dividend	(20)	(12)
	230	80
Share capital: ordinary shares of £1 each	100	40
Reserves	130	40
	230	80

Lion Ltd has not yet recorded the dividend due from Cub Ltd.

Discussion

You should by now be familiar with the technique — open up a consolidated balance sheet format and the three working accounts you know you will need, then go line by line through the question entering items direct to the consolidated balance sheet or to the working accounts as appropriate.

When you come to the proposed dividends, the dividend for the holding company can go straight to the consolidated balance sheet. Of the proposed dividend of the subsidiary, £9,000 is due to the holding company and £3,000 is due to the minority. The £3,000 may be entered direct to the consolidated balance sheet as a liability. The £9,000 due to the holding company has to be cancelled but as yet this cannot be done. Therefore an entry must be made in workings:

	Dr £	Cr £
Debtors	9,000	
Profit and loss account working		9,000

The £9,000 debit to debtors may be cancelled against the £12,000 creditor in the subsidiary. (There's no need to actually make an entry for the debit of £9,000, as you are immediately going to cross it out!) The £9,000 credit to profit and loss account recognises that the group profit is understated by this amount at present — the profit and loss account balance of the subsidiary (£40,000) is after deducting a dividend, part of which will be received by another company in the group. It is therefore necessary to credit back the intra-group portion of the dividend.

Lion Ltd and its subsidiary
Consolidated balance sheet as at 30 June 19X6

	£000	£000	£000
Sundry assets			310
Creditors:			
Trade		48	
Proposed dividends:			
Holding company	20		
Minority	3	23	
	—	—	71
			239
Share capital: ordinary shares of £1 each			100
Reserves			119
			219
Minority interest			20
			239

Workings

Cost of control

	£000		£000
Cost of shares in Cub	80	75% share capital	30
		75% pre-acquisition reserves	15
		Goodwill written off	35
	—		—
	80		80
	—		—

Minority interest

	£000		£000
Balance to CBS	20	25% share capital	10
		25% reserves	10
	—		—
	20		20
	—		—

Reserves

	£000		£000
Minority interest 25% × £40,000	10	Lion	130
Cost of control: pre-acquisition		Cub	40
profit: 75% × £20,000	15	Dividend from Cub	9
Cost of control: goodwill written off	35		
Balance to CBS	119		
	—		—
	179		179
	—		—

Please study that example really thoroughly until it all seems blindingly obvious.

Here is another connected illustration using the same facts, in which the companies propose the same dividends as before but neither has yet recorded them. Their balance sheets will be:

	Lion Ltd	Cub Ltd
	£000	£000
Sundry assets	200	110
Investment in Cub Ltd	80	
Creditors: trade	(30)	(18)
	—	—
	250	92
	—	—
Share capital: ordinary shares of £1 each	100	40
Reserves	150	52
	—	—
	250	92
	—	—

The answer will be exactly as before but there must now be additional entries in the reserves working:

Reserves

	£000		£000
Proposed dividend — Lion	20	Lion	150
Proposed dividend — Cub	12	Dividend from Cub	9
Minority interest: 25% × £40,000	10	Cub	52
Cost of control: pre-acquisition			
profit: 75% × £20,000	15		
Cost of control: goodwill written off	35		
Balance to CBS	119		
	211		211

Note that in this situation you must debit the proposed dividend of the subsidiary before calculating the minority interest, because the minority's interest must be shown in the *retained* profits. All other workings and the consolidated balance sheet remain exactly as in the previous illustration.

4.2 Dividends paid out of pre-acquisition profits

If a subsidiary pays a dividend shortly after acquisition by the holding company, part of the next dividend paid may well be out of *pre-acquisition* profits (especially in examination questions). Incidentally, the dividend is taken first out of post-acquisition profits and pre-acquisition profits are only used if necessary to cover the dividend.

In view of the fact that when the holding company bought the shares it was effectively buying the net assets at that time, any dividend paid out of pre-acquisition profits must be regarded as a return of money paid for the shares, so reducing the debit to the cost of control working for the cost of those shares.

Accordingly, when a subsidiary pays a dividend partly out of pre-acquisition profits, and partly out of post-acquisition profits, it may have to be split three ways. The minority interest gets its share of the total dividend, and the group's share is divided — the pre-acquisition part is credited against the cost of the investment in the subsidiary and only the post-acquisition proportion is credited to profit and loss account.

So where is the problem? The problem lies in the fact that the examiner often introduces a deliberate mistake by saying that the holding company has credited the whole of the dividend to its profit and loss account. It is then up to you to realise that not all of it should be there and to transfer out the pre-acquisition portion, using it to reduce the cost of the investment in the cost of control working.

4.2.1   Illustration

Horse Ltd acquired a 75% interest in Foal Ltd on 31 December 19X3. At 31 December 19X4 their balance sheets were as follows:

	Horse Ltd		Foal Ltd	
	£000	£000	£000	£000
Fixed assets		140		90
Investment in Foal Ltd		100		
		——		
		240		
Current assets:				
Stock	100		30	
Debtors	80		60	
Cash at bank	40		10	
	——		——	
	220		100	
Less: creditors: trade	100	120	50	50
	——	——	——	——
		360		140
		——		——
Issued share capital:				
ordinary shares of £1 each		200		80
Reserves as at 1 January 19X4	100		20	
Profit for year	60	160	40	60
	——		——	
		——		——
		360		140
		——		——

On 31 March 19X4 Foal Ltd paid a dividend of 10% in respect of the year ended 31 December 19X3. Horse has credited this dividend to profit and loss account.

At 31 December 19X4 Foal Ltd proposes to pay a dividend of 15% and Horse one of 20%. Neither of these proposed dividends has yet been recorded in the above balance sheets.

Prepare a consolidated balance sheet as at 31 December 19X4.

Horse Ltd and its subsidiary
Consolidated balance sheet as at 31 December 19X4

	£000	£000
Fixed assets		230
Current assets:		
Stock	130	
Debtors	140	
Cash at bank	50	
	——	
	320	
Less: creditors:		
Trade	(150)	
Proposed dividends:		
Horse	(40)	
Minority	(3)	
	——	127
		——
		357
		——
Issued share capital: ordinary shares of £1 each		200
Reserves		125
		——
		325
Minority interest		32
		——
		357
		——

Cost of control

	£000		£000
Shares in Foal	100	75% share capital	60
Profit and loss: pre-acquisition		75% pre-acquisition reserves	15
dividend	(8)	Balance: goodwill written off to	
		reserves	17
	——		——
	92		92
	——		——

Minority interest

	£000		£000
Balance to CBS	32	25% share capital	20
		25% reserves	12
	—		—

Reserves

	£000		£000
Investment in Foal:		Horse	160
Pre-acquisition dividend	8	Dividend receivable from Foal	9
Proposed dividend:		Foal	60
Horse	40		
Foal	12		
Minority interest:			
25% × (£60,000 − £12,000)	12		
Cost of control: 75% × £20,000	15		
Cost of control: goodwill written off	17		
Balance to CBS	125		
	——		——
	229		229
	——		——

It is very important for you to understand how the dividends are accounted for in this example.

Foal Ltd dividend paid 31 March 19X4

This dividend relates to the pre-acquisition period and must thus be credited against the cost of the investment in Foal in Horse's records. Horse has credited it to profit and loss account and we must therefore make a correcting entry in Horse's records:

		£000	£000
Reserves	Dr	8	
Investment in Foal			8

The entry is shown in brackets immediately under the entry in the cost of control working for the investment to emphasise the nature of the adjustment — to reduce the cost of the investment.

Horse's proposed dividend

No entries have yet been made. We therefore have to debit reserves with £40,000 and include the amount in the consolidated balance sheet as a creditor.

Foal's proposed dividend

Again no entries have been made. We first allow for Foal's side of the dividend — debit reserves with £12,000. That creates a liability of £12,000. £9,000 of this cancels with the asset introduced into Horse's balance sheet when Horse recognises the dividend receivable, leaving a net £3,000 liability for the dividend to the minority. This goes into the consolidated balance sheet. Note that the minority interest in Foal is calculated on the *final* balance in the reserves of Foal — *after* the proposed dividend is allowed for.

Now for Horse's entries. Horse will receive £9,000 and may therefore credit its profit and loss account with this amount. The debtor thereby created cancels against the creditor already introduced into Foal's balance sheet as explained above.

Please study this illustration really carefully.

4.3   Summary

A clear understanding of the treatment of dividends in group accounts is utterly vital. It will take time, and the working of many illustrations, for you to develop that understanding. You must take that time, and work those illustrations, before you proceed.

The relevant practice questions are 9 to 12.

5 Consolidated balance sheet 4: Acquisition of a subsidiary during its accounting period

5.1 Introduction

So far we have dealt only with the acquisition of a subsidiary at the end of its accounting period. This is purely for the simplicity and convenience of having available a balance sheet from which it is possible to extract the net assets of the subsidiary at the date of acquisition.

It is unlikely that the date of acquisition will coincide precisely with the accounting period end of either the subsidiary or the acquiring company. Indeed it is quite likely that the two companies involved do not even have coterminous accounting periods and that the acquisition will take place at some stage during both companies' accounting periods. However, in order to illustrate the fundamental principles in the preparation of group accounts this discussion will concentrate on companies which have coterminous accounting periods.

If a subsidiary has been acquired during an accounting period then some of the net assets at the balance sheet date must be attributable to post-acquisition profits. In order to determine the net assets at the date of acquisition (assuming that proper accounts are not prepared at that date) the increase in reserves over the year must be apportioned on a time basis.

5.1.1 Example

Gonzo Ltd acquired 90% of the equity share capital of Piggy Ltd on 30 September 19X4, for £100,000. At 31 December 19X4 the following balance sheets were prepared:

	Gonzo Ltd		Piggy Ltd	
	£	£	£	£
Shares in Piggy Ltd		100,000		
Sundry assets	600,000		400,000	
Creditors	350,000		300,000	
		250,000		100,000
		350,000		100,000
Financed by:				
Share capital				
(ordinary shares of £1 each)		200,000		50,000
Profit and loss account:				
Balance 1 January 19X4	120,000		40,000	
Profit for the year	30,000		10,000	
		150,000		50,000
		350,000		100,000

You are required to prepare the consolidated balance sheet of Gonzo Ltd as at 31 December 19X4.

Solution

Cost of control account

	£		£
Shares in Piggy Ltd	100,000	90% share capital P	45,000
		Profit and loss account:	
		90% pre-acquisition	42,750
		Profit and loss account:	
		goodwill written off	12,250
	100,000		100,000

Minority interest account

	£		£
Balance to CBS	10,000	Share capital	5,000
		Profit and loss account	5,000
	10,000		10,000

Consolidated profit and loss account

	£			£
Cost of control account (W)	42,750	G		150,000
Minority interest account		P		50,000
(10% × 50,000)	5,000			
Cost of control:				
goodwill written off	12,250			
Balance to CBS	140,000			
	———			———
	200,000			200,000
	———			———

Working

Pre-acquisition profits of Piggy Ltd

	£	£
Balance at 1 January 19X4	40,000	
Add: profit to date of acquisition (9/12 × £10,000)	7,500	
	———	
Pre-acquisition retained profits	47,500 (90%)	42,750
	———	———

The resulting consolidated balance sheet would appear as follows:

Gonzo Ltd and its subsidiary
Consolidated balance sheet as at 31 December 19X4

	£	£
Sundry assets	1,000,000	
Creditors	650,000	
	———	350,000
		———
		350,000
		———
Financed by:		
Share capital		200,000
Profit and loss account		140,000
		———
		340,000
Minority interests		10,000
		———
		350,000
		———

5.2   Dividends payable by a subsidiary

5.2.1   Introduction

It has previously been established that all dividends declared by and received from a subsidiary for a period prior to acquisition must be credited to the cost of the investment. They are theoretically included in the purchase price of the shares and cannot be regarded as revenue of the holding company. In addition, any dividends (or parts of dividends) declared by a subsidiary for periods after acquisition should not be regarded as revenue by the holding company if they have been paid out of the pre-acquisition reserves of the subsidiary. Such dividends (or parts of dividends) received should be credited to the cost of the investment.

5.2.2   Dividends which are received by the holding company

Where a dividend is declared by a subsidiary and is received by the holding company (either because the shares were acquired cum div or because the dividend was declared after the date of acquisition), the dividend must be time-apportioned over the period for which it was declared and deducted from the apportioned profit out of which it was declared in order to calculate the figures of 'retained' profits at the date of acquisition. When received, the holding company will credit the pre-acquisition part of the dividend to shares in subsidiary account and the post-acquisition part to profit and loss account.

5.2.3   Example

Kermit Ltd acquired 75% of the equity share capital of Robin Ltd on 30 September 19X8, for £58,000. On 1 January 19X8 Robin Ltd had a credit balance on profit and loss account of £48,000. During the year to 31 December 19X8, Robin Ltd made a profit of £16,000 after providing for a first and final dividend of £4,000. At 31 December 19X8, the following summarised balance sheets were prepared:

	Kermit Ltd		Robin Ltd	
	£	£	£	£
Shares in Robin Ltd		58,000		
Sundry assets		160,000		120,000
Creditors	56,000		42,000	
Proposed dividend	14,000		4,000	
		(70,000)		(46,000)
		148,000		74,000
Financed by:				
Share capital				
(ordinary shares of £1 each)		40,000		10,000
Profit and loss account		108,000		64,000
		148,000		74,000

Kermit Ltd has credited its share of the dividend receivable from Robin Ltd to profit and loss account. The dividend receivable is included in sundry assets.

You are required to prepare the consolidated balance sheet of Kermit Ltd as at 31 December 19X8.

Solution

Kermit Ltd
Consolidated balance sheet as at 31 December 19X8

	£	£	£
Sundry assets		277,000	
Creditors	98,000		
Proposed dividends:			
Holding company	14,000		
Due to minority shareholders	1,000		
	———	113,000	
		———	164,000
			164,000
Financed by:			
Share capital			40,000
Profit and loss account			105,500
			145,500
Minority interests			18,500
			164,000

Workings

Cost of control account

	£		£
Shares in Robin Ltd		75% share capital R	7,500
£58,000 − £2,250	55,750	Profit and loss account:	
		75% pre-acquisition profit	45,000
		Profit and loss account:	
		goodwill written off	3,250
	55,750		55,750

Minority interest account

	£		£
Balance to CBS	18,500	25% share capital	2,500
		25% profit and loss account	16,000
	18,500		18,500

Consolidated profit and loss account

	£		£
Kermit Ltd			
Shares in Robin Ltd (W2)	2,250	K	108,000
Robin Ltd			
Cost of control account (W1)	45,000	R	64,000
Minority interest account			
(25% × £64,000)	16,000		
Cost of control account:			
goodwill written off	3,250		
Balance to CBS	105,500		
	172,000		172,000

Workings

1   Pre-acquisition retained profits

	£	£
Balance at 1 January 19X8	48,000	
Profit to date of acquisition (9/12 × £20,000)	15,000	
	63,000	
Less: dividend for 9 months (9/12 × £4,000)	3,000	
Pre-acquisition retained profits	60,000 (75%)	45,000

2   Treatment of final dividend receivable in the books of Kermit Ltd

		£
CREDIT	Shares in Robin Ltd	
	(75% × 9/12 × £4,000)	2,250
CREDIT	Profit and loss account	
	(75% × 3/12 × £4,000)	750

As Kermit has credited the whole of the £3,000 dividend to profit and loss account, it is necessary to adjust by debiting out £2,250 (credit shares in Robin).

5.2.4   Dividends which are not received by the holding company

This situation arises where a dividend is declared and paid before the date of acquisition (e.g., an interim dividend.

Where such a situation arises, it is necessary to time-apportion the total dividends for the year (as to pre-acquisition and post-acquisition) in order to determine how much of the final dividend received by the acquiring company relates to the period prior to acquisition. In such circumstances the interim dividend (not received by the acquiring company) may be treated as a payment first of all out of pre-acquisition profits.

5.2.5   Example

Zombie Ltd acquired 80% of the equity share capital of Ghoul Ltd on 1 November 19X4. Ghoul Ltd made a net profit after taxation of £72,000 for the year ended 31 December 19X4, and had retained profits of £240,000 at 1 January 19X4. Dividends for the year declared by Ghoul Ltd were:

Interim   £20,000   (paid August 19X4)
Final   £34,000   (proposed at 31 December 19X4)

Pre-acquisition profits

	£	£
Balance at 1 January 19X4	240,000	
Profit to date of acquisition (10/12 × £72,000)	60,000	
	300,000	
Less: dividends for 10 months (10/12 × £54,000)	45,000	
	255,000 (80%)	204,000

Treatment of final dividend receivable

		£	£	£
DEBIT	Ghoul Ltd current account (80% × £34,000)			27,200
CREDIT	Shares in Ghoul Ltd (10/12 × £54,000)	45,000		
	Less: interim dividend	20,000		
		25,000 (80%)		20,000
CREDIT	Profit and loss account 2/12 × £54,000 × 80%			7,200

A quicker way of calculating the pre-acquisition and post-acquisition elements of the final dividend is to calculate the post-acquisition element, and to treat the balance as pre-acquisition, as shown below:

	£
Dividend receivable (80% × £34,000)	27,200
Less: post-acquisition (80% × 2/12 × £54,000)	7,200
Dividend receivable out of pre-acquisition profits	20,000

Where the calculated post-acquisition element is *more* than the total dividend receivable, the *whole* of the dividend receivable by the investing company may be credited to the profit and loss account.

5.2.6   Example

Pinky Ltd acquired 90% of the share capital of Perky Ltd on 1 August 19X3. On 1 January 19X3 the profit and loss account of Perky Ltd showed a credit balance of £55,000. During the year to 31 December 19X3 Perky Ltd made a profit of £60,000 and in July 19X3 an interim dividend of £10,000 was paid to the existing shareholders of Perky Ltd. A final dividend of £20,000 has been declared by Perky Ltd, which Pinky Ltd has not yet taken into account.

The following balance sheets were prepared at 31 December 19X3:

			Pinky Ltd		Perky Ltd
	£	£	£	£	£
Shares in Perky Ltd			200,000		
Sundry assets		600,000			380,000
Creditors	370,000			175,000	
Proposed final dividend	40,000			20,000	
		410,000			195,000
			190,000		
			390,000		185,000
					£
Financed by:					
Share capital, ordinary shares of £1 each			200,000		100,000
Profit and loss account			190,000		85,000
			390,000		185,000

You are required to prepare the consolidated balance sheet of Pinky Ltd as at 31 December 19X3.

Solution

Pinky Ltd
Consolidated balance sheet as at 31 December 19X3

	£	£	£
Sundry assets		980,000	
Creditors	545,000		
Proposed dividends:			
Holding company	40,000		
Due to minority	2,000		
		587,000	
		393,000	
		393,000	
		£	
Share capital		200,000	
Profit and loss account		174,500	
		374,500	
Minority interests		18,500	
		393,000	

Workings

Cost of control account

	£		£
Shares in Perky Ltd		90% share capital Perky	90,000
£200,000 − £6,750	193,250	Profit and loss account:	
		90% profit	65,250
		Profit and loss account:	
		goodwill written off	38,000
	193,250		193,250

Minority interest account

	£		£
Balance to CBS	18,500	10% share capital	10,000
		10% Profit and loss account	8,500
	18,500		18,500

Profit and loss account

	£		£
Cost of control account (W1)	65,250	Pinky	190,000
Minority interest account		Dividend receivable from	
(10% × £85,000)	8,500	Perky Ltd (90% × 5/12 × £30,000)	11,250
Consolidated balance sheet	212,500	Perky	85,000
	286,250		286,250

Workings

1   Pre-acquisition profits

	£	£
Balance at 1 January 19X3	55,000	
Add: profit to date of acquisition (7/12 × £60,000)	35,000	
	90,000	
Less: pre-acquisition dividends (7/12 × £30,000)	17,500	
Pre-acquisition retained profits	72,500 (90%)	65,250

2   Treatment of dividend receivable

	£
Dividend receivable (90% × £20,000)	18,000
Less: post-acquisition (90% × 5/12 × £30,000)	11,250
Dividend receivable out of pre-acquisition profits	6,750

As Pinky has not yet taken the dividend into account, £11,250 must be credited to profit and loss account and £6,750 to cost of investment in Perky.

The double entry for these entries, which total £18,000, is the elimination of the £20,000 proposed dividend in Perky's balance sheet and the inclusion of £2,000 in the consolidated balance sheet as proposed dividend due to minority.

5.2.7   Preference dividends

The principles which apply to ordinary dividends apply equally to preference dividends.

5.3   Summary

As was said at the beginning of the book, each chapter represents a significant progression from the previous one, and sets the scene for later chapters. This is a particularly important chapter. When you have studied it really thoroughly, have a go at practice question 13.

6 Consolidated balance sheet 5: Piecemeal acquisitions

6.1 Where control already exists

Where a holding company acquires an additional block of shares in an existing subsidiary company, the reserves *attaching to the additional purchase* must be treated as pre-acquisition when the next consolidated accounts are prepared. The treatment is straightforward; it will simply reflect the increased interest of the holding company and the decreased interest of the minority shareholders. It will be necessary to write off any further goodwill arising, or adjust the capital reserve if a credit balance arises.

6.2 Where eventual control is achieved

Where a company gains control over another company by successive purchases of shares over a period of time, it is only at the end of the accounting period during which control is finally effected that the need to consolidate the subsidiary arises.

However, there is then a problem of deciding how much of the subsidiary's reserves should be considered as pre-acquisition. There are two alternatives:

(a)   to calculate pre-acquisition reserves by reference to the total proportion of shares held and the balance on reserves at the point of time when control is first gained; or

(b)   to calculate pre-acquisition reserves retrospectively by reference to the proportion of shares purchased related to the balance on reserves at the date of each purchase.

6.2.1   Illustration

The issued share capital of Sprout Ltd is £100,000, divided into ordinary shares of £1 each. Cabbage Ltd made the following purchases of shares in Sprout Ltd:

Date	Number of shares acquired	Balance on Sprout Ltd's reserves
		£
1 January 19X1	10,000	20,000
30 June 19X1	20,000	40,000
1 March 19X2	15,000	60,000
30 June 19X2	25,000	80,000
	70,000	

Calculation of pre-acquisition profits:

Under alternative (a) above

70% × £80,000   £56,000

Under alternative (b) above

	£
10% × £20,000	2,000
20% × £40,000	8,000
15% × £60,000	9,000
25% × £80,000	20,000
	39,000

The first alternative could be considered correct from a strictly legal point of view in that the necessity to consolidate does not arise until 30 June 19X2.

The second alternative, however, recognises the fact that all dividends attaching to the 10% holding in Sprout Ltd and paid out of profits earned after 1 January 19X1 may be treated as revenue income by Cabbage Ltd. In addition, under the second alternative, all dividends attaching to the 20% holding may be treated as revenue by Cabbage Ltd, so long as they are paid out of profits earned by Sprout Ltd after 30 June 19X1. Thus, as from 30 June 19X1 all dividends attaching to the cumulative holding of 30% may be treated as revenue by Cabbage Ltd, with similar adjustments for the increased percentages held at 1 March 19X2 and 30 June 19X2.

The second alternative should be used where the purchases are substantial and made with the object of securing control, while if the purchases are relatively small and spread over a long period of time the proportion can be determined at the time of the purchase which establishes the relationship of holding company and subsidiary.

On the whole, and in the absence of indications to the contrary in the question, examiners tend to prefer the second alternative. If you decide to use the first alternative, you should make a note to the examiner to justify your treatment.

Now arm yourself with some paper, clear the desk for action and have a go at the following question.

6.2.2   Question

The following is a summary of the balances in the records of two companies on 31 December 19X2:

	Odds Ltd £	Ends Ltd £
Fixed assets	247,000	232,400
120,000 ordinary shares in Ends Ltd	141,100	
Bills receivable (accepted by Odds Ltd)		600
Other current assets	161,700	113,000
	549,800	346,000

	£	£
Share capital authorised and issued		
Shares of £1 each, fully paid:		
Ordinary	300,000	160,000
5% preference		48,000
Dividend received from Ends Ltd for 19X1	12,000	
Provision for depreciation of fixed assets	64,000	51,000
Profit and loss account	51,000	25,000
Bills payable (drawn by Ends Ltd)	1,800	
Other current liabilities	121,000	62,000
	549,800	346,000

Note to the balance sheet of Ends Ltd:

There is a contingent liability in respect of a discounted bill for £1,200 accepted by Odds Ltd.

Odds Ltd acquired its holding of ordinary shares in Ends Ltd, cum div, as follows:

90,000 shares on 31 December 19X0 for £112,100.
30,000 shares on 31 December 19X1 for £38,000.

Ends Ltd provided in its accounts for dividends of 5% on its preference capital and 10% on its ordinary capital for each of the years 19X0 and 19X1, such dividends being paid in February following the end of the accounting year. Odds Ltd made no entry in its books in respect of the dividend from Ends Ltd until the date of receipt. The directors of Ends Ltd have recommended the payment of the preference dividend for 19X2. No ordinary dividends for 19X2 are proposed by either company.

The balance on the profit and loss account of Ends Ltd on 31 December 19X2 is made up as follows:

	£	£	£
Retained balance at 31 December 19X0			14,400
Profit, 19X1		20,000	
Less: dividends paid for 19X1:			
Preference	2,400		
Ordinary	16,000	18,400	1,600
			16,000
Profit 19X2			9,000
			25,000

You are required to prepare the consolidated balance sheet of Odds Ltd as at 31 December 19X2.

Discussion

Before attempting to answer, it is essential to clarify the position of the dividend. Odds Ltd has a credit balance of £12,000 dividend received from Ends in respect of 19X1, which is 10% of the £120,000 nominal of shares held at 31 December 19X1.

£3,000 of this dividend relates to the 30,000 shares acquired on 31 December 19X1 and must be deducted from the cost of the shares. The remaining £9,000, relating to the 90,000 shares, is post-acquisition and can be credited to Odds Ltd's profit and loss account.

A related problem is the make-up of the £141,100 shown in Odds Ltd's balance sheet as the cost of 120,000 shares in Ends Ltd. This is £103,100 for the 90,000 shares purchased on 31 December 19X0 plus £38,000 for the 30,000 purchased on 31 December 19X1. A further adjustment is needed for the pre-acquisition dividend on the 30,000 shares, as shown below:

	31 December 19X0 90,000 shares £		31 December 19X1 30,000 shares £	Total £
Cost	112,100		38,000	
Less: pre-acquisition dividend year ended 31 December 19X0	9,000	Less: pre-acquisition dividend year ended 31 December 19X1	3,000	
	103,100		35,000	138,100

Answer

Odds Ltd
Consolidated balance sheet as at 31 December 19X2

	£	£	£
Fixed assets:			
Tangible assets:			
Cost		479,400	
Depreciation		115,000	
			364,400
Current assets		274,700	
Creditors: amounts falling due within one year:			
Bills of exchange payable (W5)	1,200		
Dividend due to minority (preference shares)	2,400		
Other creditors	183,000		
		186,600	
Net current assets			88,100
Total assets less current liabilities			452,500
			£
Capital and reserves			
Called-up share capital			300,000
Profit and loss account			58,850
			358,850
Minority interests			93,650
			452,500

Workings

1   **Cost of control account**

		£		£
Cost of shares in Ends Ltd			75% share capital Ends	120,000
112,100	38,000		Profit and loss account:	
9,000	3,000		75% pre-acquisition profit	11,100
103,100	35,000	138,100	Profit and loss account:	
			goodwill written off	7,000
		138,100		138,100

2 Minority interest account

	£			£
Balance to CBS	93,650	Share capital:		
		100% preference		48,000
		25% ordinary		40,000
		25% profit and loss account		5,650
	93,650			93,650

3 Consolidated profit and loss account

	£			£
Proposed preference dividend	2,400	O		51,000
Cost of control account (W1)	11,100	Dividend received from		
Minority interest account		Ends Ltd (9/16 × £16,000)		9,000
(4/16 × (£25,000 − £2,400))	5,650	E		25,000
Cost of control account:				
goodwill written off	7,000			
Balance to CBS	58,850			
	85,000			85,000

4 Pre-acquisition profits

Pre-acquisition profits must be calculated in two stages:

	£
Re 90,000 shares:	
9/16 × £14,400 balance at acquisition 31 December 19X0	8,100
Re 30,000 shares:	
3/16 × £16,000 balance at acquisition 31 December 19X1	3,000
	11,100

5 Bills of exchange

Bills payable (£1,800) are cancelled against bills receivable (£600), leaving the £1,200 discounted bill which must appear as a liability in the consolidated balance sheet.

6.3 Summary

This short chapter deals with a point often encountered in examination questions. Be sure you understand the two methods explained — you will be needing them when we look at indirect subsidiaries in the next chapter. Practise with question 14.

7 Consolidated balance sheet 6: More complex group structures

7.1 Fellow subsidiaries

So far we have been dealing with straightforward group structures where one company owns more than 50% of another company. A variation on this basic group structure arises where the holding company controls more than one company, for example:

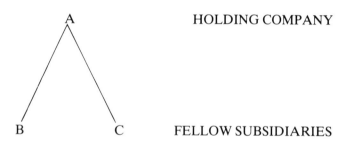

In this situation the techniques employed are identical to those already dealt with, but they must be employed for each subsidiary company. The adjustments, however, may all be effected through one cost of control account and one minority interest account, which will produce respectively a net figure for the goodwill to be written off, or capital reserve, and a total of all the minority shareholders' interests.

It is suggested in some books that when a goodwill balance arises in relation to one subsidiary, and another has a capital reserve, it is not permissible to offset them because it would contravene the Companies Act 1985, sch. 4, para. 5, which prohibits the set-off of assets against liabilities. However, the capital reserve arising on an acquisition is not a liability, and appendix 2 to SSAP 22 suggests that goodwill may be written off against 'negative goodwill' (which is nothing more than a capital reserve arising on an acquisition). It therefore seems reasonable to calculate a single net figure for goodwill or capital reserve covering all subsidiaries.

Bearing the above in mind, you should be confident enough to tackle the following question.

7.1.1 Question

The following trial balances were extracted from the records of three companies at 30 June 19X4:

	Hand Ltd	Finger Ltd	Thumb Ltd
Debits	£	£	£
Fixed assets	119,700	88,400	115,000
Current assets	171,000	40,200	96,000
Investment in subsidiary companies	204,000		
Dividends receivable:			
Finger Ltd	5,100		
Thumb Ltd	12,000		
	511,800	128,600	211,000
Credits			
Share capital:			
Ordinary shares of £1 each	100,000	50,000	70,000
6% preference shares of £1 each	30,000	20,000	—
Share premium account	10,000	5,000	—
Profit and loss account	205,000	30,000	84,000
Current liabilities	165,000	17,000	43,000
Proposed dividends:			
Ordinary	—	6,000	14,000
Preference	1,800	600	—
	511,800	128,600	211,000

The following additional information is relevant:

(a)   The investments were all acquired cum div as follows:

	Date	Retained profit and loss account balance £	Cost £
Finger Ltd:			
40,000 ordinary shares	30 June 19X0	20,000	55,000
10,000 6% preference shares	30 June 19X1	24,000	9,000
Thumb Ltd:			
60,000 ordinary shares	30 June 19X2	63,000	146,000
			210,000

(b)   The preference dividend of Finger Ltd for the half year to 30 June 19X1 was received by Hand Ltd on 4 July 19X1; and an ordinary dividend of £4,000 was received in 19X1 from Finger Ltd for the year to 30 June 19X0. Both these dividends were credited to the profit and loss account of Hand Ltd.

In July 19X2 Hand Ltd received from Thumb Ltd an ordinary dividend of £6,000 for the year to 30 June 19X2. This dividend was credited against the cost of shares in Thumb Ltd.

(c)   The share premium account of Finger Ltd was created on incorporation.

(d)   Adjustment is to be made in the accounts of Hand Ltd for a proposed ordinary dividend of £15,000.

You are required to prepare the consolidated balance sheet of Hand Ltd and its subsidiaries as at 30 June 19X4.

Answer

Hand Ltd and its subsidiaries
Consolidated balance sheet as at 30 June 19X4

	£	£	£
Fixed assets: tangible assets			323,100
Current assets		307,200	
Creditors: amounts falling due within one year:			
Sundry creditors	225,000		
Dividend due to minority	3,500		
Proposed dividend (£15,000 + £1,800)	16,800		
	———	245,300	
Net current assets			61,900
Total assets less current liabilities			385,000
Capital and reserves:			
Called-up share capital:			
£1 ordinary shares			100,000
£1 6% preference shares			30,000
Share premium account			10,000
Profit and loss account			196,000
			336,000
Minority interests			49,000
			385,000

Cost of control

	£		£
Investment in Finger Ltd:		Finger Ltd:	
Ordinary (£55,000 − £4,000)	51,000	Share capital:	
Preference (£9,000 − £300)	8,700	80% ordinary	40,000
		50% preference	10,000
		80% profit and loss account	16,000
		80% share premium account	4,000
Investment in Thumb Ltd	140,000	Thumb Ltd:	
		6/7ths share capital	60,000
		6/7ths profit and loss account	54,000
		Profit and loss account:	
		goodwill written off	15,700
	199,700		199,700

Minority interest

	£		£
Balance to CBS	49,000	Finger Ltd:	
		Share capital:	
		20% ordinary	10,000
		50% preference	10,000
		20% profit and loss account	6,000
		20% share premium account	1,000
		Thumb Ltd:	
		1/7th share capital	10,000
		1/7th profit and loss account	12,000
	49,000		49,000

Profit and loss account

	£		£
Hand Ltd:		H	205,000
Investment in Finger Ltd			
(pre-acquisition dividends):			
Ordinary 4,000			
Preference 300			
	4,300		
Proposed dividend	15,000		
Finger Ltd:		F	30,000
Cost of control account			
(80% × £20,000)	16,000		
Minority interest account			
(20% × £30,000)	6,000		
Thumb Ltd:		T	84,000
Cost of control account			
(6/7 × £63,000)	54,000		
Minority interest account			
(1/7 × £84,000)	12,000		
Cost of control: goodwill			
written off	15,700		
Balance to CBS	196,000		
	319,000		319,000

Share premium account

	£		£
Hand Ltd:		H	10,000
Finger Ltd:		F	5,000
Cost of control account			
(80% × £5,000)	4,000		
Minority interest account			
(20% × £5,000)	1,000		
Balance to CBS	10,000		
	15,000		15,000

Proposed dividends due to the minority shareholders

	£
Finger Ltd:	
Ordinary (20% × £6,000)	1,200
Preference (50% × £600)	300
Thumb Ltd (1/7 × £14,000)	2,000
	3,500

7.2 Sub-subsidiaries

A 'sub-subsidiary' is a company in which a subsidiary owns a controlling shareholding. Sub-subsidiaries must be covered by consolidated accounts, requiring a minor addition to the technique we have been using so far.

One approach would be to consolidate the subsidiary (S) with its own subsidiary (SS), to produce the consolidated accounts for that subgroup, then consolidate the result with the holding company to produce the overall group accounts. This may be called the two-stage method.

However, it is much quicker, less likely to lead to error and equally correct to consolidate all three companies in one operation — the one-stage method. To do this it is necessary first to work out the *group's percentage ownership of the sub-subsidiary*. Here is a diagram showing two sub-subsidiaries:

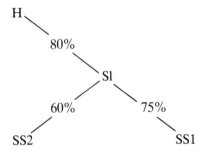

H owns 80% of S1, S1 owns 75% of SS1. Clearly therefore the group owns 80% of 75% (= 60%) of SS1. What about SS2? The group owns 80% of 60% (= 48%) of SS2. Although this is less than 50%, SS2 is still counted as a subsidiary requiring consolidation by virtue of the fact that H controls S1 which in turn controls SS2. The group accounts will ultimately cover H, plus 80% of S1, plus 60% of SS1, plus 48% of SS2.

The workings are the same as in previous examples except for one vital point. When it comes to entering the cost of the investment of the sub-subsidiary into the cost of control working, only *the proportion attributable to H's share in S1* (80% in this case) is entered. The remaining 20% is debited to the *minority interest* working. This is correct from the point of view of the minority, because the minority interest working would already have been credited with 20% of the share capital and reserves of S1, figures which include the value of the investments in SS1 and SS2. If the minority interest's proportion of the costs attributable to these investments was not eliminated, the minority interest would be overstated.

The share capital and reserves are divided according to the *group's ultimate share in the sub-subsidiaries' net assets* (60% for SS1 and 48% for SS2).

7.2.1 Illustration

London Ltd owns 80% of the ordinary share capital of Paddington Ltd and Paddington Ltd owns 75% of Train Ltd. Both investments had been acquired on 1 January 19X5, when the reserves of Paddington were £20,000 and those of Train £10,000

The balance sheets of the three companies as at 31 December 19X8 were as follows:

	London Ltd £000	Paddington Ltd £000	Train Ltd £000
Sundry fixed assets	100	100	60
Investments:			
Shares in Paddington	60		
Shares in Train		40	
Sundry current assets less liabilities	80		40
	240	140	100
Capital and reserves:			
Issued share capital: £1 ordinary shares	120	80	40
Profit and loss account	120	60	60
	240	140	100

At 31 December 19X8 the following dividends were proposed:

London	20%
Paddington	10%
Train	10%

None of these had yet been reflected in the above balance sheets.

Prepare a consolidated balance sheet for the group as at 31 December 19X8.

Discussion

It is first necessary to establish the group's interest in Train. This is clearly 80% of 75%, or 60%.

Attempt your own answer before studying the one which follows.

London Ltd and its subsidiaries
Consolidated balance sheet as at 31 December 19X8

	£000	£000
Sundry fixed assets		260
Sundry assets less current liabilities	120	
Proposed dividends:		
London	(24)	
Minority Paddington	(1.6)	
Minority Train	(1)	
		93.4
		353.4
Capital and reserves:		
Issued share capital: ordinary shares of £1 each		120
Capital reserve arising on consolidation		18
Profit and loss account		158
		296
Minority interest		57.4
		353.4

Cost of control

	£000		£000
Shares in Paddington	60	80% share capital Paddington	64
Shares in Train 80%	32	60% share capital Train	24
Capital reserve	18	80% pre-acquisition reserves Paddington	16
		60% pre-acquisition reserves Train	6
	110		110

Minority interests

	£000		£000
Shares in Train 20%	8	20% share capital Paddington	16
Balance to CBS	57.4	40% share capital Train	16
		20% profit and loss Paddington	11
		40% profit and loss Train	22.4
	65.4		65.4

Profit and loss

	£000		£000
Proposed dividend: London	24	London	120
		Dividend receivable: Paddington 80%	6.4
Proposed dividend: Paddington	8	Paddington	60
Minority interest 20% × £55,000	11	Dividend receivable: Train 75%	3
Cost of control: 80% × £20,000	16		
Proposed dividend: Train	4	Train	60
Minority interest: 40% × £56,000	22.4		
Cost of control: 60% × £10,000	6		
Balance to CBS	158		
	249.4		249.4

7.3   Direct and indirect holdings

The group structure examined in 7.2 was:

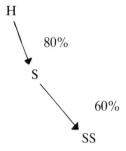

What if H owns shares in SS as well as S? Like this, for example:

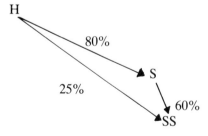

Exactly the same technique may be used. The further difficulty which may arise is that the shares in SS held by H and those held by S may have been acquired at different times. If this is the case, care is needed to choose the correct figures for reserves when calculating the pre-acquisition profit.

First the extent of H's interest in SS must be calculated. This is:

	%
Direct H in SS	25
Indirect (through S) 80% × 60%	48
	73
Minority interest	27
	100

Now let us consider the problem of calculating pre-acquisition profit. In the illustration which follows, H first acquired a 25% interest in SS on 31 December 19X2 then later acquired 80% of S on 31 December 19X4. S acquired its shares in SS on 31 December 19X3. When did SS enter the *H* group? Clearly not on 31 December 19X2, because at that time only 25% of the shares were owned. When H acquired S, S already owned 60% of SS. That means that SS became a subsidiary of H on 31 December 19X4, the date H acquired the 80% holding in S. When answering a question, draw up a time chart if this helps your thinking. (For the purposes of this illustration, H did not account for SS as an associated company between 31 December 19X2 and 31 December 19X4. Associated companies will be considered in detail in a later chapter.)

7.3.1 Illustration

The following summarised balance sheets have been prepared at 31 December 19X5:

	H Ltd £	S Ltd £	SS Ltd £
Investment in subsidiary companies:			
80,000 shares in S Ltd	165,000		
2,500 shares in SS Ltd	2,000		
6,000 shares in SS Ltd		11,000	
Sundry assets	398,000	359,000	110,000
	565,000	370,000	
Creditors	275,000	190,000	94,000
	290,000	180,000	16,000
Financed by:			
Share capital, ordinary shares of £1 each	150,000	100,000	10,000
Revenue reserves	140,000	80,000	6,000
	290,000	180,000	16,000

The investments were acquired as follows:

	Date	Balance on reserves S Ltd	SS Ltd
		£	£
H Ltd			
80,000 shares in S Ltd	31.12.X4	70,000	5,000
2,500 shares in SS Ltd	31.12.X2		1,000
S Ltd			
6,000 shares in SS Ltd	31.12.X3		3,600

There are no dividend complications.

You are required to prepare the consolidated balance sheet of H Ltd and its subsidiaries as at 31 December 19X5.

Discussion

Before beginning the answer to a complex question of this kind, three preliminary steps are necessary:

(a) Define group structure and percentage holdings.
(b) Establish the timing of acquisitions and hence relevant reserve balances.
(c) Understand and make any necessary adjustments for dividends.

For this question we have a flying start. We already know the group structure because we discussed it before the illustration, as we did the timing of acquisitions. It may help to draw up a time chart thus:

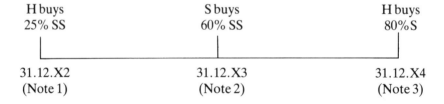

H buys 25% SS	S buys 60% SS	H buys 80% S
31.12.X2	31.12.X3	31.12.X4
(Note 1)	(Note 2)	(Note 3)

Notes

1   At 31.12.X2, no company is a subsidiary of any other. But H's acquisition of shares in SS is the first stage of the piecemeal acquisition continued at 31.12.X4. In the consolidation we therefore calculate the pre-acquisition profits for H's 25% holding using the £1,000 reserve figure.

2   At 31.12.X3, S's acquisition of 60% of SS means that this could be a relevant date *if* we were only consolidating S and SS. In the present case S and SS do not enter the H group until 31.12.X4. We are therefore not interested in the balance at 31.12.X3.

3   At 31.12.X4, H buys 80% of S. This is the moment at which H first acquires subsidiaries. The relevant reserves are therefore:

	£
H's acquisition of 80% of S	31.12.X4 70,000
H's indirect acquisition of 48% of SS	31.12.X4 5,000

The third preliminary step, to sort out any dividend problems, does not arise here.

Answer

Cost of control account

	£		£
Investment in S Ltd	165,000	S Ltd	
		80% share capital	80,000
		80% pre-acquisition revenue reserves	56,000
Investment in SS Ltd (direct)	2,000	SS Ltd:	
Investment in SS Ltd (indirect)		73% share capital	7,300
(80% × £11,000)	8,800	Revenue reserves	2,650
		Revenue reserves: goodwill written off	29,850
	175,800		175,800

Minority interest account

	£		£
		S Ltd:	
		20% share capital	20,000
		20% revenue reserves	16,000
Investment in SS Ltd		SS Ltd:	
(20% × £11,000)	2,200	27% share capital	2,700
Balance to CBS	38,120	27% revenue reserves	1,620
	40,320		40,320

Consolidated revenue reserves

	£			£
			H	140,000
Cost of control account			S	80,000
(80% × £70,000)	56,000			
Minority interest account				
(20% × £80,000)	16,000			
Cost of control account: £			SS	6,000
H in SS (25% × £1,000) 250				
S in SS (48% × £5,000) 2,400				
	2,650			
Minority interest account				
(27% × £6,000)	1,620			
Cost of control account:				
goodwill written off	29,850			
Balance to CBS	119,880			
	226,000			226,000

The final balance sheet would appear as follows:

H Ltd
Consolidated balance sheet as at 31 December 19X5

	£	£
Sundry assets	867,000	
Creditors	559,000	
		308,000
		308,000
Financed by:		
Share capital, ordinary shares of £1 each		150,000
Revenue reserves		119,880
		269,880
Minority interests		38,120
		308,000

Before leaving this question it may help to illustrate the division of the revenue reserves of SS Ltd in the form of a diagram:

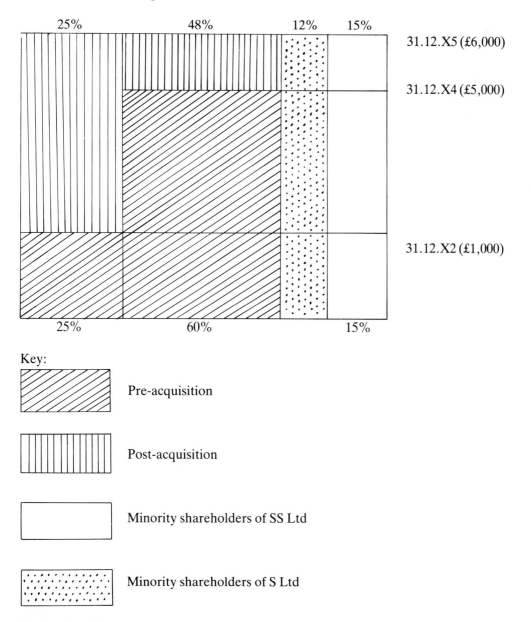

Key:

Pre-acquisition

Post-acquisition

Minority shareholders of SS Ltd

Minority shareholders of S Ltd

Notice that this is effectively a piecemeal acquisition and therefore two calculations of pre-acquisition profits are required.

7.4 Summary

Questions in the more advanced accounting examinations are usually based on the types of group structure dealt with in this chapter. Especially significant points for you to understand are:

(a)   The concept of the one-stage consolidation and the calculation of the percentages attributable to the group.

(b)   The calculation of the minority interest — the debiting of minority interest account with a proportion of the cost of shares in the sub-subsidiary.

(c)   Determination of dates when subsidiaries enter the group when there are indirect holdings.

Practice with questions 15 to 17, then work the revision questions 18 and 19 which include earlier work also. Question 19 is a particularly important one.

8 Consolidated profit and loss account

8.1 Introduction

The object of the consolidated profit and loss account is to show the total profits of the companies in the group and the group's share of those profits. It is prepared by cross-casting the figures for the individual companies, deducting inter-company transactions and eliminating unrealised profit on stock etc. as you go.

8.2 Minority interests

What about minority interests? If there are minority interests, you still cross-cast as before, down to *profit after taxation*. At this point, the minority interest's share in the profits or losses of subsidiaries is calculated and deducted.

If the subsidiaries with minority interests have ordinary share capital only, it is a simple matter of taking the appropriate percentage of their post-tax profit. If they have preference share capital, it is necessary to proceed in two stages. The minority interest (MI) in such a company consists of two parts:

(a) MI percentage of preference capital × *preference dividend* for year.
(b) MI percentage of ordinary share capital × *balance of profits* for year.

Once minority interest has been deducted from profit after taxation, only *the group's share* of subsequent items is included. Thus only the group's share of the extraordinary items of subsidiaries is included.

8.3 Dividends and retained profit

The dividend deducted is the holding company's dividend only. Retained profits brought forward and carried forward are based on the group's share, including only post-acquisition profits of subsidiaries, of course. Finally, a note shows how much of the year's profit is dealt with in the separate profit and loss account of the holding company. If this is done, it is not necessary for the holding company to publish its own profit and loss account (Companies Act 1985, s. 228).

The following pro forma shows the basic layout and methods of computation.

	£000	
Turnover	1,000	
Cost of sales	(700)	
	———	
Gross profit	300	
Distribution costs	(100)	
Administration expenses	(80)	H + S − IG
(Other income and expenses as required)		
	———	
	120	
Tax on profit on ordinary activities	(40)	
	———	
Profit after taxation	80	
Minority interest	(20)	
	———	
	60	
Extraordinary items (net of tax)	(10)	← H + group's
	—	share of S
Profit for financial year	50	
Dividends proposed	(30)	← H only
	———	
	20	
Retained profit brought forward	100	← H + group's share
	———	of S post acquisition
Retained profit carried forward	120	
	———	

Down to the calculation of profit after taxation, we take the sum of the holding company (H) and subsidiaries (S), adjusting where necessary for intra-group transactions (IG). We then calculate and deduct the minority interest, and from that point on we must include only *the group's share of S*. The dividend taken is that of H only because the subsidiary's dividend cancels as explained in note 2 to illustration 8.3.1.

8.3.1   Illustration

The share capital of Minnow Ltd consists of 100,000 ordinary shares of which Whale Ltd acquired 80% when the reserves of Minnow were £20,000. The profit and loss accounts of the two companies for the year ended 31 December 19X2 are as follows:

	Whale	Minnow
	£000	£000
Sales	1,000	400
Cost of sales	(600)	(200)
Gross profit	400	200
Distribution costs	(80)	(30)
Administration expenses	(70)	(50)
Operating profit	250	120
Taxation	(80)	(40)
Profit after taxation	170	80
Extraordinary items (net of tax)	15	10
	185	90
Dividends proposed	(100)	(50)
	85	40
Retained profit brought forward	260	100
	345	140

Whale had sold goods to Minnow during the year for £100,000 charging cost plus 25%. At the balance sheet date Minnow still had £10,000 of these goods in stock. Whale has not yet taken the dividend receivable from Minnow into account in its records.

Prepare a consolidated profit and loss account for the year.

Whale Ltd and its subsidiary
Consolidated profit and loss account for the year ended 31 December 19X2

	£000
Turnover (H + S − IG)	1,300
Cost of sales (H + S − IG + unrealised profit on stock)	(702)
	598
Distribution costs (H + S − IG)	(110)
Administrative expenses (H + S − IG)	(120)
Operating profit	368
Taxation (H + S)	(120)
Profit after taxation	248
Less: minority interest (20% × 80)	(16)
	232
Extraordinary items (H + group's share of S)	23
	255
Dividends proposed (H only)	(100)
	155
Retained profit brought forward (H + group's share of S post-acquisition)	324
	479

The amount of profit dealt with in the accounts of the holding company was £225,000 (£185,000 plus dividend from Minnow 80% × £50,000).

Notes

1   Cost of sales. It is easy to make a mistake here. The figure eliminated from cost of sales for the inter-company sales is the *same* as that eliminated from turnover. Why? Because that is the figure included in Minnow's purchases. Do not be tempted to adjust for the cost to Whale.

It is also necessary to allow for the £2,000 of unrealised profit on the stock retained by Minnow, which is 25/125 × £10,000 or £2,000. This adjustment reduces the value of the closing stock and thus *increases* cost of sales. If there is already an opening provision for unrealised profit, the adjustment in the consolidated profit and loss account must be for the net movement required in the provision during the year.

2   Dividends. Only the holding company's dividend is included in the consolidated profit and loss account. What happens to the subsidiary's dividend of £50,000? It cancels. £40,000 of it would be credited by Whale to its profit and loss account and the remaining £10,000 is included in the minority interest adjustment (20% × £80,000). If Whale had already credited its share of £40,000 to profit and loss account this could have been ignored for the same reason when preparing the consolidated profit and loss account.

3 Directors' remuneration. If separate figures are given for each company's directors' remuneration, the amount for the consolidated profit and loss account is simply the sum of all the figures. But the notes giving the breakdown of the remuneration, highest paid director etc. must deal with remuneration received *by the directors of the holding company* from all companies in the group.

It is possible, though not always necessary in examination questions, to arrive at the final balance of the consolidated profit and loss account by constructing the profit and loss account working which would form part of the answer to a consolidated balance sheet question:

Profit and loss account

	£000		£000
Minority interest: 20% × 140	28	Retained profit brought forward:	
Pre-acquisition profit: 80% × 20	16	Whale	260
Unrealised profit on stock	2	Minnow	100
Balance	479	Retained profit for year:	
		Whale	85
		Minnow	40
		Dividend from Minnow:	
		80% × £50,000	40
	525		525

Study that answer, including the profit and loss account working above, until you really understand the logic of every item.

8.4 Subsidiary acquired part way through the year

If a subsidiary is acquired during the current year, only its post-acquisition profit can come into the group profit and loss account. The easiest way to handle this is to continue to cross-cast all figures exactly as before, down to the calculation of profit after tax. The minority interest is deducted, again exactly as before, to give the group's share of the profit, then the pre-acquisition portion is deducted. Remember that the minority interest adjustment must come first, then the pre-acquisition profit adjustment. The logic of this is, of course, that the minority interest is entitled to its share of the *total* profit, whereas the pre-acquisition profit adjustment relates to the *group's* share of the profit and must therefore be calculated on the balance remaining after deducting the minority interest in the profit.

It is also possible to arrive at the same answer by including the appropriate proportion of turnover and expenses in the consolidated profit and loss account. It is then not necessary to deduct the pre-acquisition profit after taking out the minority interest, and the minority interest deduction is based on the post-acquisition profit of the subsidiary only. The answer to practice question 20 illustrates both methods.

To provide an illustration, let us take the previous one (Whale and Minnow). We will assume that Whale had acquired its interest on 30 June 19X2, that profits accrue evenly, that all sales from Whale to Minnow occurred after the acquisition and that Minnow's extraordinary items all relate to the post-acquisition period:

	£000	£000	
Turnover		1,300	
Cost of sales		(702)	
		598	
Distribution costs		(110)	Exactly as
Administrative expenses		(120)	before*
		368	
Taxation		(120)	
		248	
Less: minority interest	(16)		
Pre-acquisition profit: ½(£80,000 − £16,000)	(32)		
	—	(48)	
		200	
Extraordinary items		23	
		223	
Dividends proposed		100	
		123	
Retained profit brought forward (W only as M was not a subsidiary at the beginning of the year)		260	
		383	

The amount of profit dealt with in the accounts of the holding company was £205,000 (£185,000) plus £20,000).

*The turnover and cost of sales remain the same as in the original illustration because we have assumed that all sales by Whale to Minnow occurred post acquisition. If we had assumed that only half the sales related to the post-acquisition period, we should have had to adjust for the post-acquisition sales only. In that case we should have had:

	£000
Turnover (£1,000,000 − £50,000 + £200,000)	1,150
Cost of sales (£600,000 + £100,000 − £50,000 + £2,000)	652
Gross profit	498

The answer can be proved by constructing the profit and loss account working:

Profit and loss account

	£000		£000
Minority interest	28	Retained profit brought forward:	
Pre-acquisition profit (Working)	92	Whale	260
Unrealised profit on stock	2	Minnow	100
Balance	383	Retained profit for year:	
		Whale	85
		Minnow	40
		Dividend from Minnow:	
		½ × 80% × 50 (the post- acquisition proportion)	20
	505		505

Working

Calculation of pre-acquisition retained profits

	£000
Retained profit at beginning of year	100
Profit to date of acquisition ½ × £80,000	40
Less: dividend: ½ × £50,000	25
	115
80% × £115,000	92

Note

Here is the alternative way to present the consolidated profit and loss account when a subsidiary is acquired part way through the year — to include in turnover, expenses, and taxation the *post-acquisition* proportion only.

Reworking the Whale and Minnow question in this style gives:

	£000
Turnover (£1,000,000 − £100,000 + £200,000)	1,100
Cost of sales (£600,000 + £100,000 − £100,000 + £2,000)	602
Gross profit	498
Distribution costs (£80,000 + £15,000)	(95)
Administrative expenses (£70,000 + £25,000)	(95)
	308
Tax (£80,000 + £20,000)	100
	208
Less: minority interest ½ × 20% × £80,000	8
Profit after taxation	200
Extraordinary items (net of tax)	23
	223
Dividends proposed	(100)
	123
Retained profit brought forward (W only as M was not a subsidiary at the beginning of the year)	260
	383

The amount of profit dealt with in the accounts of the holding company was £205,000 (£185,000 plus £20,000).

8.5   Sub-subsidiaries

The procedure for the inclusion of sub-subsidiaries is relatively straightforward. The main point to watch is the effect on the minority interests in dividends paid by a sub-subsidiary.

8.5.1   Illustration

A Ltd owns 75% of B Ltd, and B Ltd owns 90% of C Ltd. Abridged profit and loss accounts for the year 19X3 are as follows:

	A Ltd £	B Ltd £	C Ltd £
Operating profit	100,000	80,000	20,000
Dividend from B Ltd	6,000		
Dividend from C Ltd		1,800	
Profit before taxation	106,000	81,800	20,000
Taxation	40,000	30,000	7,000
Profit after taxation	66,000	51,800	13,000
Dividends paid	35,000	8,000	2,000
Retained profit for the year	31,000	43,800	11,000

The calculation of the minority interest in B Ltd's profit must exclude the dividend received from C Ltd because this will be taken into account when computing the minority share of C Ltd's profit. To give B Ltd's minority their share of the dividend received from C Ltd would be double-counting.

The minority interest calculation would be as follows:

	£	£
In B Ltd (25% × (£51,800 − £1,800))		12,500
In C Ltd:		
Direct (10% × £13,000)	1,300	
Indirect (25% × 90% × £13,000)	2,925	
Aggregate minority interest in C Ltd (32.5% × £13,000)		4,225
		16,725

From the information given the consolidated profit and loss account would appear as follows:

	£
Profit before taxation	200,000
Taxation	77,000
Profit after taxation	123,000
Minority interests	16,725
Profit attributable to the group	106,275
Dividends paid	35,000
Retained profit for the year	71,275

8.5.2   Illustration

H Ltd acquired 80% of the share capital of S Ltd on 1 August 19X4. During the year to 31 December 19X4, H Ltd made a profit of £160,000 before a taxation charge of £65,000; and S Ltd made a profit of £72,000 before a taxation charge of £30,000.

Dividends declared for the year were:

	£
H Ltd: final (proposed)	20,000
S Ltd:	
Interim (paid 1 July 19X4)	6,000
Final (proposed)	9,000
	15,000

The balances on profit and loss account at 1 January 19X4 were H Ltd £400,000 and S Ltd £200,000.

Using only the information given, you are required to prepare the consolidated profit and loss account of H Ltd for the year ended 31 December 19X4, disclosing also the amount of the group profit which has been dealt with in the accounts of H Ltd.

H Ltd and its subsidiary
Consolidated profit and loss account for the year ended 31 December 19X4

	£	£
Profit before taxation (£160,000 + £72,000)		232,000
Taxation		95,000
Profit after taxation		137,000
Less: minority interest: 20% × £42,000	8,400	
Pre-acquisition profit: 7/12 × (£42,000 − £8,400)	19,600	
		28,000
Profit attributable to the group (Note 1)		109,000
Proposed dividend		20,000
		89,000
Retained profits brought forward		400,000
Retained profits carried forward		489,000

Note 1. Profit dealt with in the accounts of H Limited was £100,000 (see working).

Working

Profit dealt with in the accounts of H Ltd

	£
H Ltd profit after tax	95,000
Dividend from S Ltd (post-acquisition portion only):	
80% × 5/12 × £15,000	5,000
	100,000

8.6   Summary

Students often neglect the consolidated profit and loss account and concentrate on the consolidated balance sheet only. This is folly — examination questions often ask for consolidated profit and loss accounts or indeed both balance sheet and profit and loss account. Relevant practice questions are 20 to 22.

9   Associated companies

9.1   Introduction

A substantial investment in a company may give the investing company considerable influence even though the holding does not give control. Such influence may justify treating the company in a special way. SSAP 1, issued in 1971, amended in 1974 and revised in 1982, calls such companies 'associated companies' and seeks to define them and lay down a special accounting treatment for them in group accounts. The definition of an associated company is similar to that of a related company in the Companies Act 1985 (see 9.3).

9.2   Definition of associated company

SSAP 1 defines an associated company as:

> . . . a company not being a subsidiary of the investing group or company in which:
>
> (a)   the interest of the investing group or company is effectively that of a partner in a joint venture or consortium and the investing group or company is in a position to exercise a significant influence over the company in which the investment is made; or
>
> (b)   the interest of the investing group or company is for the long term and is substantial and, having regard to the disposition of the other shareholdings, the investing group or company is in a position to exercise a significant influence over the company in which the investment is made.

Significant influence over a company essentially involves participation in the financial and operating policy decisions of that company (including dividend policy) but not necessarily control of those policies. Representation on the board of directors is indicative of such participation, but will neither necessarily give conclusive evidence of it nor be the only method by which the investing company may participate in policy decisions.

Where the interest of the investing group or company is not effectively that of a partner in a joint venture or consortium, an interest of *20% or more* in the equity voting rights is deemed to carry the ability to exercise significant influence unless it can clearly be demonstrated otherwise, and an interest of less than 20% in the equity voting rights is assumed not to carry such an ability unless it can clearly be demonstrated otherwise.

9.3   Related companies under the Companies Act 1985

The Companies Act 1985, sch. 4, para. 92, defines a related company as one in which the investing company holds, on a long-term basis, 20% or more of the voting equity share capital for the purpose of securing a contribution to that company's own activities by the exercise of any control or influence arising from that interest. The Companies Act 1985 requires certain disclosures in the accounts of a company which has related companies (as defined in the preceding paragraph). These disclosure requirements do not have to be met if all the related companies are accounted for as associated companies in accordance with SSAP 1.

9.4   Treatment of associated companies in consolidated accounts

The profit and loss account of a company with investments will be credited with the dividends received from those investments, while its balance sheet will normally show those investments at cost.

SSAP1 requires a company with associated companies as defined in 9.2 to account for them differently:

(a)   In the profit and loss account to bring in the appropriate *share of the associates' profit* in place of dividends received.

(b)   In the balance sheet, to value the investment at cost plus the appropriate share of the associates' *retained profit since acquisition*. This has the effect of recognising that the value of the investment increases by the amount of its retained profits, since the increase in retained profits is the measure of the increase in the value of its assets. This is the so-called 'equity basis of accounting', sometimes also called 'one-line consolidation'.

(c)   By note, to show the total value arrived at in (b) broken down into the following components:

   (i)   Group's share of tangible net assets of associate
   (ii)   Group's share of goodwill of associate
   (iii)   Premium or discount on the acquisition of the interest (so far as not written off).

Items (ii) and (iii) may be shown as a single figure.

What are the mechanics, or double entry, of all this? Here is how it works, stage by stage:

(a)   Introduce into the consolidated profit and loss account *the group's share* of:

   (i)   Associate's pre-tax profit.
   (ii)   Associate's tax charge.
   (iii)   Associate's extraordinary items.

(b)   Remove from the consolidated profit and loss account the dividend received from the associate. Note that this cancels with the group's share of the dividend shown as payable in the profit and loss account of the associate.

(c)   The net effect of stages (a) and (b) is to increase the group profit by the group's share of the associate's retained profit for the year. The closing retained profits in the consolidated profit and loss account must be analysed to show separately the amount included for associated companies. This amount is then debited to investment in associated companies in the consolidated balance sheet. In the previous year's consolidated balance the investment will have been shown at cost plus the group's share of retained profit to that date. By adding the group's share of the current year's profit the value is updated to its new value at the balance sheet date. If in an examination question the investment in the associate is shown at cost in the balance sheet, it will be necessary to increase the value by the group's share of the associate's retained profits for all the years since acquisition:

Debit	Investment in associate	With group's share of associate's post-acquisition retained profits.
Credit	Profit and loss account (in balance sheet)	

(d)   Calculate the further information required by SSAP 1:

(i)   Group's share of the fair value of associate's tangible assets.
(ii)   Group's share of associate's goodwill.
(iii)   Premium or discount on acquisition of the shares in the associate.

Items (i) and (ii) are taken from the associated company's balance sheet. Item (iii) is calculated by comparing fair value of net assets at acquisition with cost of shares. Items (ii) and (iii) may be shown as one amount. The total of items (i), (ii) and (iii) must and will equal the balance sheet total arrived at by adding the group's share of the associate's post-acquisition retained profits to the cost of the investment.

9.5 Specimen consolidated profit and loss account including associated companies

In the following specimen consolidated profit and loss account, the notes indicated by Arabic numerals form part of the account while the letters in parentheses refer to the comments which follow the account.

Consolidated profit and loss account for the year ended 31 December 19X1

	£000	£000
Turnover (a)		1,000
Cost of sales (a)		(400)
Gross profit (a)		600
Distribution costs (a)		(140)
Administrative expenses (a)		(160)
Other operating income (a)		50
Income from shares in related companies (b)		100*
Other interest receivable and similar income (a)		40
Interest payable and similar charges (a)		(160)
Profit on ordinary activities before taxation (note 1)		330
Tax on profit on ordinary activities (c):		
Group	100	
Related companies	30†	
	——	(130)
Profit on ordinary activities after taxation		200
Minority interests		(40)
Profit before extraordinary items attributable		
to members of holding company		160
Extraordinary loss (or profit) (d)		(10)
Profit for the financial year (note 2)		150
Dividends paid and proposed		(60)
Retained profit for the year (note 3)		90
Statement of retained profits		
Retained profit for the year		90
Retained profits at beginning of year		130
Retained profits at end of year (note 4)		220

*Group's share of associates' profit before tax.
†Tax on group's share of associates' profit.

Notes to the accounts

1   Profit on ordinary activities before taxation is stated after charging the following (e):

	£000
Depreciation of tangible fixed assets	80
Auditors' remuneration and expenses	10
Directors emoluments:	
As directors	10
Remuneration as executives	90

2   Of the group profit for the financial year £80,000 has been dealt with in the accounts of Holding Co. Ltd (f).

3   Retained profit for the year (g). The profit for the year retained by associated companies was £30,000.

4   Retained profit at the end of the year (h). The profit at the end of the year retained by associated companies was £70,000.

Comments

(a)   All items marked (a) will include only the holding company's and subsidiary's relevant amounts. This applies to turnover, cost of sales, distribution costs, administrative expenses, other operating income, other interest receivable and interest payable.

(b)   Income from related companies. This will include the *group share* of the profits before taxation of associated companies. Dividends from associated companies must be excluded from the consolidated profit and loss account since the profits of associated companies are being included in place of those dividends.

(c)   Tax on profit on ordinary activities. The tax charge must distinguish between that of the group (being holding company and subsidiary) and the share of the tax charge of associated companies.

(d)   Extraordinary items. These will consist of the holding company's extraordinary items together with the *group share* of the subsidiary and the *group share* of associated companies.

(e)   Statutory disclosures. The statutory disclosures for depreciation, auditors' remuneration, directors' emoluments etc., should not include any amounts relating to associated companies. They will consist only of the holding company and subsidiary (but don't forget the exception relating to directors' emoluments which should be only the emoluments of holding company's directors).

(f)   Profit dealt with by the holding company. This will be the profit shown by the holding company's profit and loss account including dividends receivable from both subsidiary and associated companies and is, of course, disclosed by note only.

(g) Retained profit for the year. SSAP 1 requires disclosure of profits for the year retained by associated companies. This will simply be the *group share* of the retained profits of the associated company.

(h) Retained profits at end of year. SSAP 1 also requires disclosure of the investing group's share of the post-acquisition accumulated reserves of associated companies.

9.6 Illustration

You are presented with the following information from which you are required to prepare the consolidated profit and loss account and consolidated balance sheet of Hartleys Ltd and its subsidiary company Samuel Smith Ltd. Your answer should also incorporate the results of Adnams Ltd, an associated company, in accordance with standard accounting practice.

Balance sheet as at 31 December 19X6

	Hartleys Ltd £	Samuel Smith Ltd £	Adnams Ltd £
Fixed assets	173,000	74,000	11,000
30,000 shares in Samuel Smith Ltd	35,000		
4,000 shares in Adnams Ltd	7,000		
Current assets	21,000	36,000	29,000
	236,000	110,000	40,000
Creditors	(20,000)	(32,000)	(6,000)
Corporation tax	(9,000)	(11,000)	(7,000)
Proposed dividend	(10,000)	—	(4,000)
	197,000	67,000	23,000
Capital and reserves:			
Called-up share capital (£1 ordinary shares)	100,000	40,000	10,000
General reserve	60,000	—	—
Profit and loss account	37,000	27,000	13,000
	197,000	67,000	23,000

Profit and loss account for the year ended 31 December 19X6

	Hartleys Ltd £	Samuel Smith Ltd £	Adnams Ltd £
Operating profit, after charging:	26,000	30,000	20,000
Depreciation	2,000	11,000	1,200
Auditors' remuneration and expenses	1,000	1,500	500
Directors' emoluments	9,000	2,000	3,000
Dividends from Samuel Smith Ltd	6,000		
Dividends from Adnams Ltd	4,000		
Profit before taxation	36,000	30,000	20,000
Tax	(9,000)	(11,000)	(7,000)
Profit after taxation	27,000	19,000	13,000
Dividend paid	—	(8,000)	(6,000)
Dividend proposed	(10,000)	—	(4,000)
Retained profit for the year	17,000	11,000	3,000
Retained profits brought forward	20,000	16,000	10,000
Retained profits carried forward	37,000	27,000	13,000

You are given the following additional information:

(a)   Hartleys Ltd purchased its investments two years ago when the relevant balances on the profit and loss accounts were Samuel Smith Ltd £12,000 and Adnams Ltd £8,000.

(b)   The companies do not trade with one another.

(c)   None of the directors of Hartleys Ltd is a director either of Samuel Smith Ltd or of Adnams Ltd.

Solution

Hartleys Ltd
Consolidated profit and loss account for the year ended 31 December 19X6

	£	£
Operating profit		56,000
Income from shares in related companies		8,000
		————
Profit on ordinary activities before taxation (Note 1)		64,000
Tax on profit on ordinaty activities:		
Group	20,000	
Related companies	2,800	
	———	(22,800)
		————
Profit on ordinary activities after taxation		41,200
Minority interests		(4,750)
		————
Profit attributable to members of holding company (Note 2)		36,450
Dividend proposed		10,000
		————
Retained profit for the year (Note 3)		26,450
Retained profits brought forward		23,800
		————
Retained profits carried forward		50,250
		————

Notes

1 Profit on ordinary activities before taxation is stated after charging:

	£
Depreciation	13,000
Auditors' remuneration and expenses	2,500
Directors' emoluments	9,000

2 Of the profit attributable to the members of the holding company, £27,000 has been dealt with in the accounts of Hartleys Ltd.

3 Of the retained profit for the year, £1,200 has been retained by the associated company.

Workings (to Profit and Loss Account)

1 Share of operating profit of Adnams Ltd
   40% × £20,000   £8,000

2 Share of taxation charge of Adnams Ltd
   40% × £7,000   £2,800

3   Minority interests
     25% × £19,000   £4,750

4   Retained profits brought forward

                                                                            £
     Hartleys Ltd   20,000
     Samuel Smith Ltd (75% × (£16,000 − £12,000))   3,000
     Adnams Ltd (40% × (£10,000 − £8,000))   800
                                                                      ───────
                                                                       23,800
                                                                      ═══════

5   Retained profits carried forward

                                                                            £
     Hartleys Ltd   37,000
     Samuel Smith Ltd (75% × (£27,000 − £12,000))   11,250
                                                                      ───────
                                                                       48,250
     Adnams Ltd (40% × (£13,000 − £8,000))   2,000
                                                                      ───────
                                                                       50,250
                                                                      ═══════

Hartleys Ltd
Consolidated balance sheet at 31 December 19X6

	£	£	£
Fixed assets:			
Tangible assets			247,000
Investments in related company (Note 1)			9,000
			256,000
Current assets		57,000	
Creditors: amounts falling due within one year:			
Trade creditors	52,000		
Taxation	20,000		
Proposed dividend	10,000		
		82,000	
Net current liabilities			(25,000)
Total assets less current liabilities			231,000
Capital and reserves:			
Called-up share capital (£1 ordinary shares)			100,000
General reserve			60,000
Capital reserve arising on consolidation			4,000
Profit and loss account (Note 2)			50,250
			214,250
Minority interests			16,750
			231,000

Notes

1 Investment in related company. Hartleys Ltd owns 40% of the ordinary share capital of Adnams Ltd which has been treated as an associated company under SSAP 1 using the equity method of accounting. The investment is stated at:

	£
Group share of net assets (40% × £23,000)	9,200
Discount on acquisition (£7,000 − 40% × £18,000)	(200)
	9,000

2 Profit and loss account. Retained profits at 31 December 19X6 include £2,000 retained by the associated company.

Workings (to Balance Sheet)

Cost of control account

	£		£
Investment in Samuel Smith Ltd	35,000	Share capital	30,000
Capital reserve arising	4,000	Profit and loss account	9,000
	39,000		39,000

Minority interest account

	£		£
Consolidated balance sheet	16,750	Share capital	10,000
		Profit and loss account	6,750
	16,750		16,750

Consolidated profit and loss account

	£		£
Hartleys Ltd		Balance brought forward	37,000
		Share of post-acquisition	
		Profits of Adnams Ltd	2,000
Samuel Smith Ltd			
Cost of control account		Balance brought forward	27,000
(75% × £12,000)	9,000		
Minority interest account			
(25% × £27,000)	6,750		
Consolidated balance sheet	50,250		
	66,000		66,000

Not all the above workings are necessary, because, having already prepared the consolidated profit and loss account, the only figures left to calculate are the capital reserve arising on consolidation and the minority interests to be included in the consolidated balance sheet. Therefore the only *necessary* additional workings would be shown as follows:

Adjustment account

	£		£
Shares in Samuel Smith Ltd	35,000	Share capital	30,000
Capital reserve arising	4,000	Profit and loss account	
		(75% × £12,000)	9,000
	39,000		39,000

Minority interest account

	£		£
Consolidated balance sheet	16,750	Share capital	10,000
		Profit and loss account	
		(25% × £27,000)	6,750
	16,750		16,750

9.7   Accounts of companies with associates but without subsidiaries

If a company has associates but no subsidiaries, it will not prepare group accounts. SSAP 1 still requires it to disclose information about associates by preparing a separate profit and loss account or by adding the information in supplementary form to its own profit and loss account in such a way that its share of the profits of the associated companies is not treated as realised.

In such a situation then, the profit and loss account is credited with dividends receivable only and a supplementary statement may be added showing the interest in the associate as in the following illustrative note. (The related profit and loss account is not reproduced.)

9.7.1   Illustration

Company's interest in Assoc Ltd. The company has a 25% holding in Assoc Ltd. The above profit and loss account only includes dividends receivable from this investment. The company's share of profit of Assoc Ltd is as follows:

25% share of:	£000
Profit before taxation	75,000
Taxation	24,000
	59,000
Extraordinary items	4,000
	63,000
Dividends	40,000
Retained profit	23,000

9.8   Summary

Associated companies appear very frequently in examination questions. It is essential for you to understand the treatment required by SSAP 1 and to practise it. Attempt practice questions 23 to 27, then try revision questions 28 to 30.

10 Requirements of the Companies Act 1985, SSAP 14 and the EEC Seventh Directive

10.1 Introduction

Some working definitions of 'holding company', 'subsidiary company' and other relevant terms were given in chapter 2. These have been sufficient for the purpose of our studies so far, but it is now necessary to add the more elaborate statutory definitions and the other requirements of the Companies Act 1985, SSAP 14 and the EEC Seventh Directive.

10.2 Companies Act 1985

10.2.1 Requirement to prepare group accounts

The Companies Act 1985, s. 229, requires a company with subsidiaries to prepare group accounts, subject to the following exceptions:

(a) A company which is itself the *wholly owned* subsidiary of another body corporate incorporated in Great Britain need not do so (s. 229(1)). This subsection exempts from the requirement a company in the following situation:

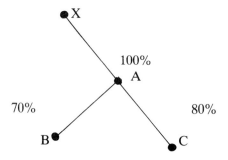

X has to prepare group accounts for the four-company group XABC, but A does not have to prepare separate group accounts for the subgroup ABC, because X owns 100% of A and there is thus no minority with an interest in the separate affairs of ABC. If the structure is:

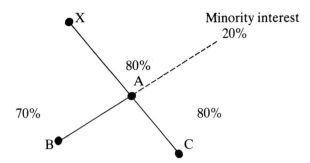

then clearly the 20% minority interest in A has a legitimate interest in seeing group accounts covering the subgroup ABC.

(b)   Group accounts need not deal with a subsidiary if the holding company's directors are of the opinion that:

    (i)   it is impracticable, or would be of no real value to the holding company's members, in view of the insignificant amounts involved, or

    (ii)   it would involve expense or delay out of proportion to the value to members, or

    (iii) the result would be misleading, or harmful to the business of the holding company or any of its subsidiaries, or

    (iv)   the business of the holding company and that of the subsidiary are so different that they cannot reasonably be treated as a single undertaking.

The approval of the Department of Trade and Industry is required if exemption is based on the ground that the result would be harmful or on the ground of difference between the business of the holding company and that of the subsidiary. The accounting treatment to be adopted when subsidiaries are excluded from consolidation is dealt with in SSAP 14 (see 10.3).

If subsidiaries are excluded from consolidation, para. 69 of sch. 4 to the Companies Act 1985 requires the group accounts to disclose by note:

(a)   the reasons for any non-consolidation;

(b)   details of any audit qualification that is material for the members of the holding company;

(c)   holding company's aggregate total investment in the shares of the subsidiaries, valued under the equity method of accounting.

See also 10.3.2 for details of disclosures required in this situation by SSAP 14.

The Companies Act 1985, s. 229, states that the normal form of group accounts should be a consolidated profit and loss account and balance sheet. However, if the directors are of the opinion that the information needs of the members of the holding company would be better served by some other method of presentation, group accounts could consist of:

(a)   More than one set of consolidated accounts covering different groups of subsidiaries.
(b)   Separate accounts for each subsidiary.
(c)   Statements expanding the information in the holding company's own financial statements.

10.2.2   Definition of subsidiary company

The working definition of 'subsidiary' given in chapter 2 was any company in which more than 50% of the called-up equity share capital was held. This is virtually always the only relevant part of the statutory definition for computational questions on group accounts. However, s. 736 of the Companies Act 1985 states that a company will also be a subsidiary of another company if that other company:

(a)   holds more than half in nominal value of its equity share capital, or
(b)   is a member of it and controls the composition of its board of directors, or
(c)   is the holding company of the subsidiary's own holding company (the sub-subsidiary situation).

Nominee shareholdings are included in the reckoning, but shares held in a fiduciary capacity (e.g., as trustee) are not.

These definitions as incorporated in Companies Act 1985 have remained unchanged since 1948, and some companies have in recent years exploited the loopholes in these requirements by establishing entities outside the statutory definition which are then excluded from the group accounts. For example, an unincorporated body will legally be excluded. It has proved very difficult to establish a clear definition which prevents such abuses.

10.2.3   Accounting dates of group companies

The Companies Act 1985, s. 227(4), requires the directors of a holding company to secure that all group companies have the same accounting date, unless 'in their opinion there are good reasons against it'. Paragraph 70 of sch. 4 to the Act requires the disclosure by note to the company's accounts (or group accounts) of the directors' reasons for maintaining different accounting dates, and also the dates of the subsidiaries' financial years ending last before that of the holding company (or the earliest and latest of such dates where there are many of them).

The discretion granted to directors by s. 227(4) means that some group companies may have differing accounting dates. To cover this situation, s. 230(7) provides that where accounting dates differ, the group accounts should normally include the subsidiary's accounts for its financial year ending last before the holding company's accounting date. This rule may be modified, subject to approval by the Department of Trade and Industry, if the circumstances justify it.

10.2.4   Disclosure requirements as regards group accounts

Some of the points listed in this section have already been mentioned earlier. They are repeated here for convenience so that you can refer to all relevant disclosure requirements in one place.

In general, group accounts must combine the information contained in the separate accounts of the group companies, with any adjustments that the directors of the holding company consider necessary. In other words, the disclosure requirements for a group are the same, so far as practicable, as those for an individual company.

Some points to note are:

(a)   Details of subsidiaries. Names of principal subsidiaries, their country of incorporation and proportion of shares held must be disclosed by note unless, with the agreement of the Department of Trade and Industry, it is considered that to do so would be harmful to the business of a group company.

(b)   Reasons for differences in accounting date of group companies. The directors' reasons for not standardising the accounting dates of group companies must be stated, along with the actual accounting dates (or earliest and latest if there are many) of group companies with differing accounting dates.

(c)   For subsidiaries not consolidated there must be disclosed:

    (i)   Reasons for non-consolidation.

    (ii)   Details of any audit qualification on the accounts of such a subsidiary, if material to the members of the holding company.

    (iii)   Holding company's aggregate total investment in the shares of the subsidiaries, valued by the equity method of accounting.

(d)   Although the consolidated profit and loss account will include among the expenses the aggregate directors' remuneration for all directors of all group companies, the note giving further details of directors' remuneration (highest-paid director, bands of £5,000 etc.) should relate to amounts received by the *directors of the holding company from all group companies*. Those interested in information about the directors of subsidiaries will obtain the information from the individual accounts of those subsidiaries. See 10.3.4 for the disclosure requirements of SSAP 14.

10.3   SSAP 14 'Group Accounts'

10.3.1   Basic requirements

SSAP 14 was introduced in 1978 and compliance with its provisions ensures compliance with International Accounting Standard 3 'Consolidated financial statements' (IAS 3). In some respects it merely reiterates points already required by the Companies Act 1985 but it does add some useful points of its own:

(a)   Format of group accounts. Group accounts should normally be prepared in the form of consolidated financial statements (s. 229 of the Companies Act 1985 allows other possibilities — see 10.2.1 — but it is rare in practice to find other forms).

(b)   Uniform accounting policies. A holding company should normally follow uniform group accounting policies when preparing consolidated financial statements. This is normally achieved in practice by requiring the subsidiaries to follow uniform accounting practices in preparing their own financial statements. If they do not, the holding company will need to make appropriate adjustments in preparing the group financial statements. If, exceptionally, the adoption of uniform accounting policies is not practicable in the group financial statements, there must be disclosure of:

   (i)   the different accounting policies used;

   (ii)   the amounts of assets and liabilities involved, and if possible an indication of the effect on results and net assets of the adoption of the different policies;

   (iii) the reasons for the different treatment.

(c)   Group accounting periods and dates. The Companies Act 1985, s. 227(4), requires directors to ensure that group companies have the same accounting period and date, but gives discretion for the directors to depart from the requirement as long as the reasons and actual accounting dates are disclosed. SSAP 14 reiterates this requirement and adds a requirement for 'appropriate adjustments to be made to the consolidated financial statements for any abnormal transactions in the intervening period'. (This should prevent 'window-dressing' transactions between group companies, by which, for example, the same asset could feature in two balance sheets being consolidated.) SSAP 14 further requires disclosure, for each principal subsidiary with a different accounting date, of:

   (i)   its name,
   (ii)   its accounting date,
   (iii) the reason for using a different accounting date.

(Items (ii) and (iii) are already required by the Companies Act 1985, sch. 4, para. 70).

10.3.2   Exclusion of subsidiaries from consolidation

The Companies Act 1985, s. 229, sets up the grounds on which, in law, subsidiaries may be excluded from consolidation. SSAP 14 deals with four situations in which subsidiaries are to be excluded:

   (a)   dissimilar activities,
   (b)   lack of effective control,
   (c)   severe restrictions on control,
   (d)   when control is temporary.

It is not open to an SSAP to add to a limited statutory list of grounds for exclusion, so items (b) to (d) must be regarded as examples of situations when it would be misleading to consolidate.

Dissimilar activities

Many groups are diversified with subsidiaries operating in different industries. Such diversification is not sufficient to justify exclusion on grounds of dissimilar activities. What the standard envisages here is some gross dissimilarity in the businesses and the method of accounting for them. For example, the exclusion of an insurance subsidiary by a manufacturing group would be justified under this heading, although a simple alternative would be to include the subsidiary in the consolidated accounts but to group its assets and liabilities separately.

Where a subsidiary is excluded on this ground the standard requires the value to be included in the consolidated financial statements using the equity method of accounting. In addition, it requires the inclusion of the separate accounts of the subsidiary in the group accounts and the following information:

(a) holding company's interest in the subsidiary;

(b) particulars of intra-group balances;

(c) nature of transactions between the subsidiary and the rest of the group;

(d) a reconciliation between the appropriate share of the net assets shown in the subsidiary's own balance sheet and the value at which the investment is stated in the consolidated accounts.

Lack of effective control

In some cases, although one company is legally the subsidiary of another, the holding company is not in a position to exercise control over the subsidiary. Such a situation arises from the definition of a subsidiary contained in the Companies Act 1985, which is based on the proportion of equity share capital held without consideration of the voting power attached to the shares held.

Thus the following situation could arise: Black Ltd holds shares in another company, White Ltd, as shown below:

	Black's holding	Issued share capital of White
Voting ordinary shares	30,000	100,000
Non-voting ordinary shares	50,000	50,000
	80,000	150,000

Black holds 80,000 out of 150,000 shares and hence White is a subsidiary. However, Black holds only 30,000 out of 100,000 of the voting shares and hence is not in a position to exercise control. Indeed, another company holding between 50,000 and 70,000 of the voting ordinary shares in White would also have White as its subsidiary!

Where a subsidiary is excluded from the consolidated accounts because of lack of control, SSAP 14 requires one of two accounting treatments. If the investment is sufficient to satisfy the definition of an associated company contained in SSAP 1, the equity method of accounting must be used. If, however, this definition is not satisfied, the investment must be treated as a simple investment included at cost or valuation less any provision required.

Severe restrictions on control

Where a subsidiary operates under severe restrictions which significantly impair control by the holding company over the subsidiary's assets and operations for the foreseeable future, consolidation would be misleading and hence SSAP 14 requires exclusion. Such restrictions could, for example, be met in connection with overseas subsidiaries. The accounting treatment required here is to show the investment at the amount at which it would have appeared if the equity method of accounting had been in use at the date the restrictions came into force. If the value of the investment has fallen below that figure the investment should be written down. In addition to this treatment the standard also requires a note giving some details of the subsidiary, namely:

(a)   net assets;

(b)   profits or losses for the period;

(c)   any amount included in the consolidated accounts in respect of dividends received in the period and amounts written off.

Thus users are given some information about the particular subsidiary although, after the date the restrictions came into force, credit is only taken for dividends received. A difficult problem in practice may be deciding when restrictions become long-term.

Temporary control

For exclusion under this heading there must have been an intention that the control would be temporary at the date of acquisition. So if a company has had a subsidiary for many years and then decides to dispose of it in a few months' time this does not constitute temporary control and hence does not justify exclusion.

Where control is temporary, the investment should be shown in the consolidated accounts as a current asset at the lower of cost and market value.

10.3.3   Additional disclosures

In all cases in which subsidiaries are excluded from consolidation, SSAP 14 requires certain additional information to be disclosed:

(a)   reasons for exclusion of subsidiary;
(b)   names of the principal subsidiaries excluded;
(c)   premium or discount on acquisition;
(d)   additional information required by the Companies Act 1985 (see 10.2.1).

This last point reiterates the requirement that companies must comply not only with the provisions of SSAP 14 but also with the provisions of the Companies Act 1985.

10.3.4   Changes in the composition of a group

SSAP 14 sets out three standard practices to be used when companies enter or leave a group:

(a)   It defines the effective date of such an event.

(b)   It requires disclosure of the effect of material acquisitions and disposals in the consolidated financial statements.

(c)   It defines how, on an acquisition, the purchase consideration is to be allocated among the underlying assets acquired.

Effective date of acquisition or disposal

SSAP 14 defines the effective date of acquisition or disposal of a subsidiary as the earlier of:

(a)   the date on which consideration passes; or
(b)   the date on which an offer becomes unconditional.

This clear definition prevents an abuse previously practised by some companies whereby an acquisition during an accounting period has been backdated so that the whole of the year's profits of the acquired company were included in consolidated profit and loss account instead of merely the post-acquisition proportion.

Disclosure of effects of acquisition or disposal

In the case of material additions to or disposals from the group, the consolidated financial statements should contain sufficient information about the results of the subsidiaries acquired or sold to enable shareholders to appreciate the effect on the consolidated results.

Where there is a material disposal, the consolidated profit and loss account should include:

(a)   the subsidiary's results up to the date of disposal; and

(b)   the gain or loss on the sale of the investment, being the difference at the time of sale between:

(i)   proceeds of sale,

(ii)   holding company's share of its net assets together with any premium (less any amounts written off) or discount on acquisition.

The above provisions of SSAP 14 need to be considered in conjunction with those of SSAP 6 (revised 1986). SSAP 6 requires the profit or loss *from* a terminated activity to be regarded as part of the ordinary activities of the business, with separate disclosure to enable the results of continuing operations to be ascertained. Item (a) above, the sold subsidiary's results up to the date of disposal, would form part of the profit or loss on ordinary activities, with separate disclosure of the amount, if material, to satisfy both SSAP 14 and SSAP 6.

SSAP 6 gives the profit or loss on *disposal of* a subsidiary as an example of an extraordinary item, thus item (b) above will normally be included as such in the consolidated profit and loss account.

Allocation of purchase consideration on acquisition

SSAP 14 requires the purchase consideration on an acquisition to be allocated between the underlying net tangible and intangible assets other than goodwill on the basis of their *fair value to the acquiring company*. Any difference between the purchase consideration and the value ascribed to net tangible and identifiable intangible assets, such as trade marks, patents or development expenditure, will represent premium or discount on acquisition. SSAP 22 'Accounting for goodwill' (issued 1984) requires any premium so arising (goodwill) to be eliminated from the accounts either by immediate write-off against reserves (the preferred method) or by amortisation through the profit and loss account over its useful economic life. A discount on acquisition (called in SSAP 22 'negative goodwill') should be credited directly to an unrealised reserve.

10.3.5   Sundry matters dealt with in SSAP 14

Disclosure of principal subsidiaries

The names of the principal subsidiaries should be disclosed, with the proportion of the nominal value of the shares issued held by the group (as in Companies Act 1985, see 10.2.4). SSAP 14 also requires an indication of the nature of each subsidiary's business.

Outside or minority interests in the consolidated balance sheet

Minority interests should be disclosed separately in the consolidated balance sheet and should not be shown as part of shareholders' funds. Debit balances should be recognised only if there is a binding obligation on minority shareholders to make good losses incurred, which they have the resources to meet.

Outside or minority interests in the consolidated profit and loss account

Profits and losses attributable to minority interests should be shown separately in the consolidated profit and loss account after arriving at group profit or loss after tax but before extraordinary items. Minority interests in extraordinary items should be deducted from the related amounts in the consolidated profit and loss account.

Restrictions on distributions

The extent of any restrictions on the ability of the holding company to distribute retained profits of the group (other than those shown as non-distributable) because of statutory, contractual or exchange control restrictions should be indicated.

10.4   The EEC Seventh Directive

The EEC Seventh Directive was passed by the EEC Council of Ministers in June 1983, and should become law in member States by 1 January 1988, to apply to company accounts for periods commencing in 1990 at the latest. At the time of writing (October 1987) it appears that legislation is unlikely to be introduced in the UK before late 1988 or early 1989.

The Seventh Directive will make a number of fairly small changes to UK law and practice:

10.4.1   Definition of 'control' and requirement to consolidate

The Seventh Directive requires consolidation when the parent company:

(a)   has a majority of voting rights; *or*

(b)   is a member and has the right to appoint or remove a majority of the directors; *or*

(c)   is a member and has a right to exercise a dominant influence as a result of a 'control contract'; *or*

(d)   is a member and as the result of an agreement with other shareholders has the right to control alone a majority of voting rights.

Items (c) and (d) have little relevance to practice in the UK. Note the difference in (a) from the requirements of the Companies Act 1985 (see 10.2.2) — the Seventh Directive refers to *voting rights* whereas the Companies Act 1985, s. 736, refers to *equity holdings*.

Nominee shareholders must be included.

The Seventh Directive *requires* the consolidation of foreign subsidiaries and of sub-subsidiaries.

10.4.2   Exemption from consolidation

'Small' groups of companies

Exemption *may* be granted to unlisted companies which meet two out of the three criteria for 'medium-sized' companies:

(a)   Turnover not over £8 million.
(b)   Balance sheet total not over £3.9 million.
(c)   Number of employees not over 250.

For 10 years from 1 January 1990 the first two limits may be mutiplied by 2.5 and the employee limit raised to 500.

Such companies would not be required to produce group accounts at all. It remains to be seen whether this exemption will be adopted in the UK legislation.

Wholly owned subsidiaries

Exemption *must* be granted to wholly owned subsidiaries and extended to 90% subsidiaries if the minority agrees. Companies have until the year 2000 to apply the exemption to 90% subsidiaries. Listed companies need not be exempted.

Exclusion of subsidiaries from consolidation

Subsidiaries need not be consolidated:

(a)   Where the amounts are not material.
(b)   If there are severe long-term restrictions on control.
(c)   If consolidation would result in undue expense or delay.
(d)   If shares are held for subsequent resale.

Different nature of business

If the nature of its business is different the subsidiary *must not* be consolidated. This provision does not apply to cases where two different manufacturing businesses are carried on, or where one company is engaged in retailing while another is in manufacturing. The object is to exclude banking companies or insurance companies from consolidation with trading companies, for example. The reason for non-consolidation must be stated.

10.4.3   Consolidation procedures

The Seventh Directive requires the application of certain consolidation procedures, most of which are normal UK practice.

Assets and liabilities in consolidated balance sheet

Assets and liabilities should be incorporated in the balance sheet in full (i.e., no proportional consolidation), though proportional consolidation is permitted if there is joint management of a company by more than one company (e.g., a consortium). Any minority interest has to be shown separately.

Profits and losses in consolidated profit and loss account

The consolidated profit and loss account *must* include the full amount of income and expenditure of companies in the group, with deduction of minority interest.

Piecemeal acquisitions

If acquisitions are piecemeal, it is acceptable to use either of the bases of computing goodwill explained in chapter 6.

Calculation of goodwill or reserve on consolidation — acquisition method

If the *acquisition* method of consolidation is used, the book value of shares issued must be set off against the proportion of capital and reserves of the subsidiary. The balance must be shown separately in the consolidated balance sheet, after first adjusting the values of under or over-valued assets. A debit balance (goodwill) would be written off either immediately or by amortisation as required by SSAP 22 and the Companies Act 1985. The Seventh Directive does, however, *allow a credit balance to be credited to consolidated profit and loss account* if it arose because of 'expectation of loss' (i.e., the company was bought at a cheap price because of expected losses, and the credit to consolidated profit and loss account offsets those losses, or if the credit corresponds to a realised gain.

Merger method of consolidation

It is permissible to use the merger method of consolidation provided at least 90% of the shares are being acquired and the cash element in the consideration does not exceed 10%. Any balance arising (see chapter 12) is to be debited or credited to consolidated reserves.

Unrealised profit on intra-group transactions

Any material unrealised profit on intra-group transactions must be eliminated. It is permissible to allow either the whole of the unrealised profit or only the group's proportion to be eliminated. Permission may be granted to exclude from this requirement a profit arising from a transaction according to normal market conditions where elimination would involve undue expense.

Date of consolidation

Consolidated accounts *must* be made up to the parent company's accounting date, except that permission may be granted to use some other date if, for example, many subsidiaries use it. If the balance sheet date of a subsidiary precedes that of the consolidated balance sheet by more than three months, interim accounts to the consolidation date must be prepared.

Changes in subsidiaries

Details of the effect of changes in subsidiaries must be disclosed, perhaps by preparing an adjusted opening consolidated balance sheet or an adjusted consolidated balance sheet.

Valuation of assets

Group assets should generally be valued as in the parent company's accounts. This could require revaluation of subsidiaries' assets.

Deferred tax

Deferred tax must be allowed for.

Associated companies

Associated companies (defined broadly as in SSAP 1) should be included in group accounts under the equity basis of accounting.

10.4.4   Disclosures to be shown by note

Notes to the consolidated accounts should disclose:

(a)   Valuation methods.

(b)   Basis of translation of foreign currency.

(c)   Names and registered offices of group companies and proportion of capital held. (This information must also be given for companies excluded from consolidation, with reasons for their exclusion.)*

(d)   Names and registered offices of associated companies and proportion of capital held (including those omitted on ground of non-materiality).*

(e)   Long-term loans (over five years).

(f)   Secured loans, with details of security.

(g)   Financial commitments not provided for in the accounts.

(h)   Turnover, analysed by activity and by geographical markets.*

(i)   Average number of employees and staff costs.

(j)   Details of deferred tax.

(k)   Emoluments of directors.

(l)   Loans to directors.

*These items need not be given if their disclosure would be 'seriously prejudicial' to the interests of the group.

10.4.5   Contents of the consolidated annual report

The consolidated annual report must provide:

(a)   A fair view of the development of the group over the period.
(b)   Details of significant post balance sheet events.
(c)   Details of the company's activities in research and development.
(d)   Details of any shares in the parent company owned by subsidiaries.

10.4.6   Audit requirement

The consolidated accounts must be audited.

10.4.7   Availability of copies

The consolidated accounts must be published, and copies must be made available at a figure not exceeding the administrative cost.

10.4.8   Comment

You can see from studying these requirements that they won't have a dramatic effect on UK consolidation practice. A few loose areas will be tightened up, and some practices which are currently in SSAPs or merely part of normal consolidation procedure will become statutory.

Notice in 10.4.2 that the grounds for non-consolidation will be modified. Some of the new grounds are already in SSAP 1. It would appear that the exemption on grounds of harm to the interests of the group may have to disappear, though the relaxation to the disclosure requirements (see 10.4.4) will limit the damage this might cause.

The specified consolidation procedures will result in some changes. Note the stipulation as to the method of preparing the consolidated profit and loss account (see 10.4.3) and the treatment to be applied to goodwill or reserve on consolidation. The most interesting provisions here are the different treatment laid down depending on whether the acquisition method or the merger method is used, and the idea of allowing a 'reserve on consolidation' to be credited directly to profit and loss account in carefully defined circumstances (see 10.4.3).

The provisions regarding dates of consolidation will require some changes, not least to reflect the requirement for interim accounts for subsidiaries whose accounting dates differ by more than three months from the consolidated balance sheet date.

10.5   Summary

Questions which are mainly computational often have a relatively small part devoted to statutory and other requirements governing group accounts. In addition, such papers as the CACA Level 2 'Regulatory framework of accounting' and Level 3 'Advanced financial accounting' often include wholly non-computational questions on group accounts and, of course, other matters. The purpose of this chapter is to provide the raw material for answers to these questions.

Practice questions 31 to 33.

11 Disposal of shares in subsidiaries

11.1 Introduction

Two forms of disposal of shares in subsidiaries must be considered:

(a)   A sale of the entire holding in the subsidiary.
(b)   A partial sale.

Partial sales may have three end results:

(a)   Control is retained with a smaller shareholding (i.e., more than 50% of the holding is retained).

(b)   The sale converts a subsidiary into an associated company (i.e., 20-50% of the holding is retained).

(c)   The sale converts a controlling interest into a simple investment (i.e., less than 20% of the holding is retained).

11.2   The regulatory background

11.2.1   SSAP 14

Methods of calculating profit or loss

SSAP 14 defines how the profit or loss on a disposal is to be calculated for the consolidated profit and loss account. Paragraph 31 states:

> . . . the consolidated profit and loss account should include . . . the gain or loss on the sale of the investment, being the difference at the time of the sale between:
>
> (i)   the proceeds of the sale and
> (ii)   the holding company's share of its net assets together with any premium (less any amounts written off) or discount on acquisition.

Date of disposal

Under SSAP 14, the date of disposal is the earlier of the date consideration passes and the date the offer becomes unconditional.

Inclusion of results of sold subsidiary

The profit or loss of the subsidiary disposed of up to the date of disposal must be included in the consolidated profit and loss account.

Inclusion of gain or loss on disposal

The gain or loss on disposal must be included in the consolidated profit and loss account, usually as an extraordinary item (see 11.2.2).

11.2.2 SSAP 6

Under SSAP 6 (revised 1986), the profit or loss made by the subsidiary must be included as part of profit on ordinary activities, and normally the profit or loss on the disposal itself must be included as an extraordinary item.

11.3 Sale of the entire holding

11.3.1 Position in the holding company's own accounts

In the holding company's own accounts, the profit or loss on the disposal is the difference between the original cost of the shares and the proceeds of sale.

It is important to make this calculation, because any tax payable on the profit will be based upon it (subject, of course, to indexation, which may certainly be ignored in answering a computational accounting question).

11.3.2 Position as regards the group

As stated in 11.2.1, under SSAP 14, the profit or loss for the group on the sale of a subsidiary is the difference, *at the time of sale*, between the proceeds of sale and the group's share of the net assets of the subsidiary, together with any premium (less amounts written off) or discount on acquisition.

This is because, in the consolidated accounts credit has already been taken, through the consolidated profit and loss account, for the group's share of the subsidiary's post-acquisition profit. Therefore, this amount must be subtracted from the profit made by the holding company to arrive at the profit to be taken as made by the group on the sale in the consolidated profit and loss account.

It is vital to appreciate that the profit disclosed under the SSAP 14 method plus the proportion of the post-acquisition profits of the subsidiary disposed of will always equal the profit calculated for the holding company's own accounts (proceeds minus cost).

If the sale is part of the way through the accounting period then the post-acquisition profit at the beginning of that period will form part of the retained profit brought forward and the profit for the current period to the date of sale will be included as part of the profit on ordinary activities of the group.

Study the illustration below.

11.3.3   Illustration

H Ltd owns 100% of S Ltd's £100,000 share capital. The shares were acquired for £180,000 at a time when the reserves of S Ltd were £60,000. At 31 December 19X6 H Ltd sells the shares for £250,000. At this date the reserves of S Ltd had risen to £100,000, of which £10,000 represented profit for the year to that date, and goodwill arising on the acquisition had not been written off.

The profit arising on the sale is clearly:

	£000
Proceeds	250
Cost	180
Profit on sale	70

To calculate the profit to be disclosed under SSAP 14, two figures must be calculated

(i)   Net assets at date of sale:

	£000
Share capital	100
Reserves	100
Net assets at date of sale	200

(ii)   Goodwill on acquisition:

	£000
Cost of shares	180
Share capital + reserves at acquisition	160
Goodwill at acquisition	20

The profit on sale in accordance with SSAP 14 is therefore:

	£000	£000
Proceeds of sale		250
Net assets at date of sale	200	
Goodwill on acquisition	20	220
Profit per SSAP 14		30

S Ltd's profit for the year of £10,000 will be reported as part of the group's profit for the year. S Ltd's post-acquisition retained profits of £30,000 will be reported as part of the group's retained profit brought forward.

These three amounts may be regarded as elements of the overall profit made on the sale (proceeds minus cost):

	£000	£000
SSAP 14 profit		30
Retained profit of S:		
Brought forward	30	
For year 19X6	10	
	—	40
Total profit		70

11.3.4 Illustration

Q Ltd has two subsidiaries R Ltd and S Ltd, both wholly owned and both acquired on 1 January 19X6. At 31 December 19X6 the balance sheets of the three companies were as follows:

	Q Ltd £000	R Ltd £000	S Ltd £000
Sundry net assets	100	40	30
Investment in R Ltd: cost	30		
Investment in S Ltd: cost	18		
	148	40	30
Share capital	100	20	10
Profit and loss account:			
At 1 January 19X6	28	5	6
Profit for year	20	15	14
	148	40	30

At 31 December 19X6 Q Ltd disposed of its entire holding in S Ltd for £40,000. Prepare a consolidated profit and loss account and balance sheet at this date.

Q Ltd and its subsidiary
Consolidated profit and loss account for the year ended 31 December 19X6

	£000
Profit for year (including S Ltd per SSAP 14)	49
Extraordinary item:	
Profit on sale of subsidiary	
(proceeds £40,000 less net assets at date of sale £30,000 + goodwill £2,000)	8
	57
Retained profit brought forward (Q only as R and S were both acquired on 1 January 19X6)	28
Retained profit carried forward	85

Consolidated balance sheet as at 31 December 19X6

	£000
Goodwill on consolidation (W1)	5
Sundry net assets (Q £100,000 + £40,000 proceeds + R £40,000)	180
	185
Share capital	100
Profit and loss account	85
	185

Workings

1   Calculation of goodwill on acquisition:

	£000
R: Cost of shares	30
Share capital + reserves at acquisition	25
	5
S: Cost of shares	18
Share capital + reserves at acquisition	16
	2
The profit made by Q Ltd is:	
Proceeds of sale	40
Cost	18
	22

This £22,000 is disclosed in the profit and loss account, complying with SSAP 14 as:

Profit for year included in profit on ordinary activities	14
Profit on sale based on net assets at date of sale	8
	22

In calculating the profit made by Q Ltd the £14,000 increase in net assets of S Ltd since acquisition forms part of the profit calculation, while in the SSAP 14 calculation the £14,000 is reported as part of the profit for the year.

11.3.5   Illustration

Let us now see the effect if the goodwill arising on consolidation had been written off immediately to reserves. The goodwill of S Ltd (£2,000) will now not enter into the SSAP 14 calculation and the profit under SSAP 14 will be £10,000. Profit and loss account will be reduced by £7,000 to write off the goodwill arising on both acquisitions, and the goodwill of £5,000 appearing in the consolidated balance sheet in illustration 11.3.4 will disappear. The consolidated accounts will become:

Q Ltd and its subsidiary
Consolidated profit and loss account for the year ended 31 December 19X6

	£000
Profit for year	49
Extraordinary item:	
Profit on sale of subsidiary (proceeds £40,000 less net assets at	
date of sale £30,000)	10
	—
	59
Retained profit brought forward (Q only)	28
	—
	87
	—

Consolidated balance sheet as at 31 December 19X6

	£000	£000
Sundry net assets		180
		—
Share capital		100
Profit and loss account	87	
Less: goodwill written off	7	80
	—	—
		180
		—

With the goodwill written off, the total group profit on the sale is £24,000:

	£000	£000
Proceeds of sale		40
Cost	18	
Less: goodwill written off	2	16
	—	—
		24
		—

	£000
This is disclosed in the profit and loss account as:	
Profit for year included in profit on ordinary activities	14
Profit on sale	10
	—
	24
	—

11.3.6   Illustration

The summarised balance sheets of H Ltd and its subsidiaries X Ltd and Y Ltd are as follows:

Summarised balance sheets 31 March 19X7

	H Ltd	X Ltd	Y Ltd
	£000	£000	£000
£1 ordinary shares	10,000	2,000	3,000
Retained earnings	5,000	2,500	1,500
	15,000	4,500	4,500
Net assets	6,000	4,500	4,500
Investments in subsidiaries at cost:			
2,000 shares in X Ltd	4,000		
3,000 shares in Y Ltd	5,000		
	15,000	4,500	4,500

When H Ltd acquired its holding in X and Y their retained profits were £500,000 and £1,000,000 respectively. The consolidated balance sheet on the same date is therefore as follows:

Consolidated balance sheet 31 March 19X7

	£000	£000
Share capital		10,000
Retained profits:		
H	5,000	
X	2,000	
Y	500	
		7,500
		17,500
Net assets		15,000
Goodwill on consolidation:		
X	1,500	
Y	1,000	
		2,500
		17,500

Let us assume that H Ltd sells the whole of its shareholding in X Ltd on 1 April 19X7, the first day after the balance sheet, for £6,500,000. This produces a profit on disposal of £2,500,000 (£6,500,000 − £4,000,000) to be included in the profit and loss account of H Ltd.

In the year ended 31 March 19X8 the results of H Ltd and Y Ltd are as follows:

Profit and loss accounts for year ended 31 March 19X8

	H Ltd £000	Y Ltd £000
Operating profit	2,000	800
Extraordinary profit on sale of shares in X Ltd	2,500	—
	4,500	800

Let us prepare the consolidated balance sheet and profit and loss account of the group at 31 March 19X8.

H Ltd and its subsidiary
Consolidated balance sheet as at 31 March 19X8

	Refer to note	£000
Net assets	1	19,800
Goodwill on consolidation (Y only)		1,000
		20,800
Share capital		10,000
Retained profits	2	10,800
		20,800

Consolidated profit and loss account for the year ended 31 March 19X8

	Refer to note	£000
Operating profit		2,800
Extraordinary item:		
Profit on sale of subsidiary	3	500
		3,300
Retained profits brought forward	4	7,500
		10,800

Notes

1 Net assets	H Ltd	Y Ltd	Total
	£000	£000	£000
As at 31 March 19X7	6,000	4,500	
Received on sale of X Ltd	6,500		
Profit to 31 March 19X8	2,000*	800	
	14,500	5,300	19,800

*We do not include the profit on the sale of X Ltd, because it is, of course, already included as part of the £6,500,000 sale receipts.

2 Retained profits	H Ltd	Y Ltd	Total
	£000	£000	£000
As at 31 March 19X7	5,000	500	
Profit to 31 March 19X8	2,000	800	
Profit on sale of X Ltd	2,500		
	9,500	1,300	10,800

3   Profit on sale of subsidiary (consolidated profit and loss account). There are two ways of calculating this figure:

    (a)   The SSAP 14 way:

	£000	£000
Proceeds of sale		6,500
Net assets at time of sale	4,500	
Goodwill at acquisition	1,500	6,000
Profit on sale		500

    (b)   Profit made by H Ltd   2,500

Less: group's share of post-acquisition profit of X Ltd
    (included in profit brought forward)   2,000

                                                500

4 Retained profits brought forward	£000
H Ltd	5,000
Y Ltd	500
X Ltd (profits to date of sale)	2,000
	7,500

Discussion

There are possibly two points requiring clarification — one minor and one fundamental to an understanding of the subject:

(a) Calculation of net assets. This is the minor point. We are usually given the balance sheets at the date we are required to prepare the consolidated balance sheet but in this case we are not. We have to calculate the net assets by adding the profit for the year and the amount received by H Ltd on the sale of X Ltd to the opening net asset figures.

(b) Treatment of the profit on the sale of X Ltd. This is the fundamental point and it can be a confusing one. We were able to obtain the figure of retained profit at 31 March 19X8 in note 2 by including the whole of the £2.5 million profit made by H Ltd on the sale of X Ltd. How can this be if we are showing only £0.5 million as the profit in the consolidated profit and loss account? The point is that all SSAP 14 is really asking us to do is to *analyse* the total profit of £2.5 million into its components:

	£000
Profit on sale calculated as required by SSAP 14 (note 3)	500
Group's share of post acquisition profit of X Ltd	
(already included in consolidated reserves)	2,000
Total profit made	2,500

Thus the whole £2.5 million finds its way to retained profits in the consolidated balance sheet. It is only in the consolidated profit and loss account that the analysis becomes significant.

In that illustration the goodwill on consolidation had not been written off. Let us see what the effect would have been if it had been written off at the acquisition of both X Ltd and Y Ltd.

The consolidated balance sheet at 31 March 19X7 would have shown retained profits of £5.0 million and the goodwill on consolidation would have disappeared.

The consolidated balance sheet at 31 March 19X8 would become:

H Ltd and its subsidiary
Consolidated balance sheet as at 31 March 19X8

	£000
Net assets	19,800
Share capital	10,000
Retained profits	9,800
	19,800

The profit on sale of the subsidiary for the consolidated profit and loss account (per SSAP 14) would become:

	£000
Proceeds of sale	6,500
Net assets at time of sale	4,500
Profit	2,000

The consolidated profit and loss account would therefore show:

H Ltd and its subsidiary
Consolidated profit and loss account for the year ended 31 March 19X8

	£000	£000
Operating profit		2,800
Extraordinary item:		
Profit on sale of subsidiary (as above)		2,000
		4,800
Retained profit brought forward (W1)		5,000
		9,800

Working

1   Retained profit brought forward

	£000
H Ltd	5,000
Y Ltd	500
X Ltd	2,000
	7,500
Less: goodwill written off	2,500
	5,000

As you can see, the writing off of the goodwill has the effect of increasing the profit to be disclosed under SSAP 14, because the goodwill element is no longer included as part of the cost of the investment.

11.3.7   Disposal during the year

In the above illustration the shares in the subsidiary were sold on the first day of the current year. Although this is a convenient starting-point it will rarely be the case in practice. If disposal occurs during the course of an accounting year, the sale proceeds include not only the post-acquisition profits of the subsidiary retained at the last balance sheet date but also profits earned and retained between that date and the date of disposal. Similarly in order to show a true and fair view of the trading activities of the group, operating profit should include profits or losses of the subsidiary from the start of the year until the date of disposal.

11.3.8   Illustration

Let us assume that the shares in X Ltd were sold for the same amount of £6,500,000 not on 1 April 19X7 but on 31 December 19X7. Let us also assume that the relevant part of the profit and loss account of X Ltd for the year to 31 March 19X8 is as shown below and that the profits accrued evenly over the year:

Profit and loss account for the year to 31 March 19X8

	£000
Operating profit	1,600

For nine months X Ltd was a member of the group. Hence three quarters of X's profit for the year should be included as part of the group operating income. This amount will also form part of the net assets at the date of sale.

The answer will become:

H Ltd and its subsidiary
Consolidated profit and loss account for the year ended 31 March 19X8

	Refer to note	£000
Operating profit	1	4,000
Extraordinary item		
Loss on disposal of subsidiary	2	(700)
		3,300
Retained profits brought forward (as before)		7,500
Retained profits carried forward		10,800

Notes

1   Operating profit

	£000	£000
As before		2,800
9/12 of X Ltd		1,200
		4,000

2   Loss on disposal of subsidiary

(a)   Per SSAP 14:

Proceeds of sale		6,500
Net assets at time of sale (£4,500,000 + 9/12 × £1,600,000)	5,700	
Goodwill at acquisition	1,500	7,200
		(700)

	£000
(b) Profit made by H Ltd	2,500
Less: group's share of post-acquisition profits of X Ltd	
(£2,000,000 + 9/12 × £1,600,000)	3,200
	(700)

11.3.9   Practical problems

Although SSAP 14 requires the inclusion of the profits or losses of subsidiaries in the consolidated profit and loss account up to the date of disposal, there may be considerable problems in achieving this. The reason is that once a holding company has sold its shares in a subsidiary it has no power to require that subsidiary to produce a copy of its financial statements. Hence it might be necessary to delay preparation of the consolidated accounts until the ex subsidiary filed its accounts with the Registrar of Companies! A further problem is that the accounting policies of the ex subsidiary may well have changed under its new ownership.

11.4   Sale of part of shareholding but with retention of control

11.4.1   Treatment in holding company's accounts

This section deals with a situation in which a holding company sells some of its shares in a subsidiary but retains sufficient shares to maintain the holding company/subsidiary company relationship. For example, a holding company with a wholly owned subsidiary may sell 25% of the equity shares to outsiders, retaining a 75% interest.

In the books of the holding company the cost of the appropriate proportion of the shares sold will be matched against the disposal proceeds to produce a profit or loss on disposal.

11.4.2   Treatment in the consolidated accounts

In the consolidated accounts it will be necessary to recognise the existence of a new or, in some cases, an increased minority interest.

11.4.3   Illustration

The summarised balance sheets of M Ltd and its subsidiary P Ltd, together with a consolidated balance sheet on 31 December 19X7 are given below. Retained profits of P Ltd on the date M Ltd acquired all the share capital were £1,000. The goodwill arising on the acquisition of the shares was written off immediately.

Summarised balance sheets 31 December 19X7

	M Ltd £	P Ltd £
Share capital (£1 shares)	10,000	4,000
Retained profits	6,000	2,000
	16,000	6,000
Net assets	8,000	6,000
4,000 £1 shares in P Ltd	8,000	
	16,000	6,000

M Ltd sells 25% of its shares in P Ltd for £3,500 on 1 January 19X8. In the accounts of the holding company this will produce a profit on disposal of £1,500 (£3,500 − £8,000/4). For the year ended 31 December 19X8, the following figures appear in the profit and loss account:

	M Ltd £	P Ltd £
Operating profit	2,100	1,400
Add: profit on sale of shares in P Ltd	1,500	—
	3,600	1,400

Taxation is ignored.

The following workings are completed in stages. Entries in the workings are numbered according to the stage at which they take place.

Stage 1   Record the position at the acquisition of P to calculate and write off goodwill.

Stage 2   Calculate the profit made by the group on the sale of the shares by deducting from proceeds the cost of the shares less goodwill written off. As the holding company retains control, minority interest is credited with the calculated cost as reduced.

Stage 3   Add to the minority interest their share of the post-acquisition profit up to the date of sale.

Stage 4   Incorporate the trading results for the year, including the minority interest transfer.

Cost of control

		£			£
Cost of shares	1	8,000	Share capital	1	4,000
			P & L pre-acquisition	1	1,000
			P & L goodwill written off	1	3,000
		8,000			8,000

Minority interest

		£				£
Balance to CBS		1,850	Sale of shares: 25% share			
			capital + pre-acquisition	2		1,250
			Retained profits: 25% of			
			post-acquisition profit	3		250
			Retained profits: 25% of			
			profit for year	4		350
		1,850				1,850

Retained profits

		£			£
Cost of control:			M Ltd	1	6,000
pre-acquisition profits	1	1,000	P Ltd	1	2,000
Cost of control: goodwill					
written off	1	3,000			
Balance c/d	1	4,000			
		8,000			8,000
Minority interest: 25% of			Balance b/d	1	4,000
post-acquisition profits £1,000	3	250	Profit on sale of P	2	2,250
25% of profit for year £1,400	4	350	Profit for year M	4	2,100
Balance c/d		9,150	P	4	1,400
		9,750			9,750

Sale of shares in P Ltd

		£			£
Minority interest	2	1,250	Proceeds of sale	2	3,500
Retained profits	2	2,250			

The 'book' profit made by the group is £2,250:

	£	£
Proceeds of sale		3,500
Less: cost (25% × £8,000)	2,000	
Less: goodwill written off (25% × £3,000)	750	1,250
		2,250

The 'SSAP 14' profit is:

	£
Proceeds of sale	3,500
Less: 25% × net assets at date of sale: 25% × £6,000	1,500
	2,000

The £250 difference is part of the £4,000 retained profit brought forward:

	£	£
Retained profit brought forward:		
M Ltd		3,000
P Ltd relating to 75% shares retained: 75% × £1,000	750	
Realised in sale 25% × £1,000	250	1,000
		4,000

Consolidated profit and loss account for the year ended 31 December 19X8

	£
Operating profit	3,500
Less: minority interest in P 25% × £1,400	350
	3,150
Extraordinary item:	
Profit on sale of shares in subsidiary	
(per SSAP 14: £3,500 − 25% × £6,000)	2,000
	5,150
Retained profit brought forward	4,000
	9,150
Retained profit carried forward	9,150

Consolidated balance sheet as at 31 December 19X8

	£
Net assets (£12,000 + £3,500 proceeds of sale + £3,500	
increase in net assets during 19X8)	21,000
	21,000
Share capital	10,000
Profit and loss account	9,150
	19,150
Minority interest	1,850
	21,000

11.4.4   Disposal during the year

Where the sale of shares occurs during the course of a year, a similar adjustment to that shown in 11.3.8 is necessary. Thus the consolidated profit and loss account will include the whole profit of the holding company and subsidiary for the year. From these will be deducted the minority interest in those profits from the date the shares were sold, that is, from the date the minority interest existed, until the end of the year. The result is that the full profits for the first part of the year have been included and 25% of these are realised in the sale proceeds.

11.4.5   Illustration continued from 11.4.3

Let us assume that the 25% of shares in P Ltd were sold for the same amount on 30 June 19X8. If the profit for the year accrued evenly during the year, the profit as required to be disclosed under SSAP 14 would become:

	£
Proceeds of sale	3,500
Group's share of net assets at the date of sale 25% × (£6,000 + ½ × £1,400)	1,675
	1,825

The profit made by the holding company remains the same at £2,250, but its analysis is now:

	£	£
Profit per SSAP 14		1,825
Post-acquisition profits of P Ltd applicable to shares sold:		
To 31.12.X7: 25% × £1,000	250	
To 30.6.X8: 25% × ½ × £1,400	175	
		425
		2,250

The consolidated profit and loss account for the year to 31 December 19X8 will then appear as follows:

Consolidated profit and loss account for the year to 31 December 19X8

	£
Operating profit	3,500
Less: minority interest: from 1 July 19X8 (25% × ½ × £1,400)	175
	3,325
Add: extraordinary item: profit on sale of shares in subsidiary	1,825
	5,150
Add: retained profits brought forward	4,000
Retained profits carried forward	9,150

11.5   Sale of part of shareholding with no retention of control

This section considers a situation in which a holding company sells part of its shareholding and retains only a minority interest. There are two possibilities here: first, the company may retain sufficient shares for the former subsidiary to be an associated company; secondly it may retain only a simple investment.

Each of these will be discussed in turn using the following summarised balance sheets, the same as those used in 11.3.6.

Balance sheets 31 December 19X7

	H Ltd £000	X Ltd £000	Y Ltd £000	Consolidated £000
£1 ordinary shares	10,000	2,000	3,000	10,000
Retained profits:				
Pre-acquisition	—	500	1,000	
Post-acquisition	5,000	2,000	500	7,500
	15,000	4,500	4,500	17,500
Net assets	6,000	4,500	4,500	15,000
Investment in subsidiaries:				
2,000 shares in X Ltd	4,000			
3,000 shares in Y Ltd	5,000			
Goodwill				2,500
	15,000	4,500	4,500	17,500

Extract from profit and loss accounts for the year to 31 December 19X8

	H Ltd £000	X Ltd £000	Y Ltd £000
Profit after taxation	2,000	1,600	800

11.5.1   Associated company

If H Ltd had sold 75% of its holding in X Ltd, the 25% retained would make X an associated company to be dealt with in accordance with SSAP 1. Thus, in the consolidated balance sheet, the investment would have to be valued at cost plus the appropriate share of retained post-acquisition profits.

Using the balance sheets given above, let us assume that H Ltd sells 75% of its shares in X Ltd for £4,300,000 on 1 January 19X8. This produces a profit on disposal of £1,300,000 (£4,300,000 − (4,000,000 × 75%)). This profit of £1,300,000 will appear in the consolidated balance sheet as:

	£000
Loss on disposal per SSAP 14 (see below)	(200)
75% × post-acquisition profits £2,000,000, included in retained profit brought forward	1,500
	1,300

The SSAP 14 result would be:

	£	£
Proceeds of sale		4,300
75% net assets at sale: 75% × £4,500	3,375	
75% goodwill not amortised: 75% × £1,500	1,125	4,500
Loss		(200)

The consolidated profit and loss account, including the group's share of the results of X Ltd as an associate, would be:

H Ltd group
Consolidated profit and loss account for the year to 31 December 19X8

	£000
Operating profit (H £2,000,000 + Y £800,000)	2,800
Share of profit after taxation of associated company: 25% × £1,600,000	400
Less: extraordinary item: Loss on sale of shares in subsidiary	(200)
	3,000
Retained profit brought forward (Working)	7,500
Retained profit carried forward	10,500

Working

Calculation of retained profit brought forward

	£000	£000
H Ltd		5,000
Y Ltd		500
X Ltd:		
75% × post-acquisition profit £2,000,000	1,500	
25% × £2,000,000 applicable to interest retained	500	
		2,000
		7,500

11.5.2   Disposal during the year

If the shares are sold during the course of a year, it is necessary to include profit up to the date of sale as ordinary operating profit. 75% of any amount so included will reduce the extraordinary profit whilst 25% will be debited to the investment in associated company in the consolidated accounts.

11.5.3   Retention of simple investment

Assume that H Ltd sells 90% of its shareholding in X Ltd for £6,000,000 on 1 January 19X8. This produces a profit on disposal of £2,400,000 (£6,000,000 − (£4,000,000 × 90%)) in the books of H Ltd and leaves an investment of 200,000 shares in X Ltd valued at their cost of £400,000. Once the sale has been made X Ltd ceases to be a subsidiary of H Ltd.

The profit on disposal is in part a realisation of the retained post-acquisition profits of X Ltd included in consolidated profit and loss accounts of previous years and included in the consolidated balance sheet on 31 December 19X7 at £2,000,000. Thus £1,800,000 (90% of £2,000,000) of the profit on disposal must be treated as a realisation of past profits.

However, the remaining 10% of £2,000,000 is the group's share in past profits, over which it now has no control or influence. One view is that this profit must be eliminated from the consolidated accounts. Since the loss of this additional £200,000 of past profits is caused by the sale of the 90% stake during the year, it would seem sensible to treat this 'consequential' loss of previously consolidated profits as part of the extraordinary item, thus reducing the group profit on disposal to £400,000. The consolidated profit and loss account for the year to 31 December 19X8 would then be:

	£000
Profit after taxation	
(H £2,000,000 + Y £800,000)	2,800
Add: extraordinary profit on disposal of shares	
in X Ltd (£2,400,000 − £1,800,000 − £200,000)	400
	3,200
Add: retained profits brought forward	7,000
Retained profits carried forward	10,200

11.5.4   Alternative treatment

An alternative view regarding the remaining 10% of £2,000,000, being the group's share in past profits in respect of the remaining 10% stake held, is that instead of being eliminated from the consolidated reserves (as part of the extraordinary item) it should be *added* to the original cost of the investment in X Ltd. This has the effect of 'revaluing' the investment to its carrying amount under the equity method at the date of disposal. No further account would be taken of profits of X Ltd and under the prudence concept it should be checked that the amount at which the investment is stated does not exceed its long-term value. The resulting consolidated profit and loss account would then be:

	£000
Profit after taxation	2,800
Add: extraordinary profit on disposal of shares in X Ltd	
(£2,400,000 − £1,800,000)	600
	3,400
Add: retained profits brought forward	7,000
Retained profits carried forward	10,400

In the consolidated balance sheet the investment in X Ltd would be stated at:

	£000
Cost (10% × £4,000)	400
Add: share of post-acquisition retained reserves up to date of disposal	
(10% × £2,000,000)	200
'Valuation'	600

11.5.5 Disposal during the year

If the shares in X Ltd had been sold during the course of 19X8, the profits would have to be shifted to the date of sale from the extraordinary profit up to the operating profit after tax to give a true and fair view of group operations for the year.

11.6 Summary

This is a tricky subject, the key to which is understanding the way in which the different calculations of 'profit' or 'loss' on disposal enter your answer. There are in fact *three* relevant figures:

(a) Proceeds of sale less cost of shares. This is the figure on which tax liability will be based, subject, of course, to CGT indexation.

(b) Proceeds of sale less cost of shares as reduced by the writing off of goodwill on acquisition. This will, of course, be the same as (a) if there has been no write-off of goodwill. This is the measure of profit which must, *in total*, enter the consolidated profit and loss account.

(c) Proceeds of sale less net assets at date of sale, adjusted for goodwill on acquisition not written off. This is the 'SSAP 14' profit which will normally be disclosed as an extraordinary item, less relevant taxation. The remainder of the profit in (b) will be included in retained profit brought forward and, if the disposal took place during the year, in profit on ordinary activities.

Practice questions are 34 and 35.

12 Consolidation by the merger method

12.1 Introduction

All our work to date has been based on consolidation according to the acquisition method of accounting, the main features of which may be summarised as follows:

(a)   Shares purchased in a subsidiary company are valued in the balance sheet of the holding company at cost, that is, at the fair market value of the consideration given to acquire them (less any dividends out of pre-acquisition profits).

There is no problem when shares are purchased for cash. However, on a share exchange, that is, where the holding company gives shares in itself in exchange for the shares in the subsidiary, it is necessary to place a value on the consideration given. If this fair value exceeds the par value of the shares issued, a share premium account is required.

(b)   Pre-acquisition profits of the subsidiary company are no longer available for distribution. They are 'frozen' at the date of acquisition and only post-acquisition profits of the subsidiary are consolidated with the distributable profits of the holding company. This is recognised in the technique for consolidation we have been using by crediting the group's share of pre-acquisition profit to cost of control account.

(c)   Assets and liabilities of the subsidiary are required by SSAP 14 to be revalued to their fair market value at the date of acquisition. The difference between the consideration and the sum of the net assets is treated as goodwill or reserve on consolidation, which is then written off or amortised as required by SSAP 22.

A frequent practical disadvantage of the acquisition method of accounting is that the right to distribute the pre-acquisition profits of a company entering a group is lost. It is argued that this could be unfair if the consideration received by the shareholders in that company consists of shares in the holding company.

In an attempt to provide an alternative treatment 'merger accounting' (called 'pooling of interests' in the USA) was developed, and codified in the USA in 1970 with the issue by the Financial Accounting Standards Board (FASB) of APB 16. In 1971 the UK Accounting

Standards Committee issued an exposure draft on the subject (ED 3 'Accounting for acquisitions and mergers') but it never became a standard because of doubts over the legality of merger accounting in UK law. In 1980 the case of *Shearer* v *Bercain Ltd* confirmed its illegality, but soon afterwards the Companies Act 1981 introduced provisions which allowed merger accounting once again to be considered. The ASC responded with ED 31 in October 1982, which in 1985 duly became SSAP 23 'Accounting for acquisitions and mergers', the provisions of which are very similar to those of the International Accounting Standard IAS 22 'Accounting for business combinations'.

12.2   Merger accounting

So what is merger accounting? It is a method of accounting for business combinations which allows pre-acquisition profits to remain distributable.

In merger accounting, it is not necessary to adjust the carrying values of the assets and liabilities of the subsidiary to fair value either in its own books or on consolidation. However, appropriate adjustments should be made to achieve uniformity of accounting policies between the combining companies.

In the group accounts for the period in which the merger takes place, the profits or losses of subsidiaries brought in for the first time should be included for the entire period without any adjustment in respect of that part of the period prior to the merger. Corresponding amounts should be presented as if the companies had been combined *throughout the previous period and at the previous balance sheet date*.

A difference may arise on consolidation between the carrying value of the investment in the subsidiary (which will normally be the nominal value of the shares issued in consideration plus the fair value of any additional consideration) and the nominal value of the shares transferred to the issuing company. Where the carrying value of the investment is *less* than the nominal value of the shares transferred, the difference should be treated as a reserve arising on consolidation. Where the carrying value of the investment is *greater* than the nominal value of the shares transferred, the difference is the extent to which reserves have been in effect capitalised as a result of the merger and it should therefore be treated on consolidation as a reduction of reserves.

Here is a simple illustration first consolidated using the 'normal' acquisition method and then using the merger method.

12.2.1   Illustration

The balance sheets of A Ltd and M Ltd are as follows:

	A Ltd £000	M Ltd £000
Net assets	200	120
Share capital: ordinary shares of £1 each	160	60
Profit and loss account	40	60
	200	120

A Ltd buys the whole of the share capital of M Ltd for £160,000 by issuing 80,000 shares at £2 each. It is agreed that the balance sheet of M Ltd correctly states the fair value of the company's net assets.

Consolidation following the acquisition method

Under the acquisition method with which you should by now be very familiar, the following working accounts would be constructed:

Cost of control

	£000		£000
Cost of shares	160	Share capital M	60
		Profit and loss account M	60
		Goodwill	40
	——		——
	160		160
	——		——

Profit and loss account

	£000		£000
Cost of control: 100%		A	40
pre-acquisition profit	60	M	60
Balance to CBS	40		
	——		——
	100		100
	——		——

A Ltd and its subsidiary
Consolidated balance sheet

	£000
Net assets	320
Goodwill	40
	——
	360
	——
Share capital	240
Share premium	80
Profit and loss account	40
	——
	360
	——

The distributable profits of M Ltd have completely disappeared, and those of A Ltd would also disappear if the goodwill of £40,000 were written off. Note, however, that the shareholders of M Ltd continue to participate in the enterprise by virtue of the shares in A Ltd they have received.

Consolidation following the merger method

Under the merger method, there is no need to consider pre-acquisition profits, and the shares issued by A Ltd are accounted for at their nominal value. The working accounts would become:

Adjustment account

	£000		£000
Nominal value of shares issued by A Ltd	80	Share capital M	60
		Profit and loss account: excess of nominal value of shares issued over share capital written off	20
	80		80

Profit and loss account

	£000		£000
Adjustment account	20	A	40
Balance to CBS	80	M	60
	100		100

A Ltd and its subsidiary
Consolidated balance sheet

	£000
Net assets	320
Share capital: 240,000 shares of £1 each	240
Profit and loss account	80
	320

The distributable profit of the combined companies is £80,000. This is £20,000 less than the £100,000 originally distributable when the companies were separate, because of the fact that the nominal value of the shares issued by A Ltd exceeded the nominal value of the shares in M Ltd which they replaced. Note that if the difference should be in the opposite direction the credit arising would be to capital reserve.

Discussion

There are in fact just three differences in the workings for the merger method compared with those for the acquisition method:

    (a)   The cost of control account is renamed the adjustment account to emphasise that this is a merger, not a take-over.

(b)   The nominal value of the shares issued by A Ltd is used, not their fair value. (If there were any other elements in the consideration, cash or debentures for example, these would be included at their fair value.)

(c)   No adjustment is made for pre-acquisition profit.

In addition, when preparing the consolidated balance sheet by cross-casting assets and liabilities, the *fair* value should be used in acquisition accounting (if given in the question) whereas in the merger method the book value might be used.

12.3   Provisions of SSAP 23

12.3.1   Introduction

Because merger accounting preserves the distributability of pre-acquisition profits, it is attractive to many companies and could lend itself to abuse if the occasions when its use was permitted were not carefully defined and controlled. SSAP 23 seeks to provide the necessary rules.

SSAP 23 *requires* the acquisition method to be used unless a combination is based principally on a share-for-share exchange, but it allows *either* merger accounting *or* acquisition accounting for combinations which are principally on a share-for-share basis.

12.3.2   Conditions to be satisfied if the merger basis is to be used

The precise conditions which must be met if the merger method is to be used are:

(a)   the business combination results from an offer to the holders of all equity shares and the holders of all voting shares which are not already held by the offeror; and

(b)   the offeror has secured, as a result of the offer, a holding of:

    (i)   at least 90% of all equity shares (taking each class of equity separately) and
    (ii)   the shares carrying at least 90% of the votes of the offeree; and

(c)   immediately prior to the offer, the offeror does not hold:

    (i)   20% or more of all equity shares of the offeree (taking each class of equity separately) or
    (ii)   shares carrying 20% or more of the votes of the offeree; and

(d)   not less than 90% of the fair value of the total consideration given for the equity share capital (including that given for shares already held) is in the form of equity share capital; not less than 90% of the fair value of the total consideration given for voting non-equity share capital (including that given for shares already held) is in the form of equity and/or non-equity share capital.

If *all* these conditions are not met, the merger method must not be used and the combination must be accounted for as an acquisition.

12.3.3 Disclosure requirements of SSAP 23

SSAP 23 contains disclosure requirements for both types of combination. All of them are listed below:

(a) Disclosure requirements for all business combinations. The financial statements for the year in which the combination takes place must disclose:

    (i) the names of the combining companies;

    (ii) the number and class of the securities issued in respect of the combination, and details of any other consideration given;

    (iii) the accounting treatment adopted for the business combination (i.e., whether it has been accounted for as an acquisition or as a merger);

    (iv) the nature and amount of significant accounting adjustments by the combining companies to achieve consistency of accounting policies.

(b) Disclosure requirements for combinations accounted for as acquisitions. The consolidated financial statements should contain sufficient information about the results of subsidiaries acquired to enable shareholders to appreciate the effect on the consolidated results. In addition, disclosure should be made of the date from which the results of major acquisitions have been brought into the accounts (that is, the effective date of those acquisitions).

(c) Disclosure requirements for combinations accounted for as mergers. The financial statements for the year in which the merger takes place should disclose:

    (i) the fair value of the consideration given by the issuing company;

    (ii) an analysis of the current year's attributable profit before extraordinary items between that of before and that of after the effective date of the merger;

    (iii) an analysis of the attributable profit before extraordinary items of the current year up to the effective date of the merger and of the previous year between that of the issuing company and that of the subsidiary; and

    (iv) an analysis of extraordinary items so as to indicate whether each individual extraordinary item relates to pre or post-merger events, and to which party to the merger the item relates.

12.3.4 Problems in the adoption of merger accounting

Critics of the use of merger accounting raise a number of objections to it. SSAP 23 and ED 31 on which it was based discuss some of these problems:

(a) Creation of instant earnings. In merger accounting, the profit and loss account includes the full year's results of the companies involved in the merger, even though the merger may not have taken place until towards the end of the year. Not only that, the corresponding figures are restated to include all companies in the enlarged group. It would be undesirable if a company could enhance its results in this way by making acquisitions for cash or loan stock. However, merger accounting is only proposed in cases where at least 90% of the consideration given is in the form of shares, so that there is a genuine merging of the interests of the shareholders, the increased earnings being attributable to a larger number of shares as a result of the fresh issue entailed in the merger. Disclosure of the pre-combination profits of the current and preceding years is required. It is also pointed out that, as far as the corresponding amounts are concerned, it would be more misleading if they were not restated, as such a presentation would indicate illusory growth. Indeed, it can be argued that acquisition accounting, rather than merger accounting, results in the presentation of figures which could indicate illusory growth.

(b)   Creation of instant distributable reserves. It is sometimes contended that merger accounting leads to the creation of instantly distributable reserves which may be paid to shareholders as dividend. To rebut this argument, it was stated in ED 31 that the total distributable reserves are no higher than the total of the distributable reserves of the individual companies prior to the merger. The protection of creditors of each company, in the form of the separate share capitals of each of the combining companies remains.

(c)   Impossibility of a true 'merger' if the size of the companies involved is very different. ED 3, back in 1971, proposed that merger accounting could only be adopted if no company in the combination was more than three times the size of any other. SSAP 23 rejects the need for a size test, pointing out that the real requirement is that the transaction must be effected by a share-for-share exchange. It is perhaps useful to point out that the 'three times' test of ED 3, in a two-company merger, meant that the shareholders from the smaller company would be in a position to block a special resolution, which requires a 75% majority.

(d)   Understatement of assets. Merger accounting may mean that the assets of 'acquired' companies are not brought into the consolidated balance sheet at their fair value. However, the consolidated balance sheet will show almost exactly the same position as would an aggregation of the balance sheets of the individual companies. Also, there is nothing to stop a revaluation of assets before or after the merger.

(e)   Effect on holding company profitability. In merger accounting, dividends paid by 'acquired' companies out of pre-acquisition profits could be credited to the holding company's profit and loss account. However, such dividends would cancel out and would not appear in the consolidated balance sheet.

(f)   Extraordinary items. Merger accounting has come into some criticism because certain companies have boosted earnings by including in operating profits the profit on the sale of assets brought into the consolidated accounts at historical cost to the company owning the asset. The disclosure requirements of SSAP 23 which call for an analysis of extraordinary items, should mean that no one will be misled.

12.4   Summary

This is another topic often neglected by students — I wonder how many were caught out by question 1 in the June 1987 Advanced Accounting Practice paper!

In fact the difference in consolidation technique compared with acquisition accounting is fairly small. Stand by too for non-computational questions or parts of questions on SSAP 23.

The practice question is from Advanced Accounting Practice June 1987 (question 36).

13 Accounting for overseas operations

13.1 Introduction

13.1.1 Foreign currency operations

A company may engage in foreign currency operations in two main ways:

(a) It may enter directly into business transactions which are denominated in foreign currencies.

(b) Foreign operations may be conducted through a foreign subsidiary company which maintains its own accounting records in terms of its own local foreign currency.

13.1.2 The need for translation

Problems then arise when these companies wish to include the overseas transactions which are effected in foreign currency, in their own accounts which are denominated in sterling. The process of changing figures in accounts expressed in one currency to another currency is referred to as 'translation'.

13.1.3 Problems of translation

The main problems in relation to translation of foreign currency values are:

(a) which rate of exchange to use;

(b) how to treat translation differences when rates of exchange vary from one accounting period to another.

13.1.4 Possible exchange rates

For any particular item there would appear to be two relevant rates of exchange:

(a) the historical rate, that is, the rate which was applicable on the date of the original transaction;

(b) the closing rate, that is, the rate of exchange on the balance sheet date.

If we take as an example a balance sheet item, raw material stock, the choice would be between the rate of exchange ruling when the stock was purchased, or the rate of exchange on the balance sheet date. If we turn to the profit and loss account, an item such as cost of sales could be translated either at the rate in force when the item of stock was acquired or at the rate in force on the balance sheet date. If the historical rate is used in practice, although depreciation is usually translated at the rate ruling when the relevant fixed asset was acquired, other items are often translated at the average rate of exchange for the period as an approximation to the true historical rate for each item.

13.1.5   Exchange rate experience

The greater the movement in rates of exchange, the greater will be the difference between the figures produced by use of the two rates discussed above. The table below emphasises the importance of the choice by showing movements in a selection of exchange rates between 1975 and 1987.

Rate to £

	December 1975	May 1983	September 1987
US dollars	2.0233	1.6061	1.633
Belgian francs	79.95	80.95	61.60
Swiss francs	5.3025	3.3702	2.4375
French francs	9.0375	12.1587	9.88
Italian lire	1,382.87	2,404.32	2,140.0
Netherlands guilders	5.4287	4.5605	3.3325
Deutschemarks	5.2987	4.0525	2.9575
Japanese yen	617.37	383.80	232.0

13.1.6   Translation methods

This chapter will deal with two of the possible methods:

(a)   The closing rate/net investment method. Under this method, assets and liabilities denominated in foreign currencies are translated using the closing rate. For revenue items there is a choice of either the closing rate of exchange or the average rate of exchange for the period.

(b)   The temporal method. Under this method, assets, liabilities, revenues and expenses are translated at the rate of exchange ruling at the date on which the amount recorded in the financial statements was established. At the balance sheet date any assets or liabilities which are carried at current values are retranslated at the closing rate.

13.1.7   Development of SSAP 20

ED 21, issued in September 1977, permitted the use of either the temporal method or the closing rate method.

ED 27, issued in October 1980, recommended that the closing rate method should normally be used when translating the accounts of an overseas subsidiary. The proposals of ED 27 were, in most respects, similar to the requirements of SSAP 20 except that ED 27 proposed the use of the average rate for the profit and loss account rather than permitting the choice of rate indicated in 13.1.6 (a).

13.2   Requirements of SSAP 20 concerning the individual company

13.2.1   Introduction

We shall deal first with the situation where a company enters directly into transactions which are denominated in a foreign currency. The results of these transactions will need to be translated into the currency in which the company reports, so that they may be entered in the accounting records.

13.2.2   Translation of profit and loss account items

Profit and loss account items (e.g., sales in French francs or expenses payable in Deutschemarks) should be translated and recorded at the rate of exchange in operation on the date of the transaction; if the rates do not fluctuate significantly, an average rate for the period may be used. Where the transaction is to be settled at a contracted rate, that rate should be used and if a trading transaction is covered by a related or matching forward contract, the rate of exchange specified in that contract may be used.

13.2.3   Translation of non-monetary assets

Non-monetary assets (e.g., fixed assets or stocks) should be translated and recorded in the company's accounting records at the rate of exchange ruling on the date of purchase. Once these items have been translated and recorded, no subsequent translations will normally be made except for foreign equity investments financed by foreign currency borrowings (see 13.2.8).

13.2.4   Translation of monetary items

Monetary items include cash held and amounts to be received or paid in money (e.g., cash, debtors, creditors, loans). These items should be translated at each balance sheet date at the closing rate of exchange or, where appropriate, the rates of exchange fixed for the transaction. Where there are related or matching forward contracts in respect of trading transactions, the rates of exchange specified in those contracts may be used.

13.2.5   Exchange differences

Exchange differences will arise because of the delay between the date of the transaction, e.g., making a sale or purchase, and the date of settlement or the balance sheet date if earlier.

13.2.6   Illustration

A UK company sells goods to a French company in August 19X0 for FFr 200,000 when the rate was FFr 9.98 to the £. Payment was received in October 19X0 when the rate was FFr 10.66. In August the company recorded a debt of £20,040 and a sale of £20,040. When payment is received in October the actual amount received is £18,762. The loss on exchange is £1,278.

13.2.7   Treatment of exchange differences

All exchange differences on settled transactions and unsettled short-term monetary items should be reported as part of the profit for the year from ordinary operations unless they result from transactions which would be treated as extraordinary items.

The effect in the illustration in 13.2.6 is to reduce the profit for the year by £1,278, which can be considered as having the effect of recording the sale at the lower figure of £18,762 (the net of £20,040 and £1,278).

It is appropriate to recognise such differences as part of the profit for the year, since the gains or losses are ultimately reflected in cash flows (i.e., the company received in sterling £18,762 and not £20,040).

Exchange differences on long-term monetary items should also be recognised in the profit and loss account; however, where there are doubts about the convertibility or marketability of the currency in question, then it is necessary to consider whether the gain or the amount by which exchange gains exceed past exchange losses on the same items should be restricted on the grounds of prudence.

13.2.8   Foreign equity investments and foreign currency borrowings

Where a company has used foreign currency borrowings to finance, or provide a hedge against, its foreign equity investments then, under certain conditions, the investments (denominated in the foreign currency) may be translated at the end of each accounting period at closing rates. Where investments are treated in this way, any exchange differences arising should be taken to reserves and the exchange differences on the foreign currency borrowings should be offset against the exchange differences on the investments. The conditions which must apply are:

(a)   In any accounting period, exchange gains or losses on the borrowings may be offset only to the extent of exchange differences arising on the equity investments.

(b)   The foreign currency borrowings concerned should not exceed the total amount of cash that the investments are expected to be able to generate, whether from profits or otherwise.

(c)   The accounting treatment should be consistent from period to period.

13.2.9   Illustration

A UK company purchased an equity investment in a German company for DM 2,000,000 in January 19X1. The company needed to make borrowings to finance this investment but found it impossible to raise funds in Deutschemarks and so it decided to attempt to reduce its exposure to currency fluctuations by borrowing SFr 1,500,000. The investment and loan still existed in the company's books at the end of 19X1. Relevant exchange rates are as follows:

	SFr to £	DM to £
January 19X1	3.62	4.07
December 19X1	3.53	4.03

This means that, when translated into sterling, the loan and investment become:

	Loan £	Investment £
January 19X1	414,365	491,400
December 19X1	424,929	496,278
	Loss of £10,564	Gain of £4,878

The company should, therefore, take the gain of £4,878 on the investment to the reserves and offset, as a reserve movement, £4,878 of the loss on the loan. The remaining loss on the loan of £5,686 should be recognised in the profit and loss account.

Note. If the gain on the investment had been, for example, £10,564 and the loss on the loan had been £4,878 then *all* of the gain on the investment would be taken to reserves and all of the loss on the loan would be offset against the gain as a reserve movement.

13.2.10   Companies Act 1985

Paragraph 12 of schedule 4 to the Companies Act 1985 requires that only profits realised at the balance sheet date shall be included in the profit and loss account. Any gains on unsettled long-term monetary items are not realised but this conflicts with the requirement of SSAP 20 that these gains should be recognised in the profit and loss account.

However, paragraph 15 of the schedule permits a departure from paragraph 12 if it appears to the directors that there are special reasons for such a departure: in this case, particulars of any departure, the reasons for it and its effect must be given in a note to the accounts. SSAP 20 considers that such gains must be shown in the profit and loss account in order to give a true and fair view of results and that this constitutes a special reason for departure under paragraph 15.

Part I of the schedule lays down the choice of formats permitted for the presentation of accounts. Distinction is drawn between operating and other income and expense. For this reason it is necessary to consider the nature of each foreign exchange gain or loss and to allocate each accordingly. Thus, SSAP 20 states that gains or losses arising from trading transactions should normally be included under 'Other operating income or expense' while those arising from arrangements which may be considered as financing should be disclosed separately as part of 'Other interest receivable/payable and similar income expense'. Exchange gains or losses which arise from events which themselves fall to be treated as extraordinary items should be included as part of such items.

13.3   Requirements of SSAP 20 concerning consolidated financial statements

13.3.1   Introduction

We shall now deal with the situation where a company has a foreign subsidiary, associate or branch which maintains its own accounting records.

13.3.2   Concept behind SSAP 20

SSAP 20 requires that, in almost all cases, the closing rate method of translation based on the 'net investment' concept should be used. This concept recognises the fact that the investment is in the net worth of the foreign enterprise rather than a direct investment in the individual assets and liabilities of that enterprise. The foreign enterprise will normally have net current assets and fixed assets which may be financed partly by local currency borrowings. In its day-to-day operations the foreign enterprise is not normally dependent on the reporting currency of the investing company. The investing company may look forward to a stream of dividends but the net investment will remain until the business is liquidated or the investment disposed of.

13.3.3   Requirement of SSAP 20: closing rate method

Amounts in the balance sheet of a foreign enterprise should be translated into the reporting currency of the holding company, using the rate of exchange ruling at the balance sheet date.

Amounts in the profit and loss account of a foreign enterprise should be translated at the closing rate or an average rate for the accounting period. The closing rate is more likely to reflect the financial results and relationships as measured prior to translation but, on the other hand, the average rate more fairly reflects the profits or losses and cash flows as they arise to the group. Either method is permitted but the one selected must be applied consistently.

All exchange differences should be recorded as a movement on reserves, because to include these differences in the profit and loss account would distort the results, as shown prior to translation.

13.3.4   Exceptions to the closing rate/net investment method

Most foreign operations are carried out through foreign enterprises which operate as separate or quasi-independent entities and, therefore, the closing rate/net investment method is appropriate in almost all circumstances.

However, there are some cases in which the affairs of a foreign enterprise are so closely interlinked with those of the investing company that its results may be regarded as being more dependent on the economic environment of the investing company's currency than on that of its own reporting currency. In such a case the financial statements of the foreign enterprise should be included in the consolidated financial statements as if all its transactions had been entered into by the investing company itself in its own currency. For this purpose the temporal method of translation should be used; the mechanics of this method are identical with those used in preparing the accounts of an individual company, as stated in 13.2 (but see also 13.6.2).

It is not possible to select one factor which of itself will lead a company to conclude that the temporal method should be adopted. All the available evidence should be considered in determining whether the currency of the investing company is the dominant currency in the economic environment in which the foreign enterprise operates. Amongst the factors to be taken into account will be:

(a)   the extent to which the cash flows of the enterprise have a direct impact upon those of the investing company;

(b)   the extent to which the functioning of the enterprise depends directly upon the investing company;

(c)   the currency in which the majority of the trading transactions are denominated;

(d)   the major currency to which the operation is exposed in its financing structure.

Examples of situations where the temporal method may be appropriate are where the foreign enterprise:

(a)   acts as a selling agency receiving stocks of goods from the investing company and remitting the proceeds back to the company;

(b)   produces a raw material or manufactures parts or subassemblies which are then shipped to the investing company for inclusion in its own products;

(c)   is located overseas for tax, exchange control or similar reasons to act as a means of raising finance for other companies in the group.

13.4 Explanatory illustration: closing rate method

13.4.1 Introduction

In the following simple example, consolidated accounts are prepared using the closing rate/net investment method. The steps to be followed are:

(a)   translate the accounts of the subsidiary into sterling (the reporting currency of the holding company);

(b)   consolidate the balance sheets and profit and loss accounts following the normal rules of consolidation; and

(c)   prepare a statement of movements on reserves including the exchange differences.

13.4.2 Illustration

A UK company, Harmony Ltd, purchased 75% of the share capital in an established overseas company, Cadence SA, for £25,000 and immediately after that transaction its summarised balance sheet was as follows:

Harmony Ltd
Balance sheet on 1 January 19X8

	£
Fixed assets:	
Tangible assets	120,000
Investment in subsidiary	25,000
Net current assets	35,000
	180,000
Capital and reserves:	
Share capital	100,000
Profit and loss account	80,000
	180,000

On 1 January 19X8 the summarised balance sheet of Cadence SA prepared in the local currency, skodas, is given in the left-hand column below. In accordance with SSAP 14 the assets have been revalued to the fair value at the date of acquisition.

Cadence SA
Balance sheet on 1 January 19X8

	Skodas	£
Fixed assets: tangible assets	100,000	33,333
Net current assets	20,000	6,667
	120,000	40,000
Long-term loan	30,000	10,000
Capital and reserves:		
Share capital	60,000	20,000
Profit and loss account and revaluation reserve	30,000	10,000
	90,000	30,000

The exchange rate on 1 January 19X8 was 3 skodas to the £ so that translation of the balance sheet of Cadence SA produces the figures in the right-hand column above.

13.4.3 Consolidated balance sheet on 1 January 19X8

The premium on acquisition or goodwill can be calculated as follows:

	£	£
Cost of investment		25,000
Net assets acquired: share capital and reserves	30,000	
Group share (75%)		22,500
Goodwill on consolidation		2,500

The consolidated balance sheet will therefore be:

Harmony Ltd
Consolidated balance sheet on 1 January 19X8

	£
Fixed assets:	
Intangible assets: goodwill	2,500
Tangible assets	153,333
	155,833
Net current assets	41,667
	197,500
Long-term loan	10,000
	187,500
Capital and reserves:	
Share capital	100,000
Profit and loss account	80,000
	180,000
Minority interests	7,500
	187,500

The minority interest is merely 25% of the translated net assets of the subsidiary (i.e., 25% × £30,000).

13.4.4 The position after one year's trading

After operating for a year the following accounts were produced for 19X8.

Summarised profit and loss accounts for the year ended 31 December 19X8

	Harmony £	Cadence Skodas
Profit before taxation	35,000	15,000
Taxation	15,000	7,000
Profit after taxation (retained)	20,000	8,000

Summarised balance sheets on 31 December 19X8

	Harmony £	Cadence Skodas
Fixed assets:		
Tangible assets	100,000	80,000
Investment in subsidiary	25,000	—
Net current assets	75,000	48,000
	200,000	128,000
Long-term loan	—	30,000
	200,000	98,000
Capital and reserves:		
Share capital	100,000	60,000
Profit and loss account and revaluation reserve	100,000	38,000
	200,000	98,000

The relevant rates of exchange are as follows:

	Rate to £
1 January 19X8	3 skodas
Average for 19X8	2.5 skodas
31 December 19X8	2 skodas

The closing rate will be used for the profit and loss account and then the average rate to show the two alternatives.

13.4.5   Translation of the balance sheet of Cadence SA on 31 December 19X8

When the closing rate method is used we could merely translate everything in the subsidiary's balance sheet at the closing rate of exchange. This seems extremely simple and, at first sight, it is difficult to see why any differences arise using this method. Let us examine what happens:

Cadence SA
Balance sheet on 31 December 19X8

	Skodas	Rate	£
Fixed assets	80,000	2	40,000
Net current assets	48,000	2	24,000
	128,000		64,000
Long-term loan	30,000	2	15,000
	98,000		49,000
Share capital	60,000	2	30,000
Reserves	38,000	2	19,000
	98,000		49,000

The translated retained profits in the balance sheet above are £19,000 but the retained profits at 1 January 19X8 were £10,000 and the profits for the year translated at the closing rate of exchange should be (8,000 Skodas ÷ 2 =) £4,000 and therefore it would seem that retained profits at the end of the year should be £14,000 and not £19,000. Thus, a translation difference of £5,000 has arisen when compared to the balance brought forward together with the translated profits for the year.

However, these are not the only differences which arise. Further differences emerge when we attempt to consolidate.

13.4.6   Calculation of goodwill (premium on acquisition)

On 1 January 19X8 the cost of investment in subsidiary was matched with the net assets at that date (representing the share capital together with reserves) to produce goodwill of £2,500.

If the share capital and pre-acquisition reserves at 31 December 19X8 are translated at the closing rate of 2 skodas to £1 the result is:

	£	£
Cost of investment		35,000
Less: share capital and pre-acquisition reserves at		
31 December 19X8: 90,000 skodas at 2 skodas to £1	45,000	
Group share (75%)		33,750
Goodwill on consolidation		1,250

Thus the movement in exchange rates has produced a further difference arising in the consolidation process. The change in the figure for goodwill would seem to be illogical. Under SSAP 14, goodwill is calculated by comparing the purchase consideration with fair value of the net assets of the subsidiary *at the date of acquisition*. Therefore, it would seem illogical to allow a *subsequent* movement in exchange rates to alter the state of affairs (and hence goodwill) *at the date of acquisition*. To avoid this situation, an adjustment must be made when computing goodwill at a date subsequent to acquisition in order to keep goodwill at a consistent figure.

SSAP 20 states that under the closing rate method all assets and liabilities should be translated at the closing rate and this would strictly include shareholders' funds and thus, the adjustment would theoretically need to be made *on consolidation*. However, an easier approach would be to hold the goodwill on consolidation constant by applying the historical rate to share capital and pre-acquisition reserves. This would produce translated accounts for the subsidiary as follows:

Cadence SA
Balance sheet on 31 December 19X8

	Skodas	Rate	£
Net assets (as before	98,000	CR: 2	49,000
Share capital	60,000	HR: 3	20,000
Reserves:			
Pre-acquisition	30,000	HR: 3	10,000
Post-acquisition	8,000	Balancing figure	19,000
	98,000		49,000

The post-acquisition reserves (which coincidentally are £19,000) are inserted in the sterling balance sheet as a balancing figure and hence will include the exchange differences arising. The figure of £19,000 represents the increase in the net assets of the subsidiary, when translated into sterling, since the date of acquisition. This increase can be shown to comprise:

(a)   the profit for the year since acquisition; and

(b)   the exchange differences arising on the retranslation of the opening net assets of the subsidiary.

The profit for the year is 8,000 skodas or £4,000 and the exchange differences on the opening net assets can be calculated as follows:

	£
Opening net assets of Cadence SA: 90,000 skodas:	
At closing rate of 2 skodas	45,000
At opening rate of 3 skodas	30,000
	15,000

This gives an analysis as follows:

	£
Profit for year	4,000
Exchange difference on opening net assets	15,000
Post-acquisition reserves	19,000

13.4.7   Consolidated balance sheet on 31 December 19X8

The consolidated balance sheet can now be produced:

Harmony Ltd
Consolidated balance sheet on 31 December 19X8

	£
Fixed assets:	
Intangible assets: goodwill	2,500
Tangible assets	140,000
	142,500
Net current assets	99,000
	241,500
Long-term loan	15,000
	226,500
Capital and reserves:	
Share capital	100,000
Profit and loss account	114,250
	214,250
Minority interest (25% × £49,000)	12,250
	226,500

The consolidated profit and loss account balance is calculated as follows:

	£
Harmony	100,000
Cadence: group share of post-acquisition retained reserves: 75% × £19,000	14,250
	114,250

13.4.8   Translation of the profit and loss account of Cadence SA

As stated above, initially the closing rate will be used for translating profit and loss account items for Cadence.

Profit and loss account for the year ended 31 December 19X8

	Skodas	Rate	£
Profit before taxation	15,000	CR: 2	7,500
Taxation	7,000	CR: 2	3,500
Profit after taxation			
(retained)	8,000		4,000

13.4.9   Consolidated profit and loss account for the year ended 31 December 19X8

The consolidated profit and loss account can now be prepared:

Harmony Ltd
Consolidated profit and loss account for the year ended 31 December 19X8

	£
Profit before taxation	42,500
Taxation	18,500
Profit after taxation	24,000
Minority interest (25% × £4,000)	1,000
Profit attributable to shareholders of Harmony Ltd	23,000

13.4.10   Movement on reserves

The statement of retained profits can now be prepared:

Harmony Ltd
Statement of consolidated reserves for the year ended 31 December 19X8

	£
Profit and loss account at 1 January 19X8	80,000
Exchange difference arising from retranslation of opening net assets of foreign subsidiary (75% × £15,000)	11,250
Retained profit for the year	23,000
Profit and loss account at 31 December 19X8	114,250

Remember that in a statement of reserves only the group share of amounts relating to subsidiaries is brought in and hence only the group share of the exchange differences calculated in 13.4.6 is taken.

13.4.11   An alternative answer using the average rate

We will now see how the use of the average rate for the profit and loss account changes the consolidated accounts. There will be no effect on the balance sheet and this will be as calculated in 13.4.7. The translation of the profit and loss account of Cadence will now be as follows:

Profit and loss account for the year ended 31 December 19X8

	Skodas	Rate	£
Profit before taxation	15,000	AR: 2.5	6,000
Taxation	7,000	AR: 2.5	2,800
Profit after taxation	8,000		3,200

The consolidated profit and loss account will show:

Harmony Ltd
Consolidated profit and loss account for the year ended 31 December 19X8

	£
Profit before taxation	41,000
Taxation	17,800
Profit after taxation	23,200
Minority interest (25% × £3,200)	800
Profit attributable to shareholders of Harmony Ltd	22,400

Since the consolidated reserves per the balance sheet will remain the same regardless of the choice of rate for the profit and loss account and since the retained profit for the year is £600 less than when the closing rate was used, this must mean that further exchange differences arise when the average rate is chosen. They may be reconciled as follows:

	£
Retained profit for the year of Cadence SA: 8,000 skodas:	
At closing rate of 2 skodas	4,000
At average rate of 2.5 skodas	3,200
Exchange difference	800
Group share (75%)	600

Under this approach the total exchange differences attributable to the group are therefore £11,250 + £600 = £11,850 (or 75% × (£15,000 + £800)), and the statement of retained profits will show:

Harmony Ltd
Statement of consolidated reserves for the year ended 31 December 19X8

	£
Profit and loss account at 1 January 19X8	80,000
Exchange differences	11,850
Retained profit for the year	22,400
Profit and loss account at 31 December 19X8	114,250

Thus, the effect of applying the average rate to the profit and loss account of a subsidiary is:

(a) it will obviously give rise to a different profit figure in sterling; and

(b) there will be an additional element of exchange differences to compute (this will simply be the difference between the retained profit of the subsidiary translated at the closing rate and the retained profit translated at the average rate).

13.4.12   The position after a further year

After operating for a further year the following accounts were produced for 19X9.

Profit and loss accounts for the year ended 31 December 19X9

	Harmony £	Cadence Skodas
Operating profit	40,000	18,000
Dividend receivable from group company	1,650	—
Profit before taxation	41,650	18,000
Taxation	16,000	8,000
Profit after taxation	25,650	10,000
Dividend (proposed)	10,000	4,950
Retained profit for the year	15,650	5,050

Harmony has brought its share of the dividend receivable from Cadence into its accounts at the closing rate of 2.25 skodas.

Balance sheets on 31 December 19X9

	Harmony £	Cadence Skodas
Fixed assets:		
Tangible assets (see note)	80,000	90,000
Investment in subsidiary	25,000	—
Net current assets	110,650	43,050
	215,650	133,050
Long-term loan	—	30,000
	215,650	103,050
Capital and reserves:		
Share capital	100,000	60,000
Profit and loss account and revaluation reserves	115,650	43,050
	215,650	103,050

The note on tangible fixed assets includes:

	£	Skodas
Net book value at 1 January 19X9	100,000	80,000
Additions during the year	—	40,000
Depreciation charge for the year	(20,000)	(30,000)
Net book value at 31 December 19X9	80,000	90,000

The rates of exchange are as follows:

	Rate to £
1 January 19X9	2 skodas
Average for 19X9	2.1 skodas
31 December 19X9	2.25 skodas

13.4.13   Translation of the accounts of Cadence SA for 19X9

Cadence SA
Balance sheet on 31 December 19X9

	Skodas	Rate	£
Fixed assets	90,000	CR: 2.25	40,000
Net current assets	43,050	CR: 2.25	19,133
	133,050		59,133
Long-term loan	30,000	CR: 2.25	13,333
	103,050		45,800
Share capital	60,000	HR: 3	20,000
Reserves:			
Pre-acquisition	30,000	HR: 3	10,000
Post-acquisition	13,050	Balancing figure	15,800
	103,050		45,800

Cadence SA
Profit and loss account for the year ended 31 December 19X9

	Skodas	Rate	£
Profit before taxation	18,000	CR: 2.25	8,000
Taxation	8,000	CR: 2.25	3,556
Profit after taxation	10,000		4,444
Dividend (proposed)	4,950	CR: 2.25	2,200
Retained profit for the year	5,050		2,244

Note that we now return to the main illustration where closing rate is used for the profit and loss account.

13.4.14   Consolidated accounts for 19X9

Harmony Ltd
Consolidated balance sheet on 31 December 19X9

	£
Fixed assets:	
Intangible assets: goodwill	2,500
Tangible assets (Note)	120,000
	122,500
Net current assets	129,783
	252,283
Long-term loan	13,333
	238,950
Capital and reserves:	
Share capital	100,000
Profit and loss account (£115,650 + 75% × £15,800)	127,500
	227,500
Minority interest (25% × £45,800)	11,450
	238,950

Note

The note on tangible fixed assets would include:

	£
Net book value at 1 January 19X9	140,000
Exchange differences (see below)	(4,444)
	135,556
Additions during the year (40,000 skodas @ 2.25)	17,777
Depreciation charges for the year (£20,000 + 30,000 skodas @ 2.25)	(33,333)
Net book value at 31 December 19X9	120,000

The exchange difference arises on the retranslation of the opening fixed assets of the subsidiary and can be calculated as:

	£
Cadence: fixed assets at 1 January 19X9: 80,000 skodas:	
At closing rate of 2.25 skodas	35,556
At opening rate of 2 skodas	40,000
Exchange loss	(4,444)

Consolidated profit and loss account for the year ended 31 December 19X9

	£
Profit before taxation	48,000
Taxation	19,556
Profit after taxation	28,444
Minority interest (25% × £4,444)	1,111
Profit attributable to shareholders of Harmony Ltd	27,333
Dividend (proposed)	10,000
Retained profit for the year	17,333

Statement of consolidated reserves for the year ended 31 December 19X9

	£
Profit and loss account at 1 January 19X9	114,250
Exchange differences (see below)	(4,083)
Retained profit for the year	17,333
Profit and loss account at 31 December 19X9	127,500

The exchange differences can be calculated as follows:

	£
Opening net assets of Cadence SA: 98,000 skodas:	
At closing rate of 2.25 skodas	43,556
At opening rate of 2 skodas	49,000
	5,444
Group share thereof (75%)	4,083

13.4.15   A possible problem with the dividend from a subsidiary

In the illustration above the dividend from the subsidiary was included as an asset in Harmony's books at the closing rate and was also translated as part of the profit of Cadence at the closing rate and, hence, no exchange difference arose. However, if the dividend had been paid (or was about to be paid) at any rate other than that used for the translation of the subsidiary's profit and loss account (closing or average rate as applicable), a further exchange difference would have arisen. For example, if the dividend of 4,950 skodas had been paid during the year when the exchange rate was 2.2 skodas to the £, then Harmony would have brought into its accounts a dividend of £1,687.50 (75% × 4,950 skodas @ 2.2 skodas) and hence its net current assets and retained profit would have increased accordingly. When the accounts of Cadence are translated at the year end, prior to consolidation, the rate used for the profit and loss account would still be the closing rate and hence the dividend, as part of the profit, is effectively brought in at £1,650 (75% × 4,950 skodas @ 2.25 skodas). There is, therefore, an exchange gain of which the group's share is £37.50.

This exchange gain will have been reflected in the cash flows of Harmony (its bank balance will be £37.50 better off) and it would, therefore, seem that the best treatment for this exchange difference is to include it as part of the profit for the year. This interpretation is based on the concepts behind SSAP 20 which are that exchange differences arising from the retranslation of a net investment (and which therefore do not affect the cash flows of the holding company) should be shown as a movement on reserves whereas exchange differences which are reflected in cash flows should be included as part of the profit.

13.5   Examination technique: closing rate method

13.5.1   Introduction

In an examination it is unlikely that the question would be presented as set out above. The information normally provided would include the accounts of the holding company and the overseas subsidiary for a particular year, say 19X9, and additional details of the position at the date of acquisition and the exchange rate at various dates since then.

13.5.2   Illustration

The basic information given would be as in 13.4.12, i.e., the profit and loss account for 19X9 and the balance sheet on 31 December 19X9. You would also be given the following information:

	Rate to £	
1 January 19X8	3	skodas
31 December 19X8	2	skodas
Average for 19X9	2.1	skodas
31 December 19X9	2.25	skodas

On 1 January 19X8, Harmony Ltd purchased the whole of the share capital of Cadence SA. The reserves of Cadence SA at that date were 30,000 skodas.

13.5.3   Problem

The consolidated balance sheet at 31 December 19X9 and the consolidated profit and loss account should not cause any problems but when we come to the statement of reserves we will not know the figure for the consolidated reserves brought forward. In an examination it will be quickest to bring in this figure as the balancing figure since we already know the retained profit for the year (from the profit and loss account) and the consolidated reserves carried forward (from the balance sheet) and the exchange differences for the year can easily be calculated in the following manner:

	Skodas
Closing net assets of Cadence SA	103,050
Less: Retained profit for the year	5,050
Opening net assets of Cadence SA	98,000

Translated:	£
At closing rate of 2.25 skodas	43,556
At opening rate of 2 skodas	49,000
Exchange loss	(5,444)
Group share (75%)	(4,083)

Having calculated this figure, the statement of reserves can be produced with the opening balance as the balancing figure.

13.5.4   Reconciling the reserves brought forward

In an examination, the priority is to produce the financial statements as quickly as possible and this involves using a balancing figure for the consolidated reserves brought forward. Having produced an answer, it is obviously vital to double-check this figure if time in the examination permits.

To produce a figure for consolidated reserves we must first produce a figure for the translated post-acquisition reserves of Cadence at 1 January 19X9, including all exchange differences to that date, i.e., a figure for the increase in net assets of the subsidiary, when translated into sterling, since the date of acquisition. This can be calculated as follows:

	£
Net assets at 1 January 19X9: 98,000 skodas @ 2 skodas	49,000
Net assets at acquisition: 90,000 skodas @ 3 skodas	30,000
Increase in net assets in sterling, i.e., post-acquisition reserves including exchange differences	19,000

The consolidated reserves are therefore:

	£
Harmony (£115,650 − £15,650)	100,000
Cadence: group share of post-acquisition retained reserves (75% × £19,000)	14,250
	114,250

13.5.5 Summary of closing rate method

(a)   Translate the profit and loss account and balance sheet of the subsidiary as follows:

   (i)   For the balance sheet, translate all items at the closing rate except for the share capital and pre-acquisition reserves which should be translated at the rate at the date of acquisition (post-acquisition reserves are the balancing figure in sterling).

   (ii)   For the profit and loss account, translate all figures at either the closing rate or the average rate as the accounting policy requires.

(b)   Produce the consolidated balance sheet and profit and loss account, incorporating the subsidiary's figures as translated in (a) above. The goodwill figure will be calculated as:

	£
Cost of investment	X
Group share of share capital and pre-acquisition reserves	
of subsidiary translated at rate at date of acquisition	(X)
Goodwill	X

The figures for minority interest will be based on the translated accounts for (a) above.

(c)   Calculate the exchange differences arising during the year. These will arise from:

   (i)   the retranslation of the opening net assets of the subsidiary at the closing rate; and,

   (ii)   if average rate was used to translate the profit and loss account, the retranslation of the retained profit of the subsidiary at the closing rate.

(d)   Produce the statement of consolidated reserves incorporating the exchange differences calculated in (c) above and putting in the reserves brought forward as a balancing figure.

(e)   If time in the examination allows, prove the consolidated reserves at the beginning of the year.

13.6   Temporal method

13.6.1   Introduction

SSAP 20 envisages that the closing rate/net investment concept is likely to be applicable in almost all circumstances. However, as stated in 13.3.4, there are circumstances when the temporal method should be used. The temporal method will now be applied to the illustration given in 13.4 to show the principles involved.

13.6.2   Mechanics of the temporal method

As stated in 13.3.4, the mechanics of the temporal method are identical with those used in preparing the accounts of an individual company. Therefore the steps to be followed are:

(a)   Translate the accounts of the subsidiary into sterling as follows:

  (i)   In the profit and loss account, turnover, purchases and most expenses will be translated at the average rate (assuming that these items accrue evenly over the period) whereas stocks and depreciation will be translated at the historical rate.

  (ii)   In the balance sheet, assets and liabilities which are stated at current values (for example, monetary items, stocks at net realisable value, fixed assets revalued at the balance sheet date) should be translated at the closing rate. All other assets and liabilities (for example, stocks at cost, investments, fixed assets) should be translated at the historical rate.

(b)   Produce the consolidated accounts using a figure for goodwill calculated in the same manner as for the closing rate method, figures for minority interest based on the translated accounts of the subsidiary and with exchange differences as part of the profit for the year.

(c)   Produce a statement of consolidated reserves. This will not include any exchange differences.

13.6.3   Consolidated balance sheet on 1 January 19X8

At the date of acquisition, the historical rate is the same as the closing rate and therefore the consolidated balance sheet will be the same as under the closing rate method (see 13.4.3).

13.6.4   The position after two years' trading

We shall now move directly to the end of December 19X9 so as to show the most likely format of an examination question. The accounts for the year ended 31 December 19X9 are as follows:

Profit and loss accounts for the year ended 31 December 19X9

	Harmony £	Cadence Skodas
Turnover	200,000	130,000
Opening stock	11,000	6,300
Purchases	120,000	75,700
	131,000	82,000
Closing stock	16,000	15,000
Cost of sales	115,000	67,000
Gross profit	85,000	63,000
Distribution and administrative expenses	(25,000)	(15,000)
Depreciation	(20,000)	(30,000)
Dividend receivable from group company	1,650	—
Profit before taxation	41,650	18,000
Taxation	16,000	8,000
Profit after taxation	26,650	10,000
Dividends (proposed)	10,000	4,950
Retained profit for the year	15,650	5,050

Balance sheets on 31 December 19X9

	Harmony £	Cadence Skodas
Fixed assets:		
Tangible assets	80,000	90,000
Investment in subsidiary	25,000	—
	105,000	90,000
Stock	16,000	15,000
Other net current assets	94,650	28,050
	215,650	133,050
Long-term loan	—	30,000
	215,650	103,050
Capital and reserves:		
Share capital	100,000	60,000
Profit and loss account and revaluation reserve	115,650	43,050
	215,650	103,050

These are the same accounts as in 13.4.12 but with further details to illustrate the temporal method. The relevant exchange rates are:

	Skodas to £
1 January 19X8 (date of acquisition of subsidiary)	3.0
30 November 19X8 (date of purchase of opening stocks)	2.1
31 December 19X8	2.0
Average for year	2.1
31 July 19X9	2.15
30 November 19X9 (date of purchase of closing stocks)	2.2
31 December 19X9	2.25

The fixed assets which were purchased during the year were bought on 31 July 19X9 for 30,000 skodas and the remaining fixed assets were held by Cadence at the time of acquisition.

13.6.5   Translation of the accounts of Cadence SA for 19X9

It is easiest to start with the balance sheet:

Balance sheet on 31 December 19X9

	Skodas	Rate	£
Fixed assets: tangible:			
Held at acquisition	60,000	HR: 3	30,000
Bought during year	30,000	HR: 2.15	13,953
	90,000		33,953
Stock	15,000	HR: 2.2	6,818
Other net current assets	28,050	CR: 2.25	12,467
	133,050		53,238
Long-term loan	30,000	CR: 2.25	13,333
	103,050		39,905
Share capital	60,000	HR: 3	20,000
Reserves:			
Pre-acquisition	30,000	HR: 3	10,000
Post-acquisition	13,050	Balancing figure	9,905
	103,050		39,905

Notice that in the translation of shareholders' funds the approach is the same as under the closing rate method, using post-acquisition reserves as a balancing figure. However, the sterling total for shareholders' funds is not the same figure as under the closing rate method since, under the temporal method, it is a function of the various rates of exchange used to translate the individual assets and liabilities on the other side of the balance sheet.

The profit and loss account is more complicated than the balance sheet as it will contain a figure for exchange differences and, as will be seen later, the exchange differences under the temporal method are not as straightforward as under the closing rate method. There the exchange differences will have to be found as a balancing figure. Below, the figures in the profit and loss account which do not cause any problems have been translated.

Profit and loss account for the year ended 31 December 19X9

	Skodas	Rate	£
Turnover	130,000	AR: 2.1	61,905
Opening stock	6,300	HR: 2.1	3,000
Purchases	75,700	AR: 2.1	36,048
	82,000		39,048
Closing stock	15,000·	HR: 2.2	6,818
	67,000		32,230
Gross profit	63,000		29,675
Distribution and administrative expenses	(15,000)	AR: 2.1	(7,143)
Depreciation:			
Assets held at acquisition	(20,000)	HR: 3.0	(6,667)
Assets bought during year	(10,000)	HR: 2.15	(4,651)
Exchange differences	—		?
Profit before taxation	18,000		?
Taxation	8,000	AR: 2.1	3,810
Profit after taxation	10,000		?
Dividend (proposed)	4,950	CR: 2.25	2,200
Retained profit for the year	5,050		?

In order to be able to calculate the exchange differences as a balancing figure, the retained profit for the year has to be found and this can be calculated as the increase in net assets in sterling over the year (i.e., the increase in the sterling figure of reserves over the year).

The closing net assets can be taken from the translated balance sheet but, to calculate the opening net assets, the opening balance sheet must be prepared under the temporal method. First, the balance sheet must be reconstructed in skodas. The balance sheet is reconstructed and translated below.

Balance sheet on 31 December 19X8

	Skodas	Rate (Note 5)	£
Fixed assets			
Tangible assets (Note 1)	80,000	HR: 3	26,667
Stocks (Note 2)	6,300	HR: 2.1	3,000
Other net monetary assets (Note 4)	11,700	CR: 2.0	5,850
Net assets at 31 December 19X8 (Note 3)	98,000		35,517

Notes

1   The opening fixed assets can be found from the fixed asset note or calculated by adjusting the closing fixed assets for additions, disposals and depreciation.

2   The opening stocks are taken from the detailed profit and loss account.

3   The opening net assets in skodas are calculated by deducting the retained profit for the year from the closing net assets:

	Skodas
Net assets at 31 December 19X9	103,050
Less: retained profit for the year	5,050
Net assets at 31 December 19X8	98,000

4   The 'other net monetary assets' are the balancing figure and do not need to be split as they will all be translated at closing rate.

5   The translation rates used are those which would have been used in translating last year's balance sheet.

The retained profit for the year in sterling can now be found as:

	£
Cadence:	
Net assets at 31 December 19X9	39,905
Net assets at 1 January 19X9	35,517
Retained profit for the year (including exchange differences)	4,388

This can be inserted in the translated profit and loss account of Cadence and the exchange differences can be put in as the balancing figure. From gross profit onwards, the profit and loss account will become:

	£
Gross profit	29,675
Distribution and administrative expenses	(7,143)
Depreciation:	
Assets held at acquisition	(6,667)
Assets bought during year	(4,651)
Exchange differences (balancing figure)	(816)
	10,398
Profit before taxation	10,398
Taxation	3,810
	6,588
Profit after taxation	6,588
Dividend (proposed)	2,200
	4,388
Retained profit for the year	4,388

13.6.6   Consolidated accounts for 19X9

Harmony Ltd
Consolidated balance sheet on 31 December 19X9

	£
Fixed assets:	
Intangible assets: goodwill	2,500
Tangible assets (see note below)	113,953
	116,453
Stock	22,818
Other net current assets	107,117
	246,388
Long-term loan	13,333
	233,055
Capital and reserves:	
Share capital	100,000
Profit and loss account (£115,650 + 75% × £9,905)	123,079
	223,079
Minority interest (25% × £39,905)	9,976
	233,055

Note

The note on tangible fixed assets would include:

	£
Net book value at 1 January 19X9	126,667
Additions during the year	18,604
Depreciation charge for the year	(31,318)
Net book value at 31 December 19X8	113,953

Consolidated profit and loss account for the year ended 31 December 19X9

	£
Turnover	261,905
Opening stock	14,000
Purchases	156,048
	170,048
Closing stock	22,818
	147,230
Gross profit	114,675
Distribution and administrative expenses	(32,143)
Depreciation	(31,318)
Exchange differences	(816)
Profit before taxation	50,398
Taxation	19,810
Profit after taxation	30,588
Minority interest (25% × £6,588)	1,647
Profit attributable to shareholders of Harmony Ltd	28,941
Dividend (proposed)	10,000
Retained profit for the year	18,941

The above consolidated profit and loss account has been shown in detail. Obviously, for the published accounts, the breakdown of cost of sales would be omitted and depreciation would have to be included in the appropriate expense headings.

Statement of consolidated reserves for the year ended 31 December 19X9

	£
Profit and loss account at 1 January 19X9 (see below)	104,138
Retained profit for the year	18,941
Profit and loss account at 31 December 19X9	123,079

The opening balance on reserves may be proved as follows:

	£	£
Harmony (£115,650 − £15,650)		100,000
Cadence: group share of post-acquisition retained reserves		
(equal to increase in net assets since date of acquisition):		
Net assets at 31 December 19X8 (per translated		
balance sheet)	35,517	
Net assets at acquisition: 90,000 skodas @ 3 skodas	30,000	
	5,517	
Group share (75%)		4,138
		104,138

13.6.7   Proof of exchange differences

In an examination it is unlikely to be worthwhile attempting to prove the exchange differences under the temporal method as the calculation can be very complicated unless the accounts are very simple. However, we shall prove below that the balancing figure in the translated profit and loss account of Cadence is correct.

Obviously, there will be no exchange differences on fixed assets and stocks in the opening balance sheet and, therefore, exchange differences will arise on opening *monetary* assets. In the case of Cadence, the situation is a little complex as some of the opening monetary assets were used to purchase fixed assets and once this has happened no further exchange differences arise on them. The opening net monetary assets of Cadence can be seen from the reconstructed balance sheet of the company at 31 December 19X8 to be 11,700 skodas. The exchange differences relating to opening net assets are therefore:

	£	£
On net monetary assets used to purchase fixed assets:		
40,000 skodas:		
At rate at date of purchase of fixed assets 2.15 skodas		18,605
At opening rate of 2 skodas		20,000
Exchange loss		(1,395)
On remaining net monetary liabilities: (28,300 skodas)		
At closing rate of 2.25 skodas	(12,577)	
At opening rate of 2 skodas	(14,150)	
Exchange gain		1,573
Net exchange gain		178

There will also be exchange differences on the profit for the year but not on that part of the profit which relates to depreciation or stocks as these items are not retranslated.

	Skodas
Net profit for year	10,000
Add: depreciation	30,000
Add: opening stock	6,300
Less: closing stock	(15,000)
	31,300

	£
31,300 skodas:	
At closing rate of 2.25 skodas	13,911
At average rate of 2.1 skodas	14,905
Exchange loss	(994)

The total exchange difference is £178 − £994, i.e., a loss of £816.

13.7   Examination technique for the temporal method

13.7.1   Introduction

The illustration in 13.6 is likely to be similar to the way in which information will be presented in an examination, i.e., it looks at one year in isolation. The techniques used in the illustration would therefore be relevant to an examination question.

13.7.2   Summary of examination approach

(a)   Translate the balance sheet of the subsidiary as follows:

    (i)   monetary items at closing rate;
    (ii)   non-monetary items at historical rate;
    (iii)   share capital and pre-acquisition reserves at rate at date of acquisition (post-acquisition reserves are the balance figure in sterling).

(b)   Produce the consolidated balance sheet with goodwill calculated by reference to share capital and pre-acquisition reserves translated at rate at date of acquisition.

(c)   Reconstruct the subsidiary's opening balance sheet in the foreign currency and then translate to find the subsidiary's translated net assets in sterling at the beginning of the year.

(d)   Translate the profit and loss account of the subsidiary as follows:

(i)   sales, purchases, expenses and taxation at average rate;
(ii)   opening and closing stock and depreciation at historical rate;
(iii)   dividends at actual rate (or closing rate for proposed dividends).

The retained profit for the year is the difference between opening and closing net assets in sterling. The exchange differences are found as the missing figure in the profit and loss account.

(e)   Produce the consolidated profit and loss account which will include exchange differences as determined above.

13.8   Foreign currency loans in group accounts

13.8.1   Paragraph 57 of SSAP 20

This paragraph states:

Where foreign currency borrowings have been used to finance, or provide a hedge against, group equity investments in foreign enterprises, exchange gains or losses on the borrowings, which would otherwise have been taken to the profit and loss account, may be offset as reserve movements against exchange differences arising on the retranslation of the net investments provided that:

(a) the relationships between the investing company and the foreign enterprises concerned justify the use of the closing rate method for consolidation purposes;

(b) in any accounting period, the exchange gains and losses arising on foreign currency borrowings are offset only to the extent of the exchange differences arising on the net investment in foreign enterprises;

(c) the foreign currency borrowings, whose exchange gains or losses are used in the offset process, should not exceed, in the aggregate, the total amount of cash that the net investments are expected to be able to generate, whether from profits or otherwise; and

(d) the accounting treatment is applied consistently from period to period.

It is important to note that the offset is only available when the closing rate method is being used, that the borrowings do not need to be in the same currency as the investment, and that the borrowings can be made by any of the group companies and do not need to be made by the holding company.

13.8.2   Illustration

Holding plc purchased a 75% interest in Subsidiary SA for £5,000 on 1 January 19X7 when the
net assets of Subsidiary SA were FFr 66,000 and the exchange rate was 10 francs to the £.
Holding plc raised a loan of FFr 33,000 on that day in order to part-finance the investment. The
summarised accounts for the year to 31 December 19X7 are:

Profit and loss accounts for the year ended 31 December 19X7

	Holding £	Subsidiary FFr
Profit before taxation (including gain on retranslation of loan of £300)	60,000	27,500
Taxation	25,000	11,000
Profit after taxation	35,000	16,500

Balance sheets on 31 December 19X7

	Holding £	Subsidiary FFr
Investment in Subsidiary SA (at cost)	5,000	—
Net current assets	173,000	82,500
Loan in French francs	(3,000)	—
	175,000	82,500
Share capital	100,000	30,000
Profit and loss account at 1 January 19X7	40,000	36,000
Profit for the year	35,000	16,500
	175,000	82,500

The rate at 31 December 19X7 was 11 francs to the £ and the loan in the holding company's
balance sheet has already been retranslated at the balance sheet date: the gain on retranslation
of £300 is included in the profit before taxation.

13.8.3   Translation of the accounts of Subsidiary SA

Profit and loss account for the year ended 31 December 19X7

	FFr	Rate	£
Profit before taxation	27,500	CR: 11	2,500
Taxation	11,000	CR: 11	1,000
Profit after taxation	16,500		1,500

Balance sheet 31 December 19X7

	FFr	Rate	£
Net assets	82,500	CR: 11	7,500
Share capital and pre-acquisition reserves	66,000	HR: 10	6,600
Post-acquisition reserves	16,500	Balancing figure	900
	82,500		7,500

13.8.4 Calculation of exchange differences

The exchange difference on the loan in Holding's accounts is a gain of £300 and is, at present, included in the profit before taxation.

The exchange difference on retranslation of the opening net assets of Subsidiary SA is:

	£
Opening net assets FFr 66,000:	
At closing rate of 11 francs	6,000
At opening rate of 10 francs	6,600
Exchange loss	(600)
Group share (75%)	(450)

Therefore, the whole of the exchange difference on the loan may be offset against the exchange difference on the net investment. The figure for exchange differences which goes to reserves is a loss of £150.

13.8.5 Consolidated accounts

The goodwill on consolidation will be calculated as follows:

	£
Cost of investment	5,000
Less: net assets acquired 75% × FFr 66,000 @ 10 francs	4,950
Goodwill	50

Consolidated profit and loss account for the year ended 31 December 19X7

	£
Profit before taxation (£60,000 − £300 + £2,500)	62,200
Taxation (£25,000 + £1,000)	26,000
Profit after taxation	36,200
Minority interest (25% × £1,500)	375
Retained profit for the year	35,825

Consolidated balance sheet on 31 December 19X7

	£
Intangible fixed assets: goodwill	50
Net current assets (£173,000 + £7,500)	180,500
	180,550
Long-term loan	3,000
	177,550
Share capital	100,000
Profit and loss account (£75,000 + 75% × £900)	75,675
	175,675
Minority interest (25% × £7,500)	1,875
	177,550

Statement of consolidated reserves for the year ended 31 December 19X7

	£
Profit and loss account at 1 January 19X7	40,000
Retained profit for the year	35,825
Exchange loss	(150)
Profit and loss account at 31 December 19X7	75,675

13.9   International and American standards

13.9.1   International Accounting Standard 21

IAS 21 'Accounting for the effects of changes in foreign exchange rates' was issued shortly after SSAP 20. It adopts the same approach as SSAP 20 and compliance with SSAP 20 will ensure compliance with IAS 21. One additional paragraph in IAS 21 which does not appear in SSAP 20 is the deferral of exchange differences on long-term monetary items in the accounts of an individual company. These deferred exchange differences would then be taken to the profit and loss account over the estimated remaining lives of the items to which they relate.

13.9.2 Statement of Financial Accounting Standards 52

FASB Statement No. 52 'Foreign currency translation' issued in December 1981 also closely follows the concepts and requirements of SSAP 20; it replaces FASB Statement No. 8 which required the use of the temporal method. One main difference from SSAP 20 is that FASB Statement No. 52 requires exchange differences to be accumulated and disclosed as a separate reserve.

13.10   Summary

This is probably the most difficult area in group accounts. If the closing rate is used, the preparation of the consolidated profit and loss account and balance sheet is relatively simple (if 'reserves' are inserted as a balancing figure!) but the calculation of exchange differences and consolidated reserve movements can get very complicated. Practice is as always the key point, and you will probably benefit by working questions 37 and 38 two or three times.

14 Practice questions and answers

14.1 Introduction

This is a set of practice questions which will enable you to develop skill and fluency at handling group accounts.

Questions for the opening chapters are mainly below examination level. From question 28 onwards, the level is that required for examinations.

It is really important to work through every question up to the level of difficulty needed for your particular examination. That means attempting the questions as you complete your study of each chapter — and without looking at the answer first. Answers to the more advanced questions are accompanied by detailed discussions and notes which explain the difficult parts. You will find it helpful to rework questions at intervals.

14.2 Index of practice questions

14.3   Questions

2   Consolidated balance sheet 1: definitions and basic techniques

1   The following balances relate to Park Ltd and Gate Ltd at 31 December 19X4.

	Park Ltd £	Gate Ltd £
Issued share capital (£1 ordinary shares)	200,000	80,000
Retained profits at 31 December 19X3	45,100	37,500
Profit for 19X4	17,600	28,500
Unsecured loan repayable 19X8	—	30,000
Current liabilities	53,700	26,000
	316,400	202,000
Freehold property, net of depreciation	—	99,000
Other fixed assets, net of depreciation	182,300	35,000
48,000 shares in Gate Ltd at cost	72,000	—
Current assets	62,100	68,000
	316,400	202,000

Park Ltd acquired its shares in Gate Ltd on 31 December 19X3.

Required:

The consolidated balance sheet of the group at 31 December 19X4 presented in good style so far as the information permits.

(Chartered Institute of Bankers)

2   On 30 June 19X4, Redan Ltd acquired 60% of the ordinary share capital and 20% of the preference share capital of Pyrton Ltd for £95,000 and £15,000 respectively. At that date Pyrton Ltd had a profit and loss account balance of £50,000 and a share premium account balance of £9,000.

The following balance sheets have been prepared at 30 June 19X8:

	Redan Ltd		Pyrton Ltd	
Fixed assets:	£	£	£	£
Tangible assets		220,000		170,000
Investments: shares in group companies		110,000		
		330,000		
Current assets	270,000		186,000	
Creditors: amount falling due within one year	225,000		137,000	
Net current assets		45,000		49,000
Total assets less current liabilities		375,000		219,000
Capital and reserves:				
Called-up share capital:				
Preference shares of £1 each		—		40,000
Ordinary shares of £1 each		200,000		90,000
Share premium account		25,000		9,000
Profit and loss account		150,000		80,000
		375,000		219,000

You are required to prepare the consolidated balance sheet of Redan Ltd and its subsidiary as at 30 June 19X8.

3 Pig Ltd acquired 80% of the equity share capital and 30% of the preference share capital of Whistle Ltd on 31 December 19X3 when the profit and loss account of Whistle Ltd was £25,000. The following balance sheets were prepared at 31 December 19X6:

	Pig Ltd	Whistle Ltd
	£	£
Investments: shares of Whistle Ltd:		
6,000 preference shares	5,000	
8,000 ordinary shares	35,000	
	40,000	
Sundry net assets	160,000	70,000
	200,000	70,000
Capital and reserves:		
Called-up share capital:		
Preference shares of £1 each	100,000	20,000
Ordinary shares of £1 each	20,000	10,000
Profit and loss account	80,000	40,000
	200,000	70,000

You are required to prepare the consolidated balance sheet of Pig Ltd as at 31 December 19X6.

3 Consolidated balance sheet 2: cancelling

4   H Ltd owns 80% of the ordinary share capital of S Ltd. Show the adjustments necessary on consolidation to record the following transactions:

(a)   S Ltd transferred to H Ltd a fixed asset at a value of £15,000. The original cost to S Ltd was £20,000 and the accumulated depreciation at the date of transfer was £8,000. Both companies depreciate such assets at 20% per annum on cost to the company, making full provision in the year of purchase and none in the year of sale.

(b)   S Ltd manufactures jigs for industry and during the year transferred to the holding company H Ltd, a jig at a value of £20,000. The manufactured cost of the jig to S Ltd was £16,000. H Ltd depreciates such assets at the rate of 20% per annum, charging a full year's depreciation in the year of purchase and none in the year of sale.

5   Parent Ltd acquired 60,000 ordinary shares of £1 each in Subsidiary Ltd on 31 December 19X1. The summarised balance sheets of Parent Ltd and Subsidiary Ltd on that date, were:

	Parent Ltd £	Subsidiary Ltd £
Fixed assets	253,000	128,000
Investment in Subsidiary Ltd at cost: 60,000 shares of £1 each	100,000	—
Stock in hand	30,000	10,000
Bills receivable (including £700 from Subsidiary Ltd)	2,000	—
Debtors and balances at bank	20,000	17,000
	405,000	155,000
Called up share capital:		
600,000 shares of 50p each	300,000	—
80,000 shares of £1 each	—	80,000
Capital reserve	—	34,000
Revenue reserve	20,000	10,000
Profit and loss account	50,000	10,000
Bills payable (including £1,000 to Parent Ltd)	—	3,500
Creditors	35,000	17,500
Note on balance sheet of Parent Ltd:		
There is a contingent liability for bills receivable discounted of £1,200		
	405,000	155,000

You are given the following information:

(a)   On 1 January 19X2, Subsidiary Ltd utilised part of its capital reserve to make a bonus issue of one share for every four shares held and applied the balance of the reserve to write down its fixed assets.

(b) Stock in hand of Parent Ltd includes £4,800 for goods at invoice price bought from Subsidiary Ltd: when invoicing goods to Parent Ltd, Subsidiary Ltd adds 20 per cent to cost.

You are required to prepare the summarised consolidated balance sheet as on 1 January 19X2. Workings must be submitted.

6 Able plc acquired 400,000 shares in Baker plc on 30 June 19X1. The most recent balance sheets of the two companies are set out below:

Balance sheet of Able plc as at 30 June 19X2

	£		£
Share capital: ordinary shares		Fixed assets	1,365,659
of £1 each, fully paid	1,500,000	Investment in Baker plc	161,000
General reserve	60,000	Stock	115,340
Unappropriated profit:		Debtors	71,912
Balance b/d	27,000	Bank	20,450
Current liabilities	147,361		
	1,734,361		1,734,361

Balance sheet of Baker plc as at 30 June 19X2

	£		£
Share capital: ordinary shares of		Fixed assets	229,731
50p each, fully paid	250,000	Stock	138,360
General reserve	25,000	Debtors	39,950
Unappropriated profit:		Bank	2,815
balance b/d	8,000		
12% debentures	50,000		
Current liabilities	77,856		
	410,856		410,856

Additional information:

(a) Baker plc has made a profit of £10,000 for the year to 30 June 19X2, of which £4,000 has been transferred to general reserve.

(b) The stock of Baker plc includes goods purchased from Able plc for £40,000. The transfer price for this transaction was computed as cost plus 25%. Payment had not been made for these goods by 30 June 19X2.

You are required:

(a) To draft in columnar form a consolidated balance sheet for Able and Baker as at 30 June 19X2.

(b)   To explain an alternative method which can be used to account for the profit on inter-group sales, and show the effect of the alternative on the group balance sheet.

(Association of Accounting Technicians)

7   Cat Ltd owns 60% of the ordinary share capital of Mouse Ltd, having acquired the shares at a time when Mouse's reserves amounted to £8,000. The balance sheets of the two companies at 31 December 19X4 were as follows:

	Cat Ltd		Mouse Ltd	
	£000	£000	£000	£000
Fixed assets:				
Cost		100		30
Accumulated depreciation		(40)		(10)
		60		20
Investment in Mouse Ltd		20		
		80		
Current assets:				
Stock	30		10	
Debtors	20		15	
Current account: Mouse	14			
Bills receivable	12			
(including £8,000 payable by Mouse)				
Cash at bank	8		4	
	84		29	
Less: liabilities:				
Trade creditors	(40)		(2)	
Bills payable			10	
Current account: Cat		44	(10)	7
		124		27

	Cat Ltd	Mouse Ltd
	£000	£000
Issued share capital	50	20
Reserves	74	7
	124	27

On 30 December 19X4 Mouse had remitted £4,000 to Cat which was not received by Cat until 4 January 19X5.

The bills payable by Mouse include, as well as the £8,000 shown as receivable by Cat, a bill for £11,000 which had been discounted by Cat.

Prepare a consolidated balance sheet as at 31 December 19X4.

8   Dog Ltd holds 70% of the share capital of Duck Ltd. At 30 June 19X6 their balance sheets were as follows:

	Dog Ltd		Duck Ltd	
	£000	£000	£000	£000
Fixed assets:				
Cost		100		40
Less: aggregate depreciation		(40)		(16)
		—		—
		60		24
Investment in Duck		20		
Current assets:				
Stock	40		25	
Debtor	30		18	
Cash at bank	10		5	
	—		—	
	80		48	
Less: creditors	(60)	20	(20)	28
	—	—	—	—
		100		52
		—		—
Issued share capital: ordinary shares				
of £1 each		50		20
Reserves		50		32
		—		—
		100		52
		—		—

Dog had purchased the shares in Duck at a time when the reserves of that company had been £10,000.

The fixed assets of Duck include items purchased from Dog for £8,000. Their written-down value at the time of purchase in Dog's records totalled £6,000. (Cost £10,000, depreciation £4,000.) Both companies charge no depreciation in the year of sale of an asset and a full year's depreciation in the year of purchase. All assets are depreciated at 10% per annum straight line, except for the items purchased by Duck from Dog, for which a rate of 25% (straight line) is to be used. This transaction has already been reflected in the balance sheets of the companies.

The stock of Dog at 30 June 19X6 included goods sold to it by Duck for £3,000. The cost of the goods to Duck was £2,000.

Prepare a consolidated balance sheet as at 30 June 19X6.

4   Consolidated balance sheet 3: dividends

9   The summarised balance sheets of Close Ltd and Steele Ltd as at 31 December 19X2 were as follows:

	Close Ltd	Steele Ltd
	£	£
Plant, at cost less depreciation	97,000	45,000
Fixtures, at cost less depreciation	13,000	13,200
Stock, at cost	18,000	12,000
Debtors	62,700	21,100
Investments, at cost	—	2,500
Balance at bank	10,000	3,000
Current account: Close Ltd	—	3,200
Shares in Steele Ltd:		
48,000 shares, at cost	54,000	
	254,700	100,000
Authorised and issued share capital:		
ordinary shares of £1 each	120,000	60,000
Share premium account	18,000	
Capital reserve on 1 January 19X2	8,000	6,000
General reserve on 1 January 19X2	15,000	10,000
Profit and loss account on		
1 January 19X2	40,000	8,000
Profit for 19X2	16,000	5,000
Creditors	35,000	11,000
Current account: Steele Ltd	2,700	—
	254,700	100,000

The following information is relevant:

(a)   On 31 December 19X1, Close Ltd had allotted 36,000 shares at a premium of 50p each in exchange for 48,000 shares in Steele Ltd.

(b)   On 11 January 19X2, Close Ltd received a £2,000 dividend from Steele Ltd relating to the year ended 31 December 19X1, which had been credited to its profit and loss account.

(c)   The stock of Steele Ltd included £4,000 goods from Close Ltd invoiced to Steele Ltd at cost plus 25%.

(d)   A cheque for £500 from Close Ltd to Steele Ltd sent before 31 December was not received by the latter company until January 19X3.

You are required to prepare the summarised consolidated balance sheet of Close Ltd and its subsidiary Steele Ltd as at 31 December 19X2.

10 The following is a summary of the balances in the records of Black Ltd and Bird Ltd, as on 31 March 19X2.

	Black Ltd £	Bird Ltd £
Debits		
Fixed assets at cost	250,000	220,000
75,000 ordinary shares in Bird Ltd at cost	165,000	—
60,000 preference shares in Bird Ltd at cost	60,000	—
£5,000 6% debentures of Bird Ltd	5,000	—
Current assets	145,500	143,400
	625,500	363,400
Credits		
Authorised and issued capital, fully paid:		
ordinary shares of £1 each	300,000	100,000
7% non-cumulative preference shares of £1 each	—	80,000
General reserves	50,000	40,000
Profit and loss account	98,500	44,400
Provision for depreciation of fixed assets	60,000	30,000
6% debentures	—	20,000
Proposed dividends:		
On ordinary shares	30,000	10,000
On preference shares	—	5,600
Debenture interest accrued	—	1,200
Creditors	87,000	32,200
	625,500	363,400

You ascertain the following:

(a)   Black Ltd acquired the shares of Bird Ltd, cum dividend, on 31 March 19X1.

(b)   The general reserve of Bird Ltd was the same on 31 March 19X1 as on 31 March 19X2. The balance on the profit and loss account of Bird Ltd is made up as follows:

	£
Balance on 31 March 19X1	28,000
Net profit, year ended 31 March 19X2	32,000
	60,000
Less: provision for proposed dividends	15,600
	44,400

(c)   The stock-in-trade of Bird Ltd on 31 March 19X2, included £16,000 in respect of goods purchased from Black Ltd. These goods had been sold by Black Ltd to Bird Ltd at such a price as to give Black Ltd a profit of 20% on the invoice price.

(d)   The balance on the profit and loss account of Bird Ltd, on 31 March 19X1, is after providing for the preference dividend of £5,600 and a proposed ordinary dividend of £5,000, both of which were subsequently paid but had been incorrectly credited to profit and loss account in the books of Black Ltd.

(e)   No entries had been made in the books of Black Ltd in respect of the debenture interest due from, or the proposed dividend of, Bird Ltd for the year ended 31 March 19X2.

(f)   On 31 March 19X2, the authorised and issued ordinary share capital of Bird Ltd had been increased by £20,000 by capitalising part of the general reserve and issuing 20,000 £1 shares to the existing shareholders in proportion to their existing holdings. This transaction has not yet been shown in the books of Bird Ltd or Black Ltd.

You are required to prepare the consolidated balance sheet of Black Ltd and its subsidiary company Bird Ltd as on 31 March 19X2.

11   Bough Ltd made an offer to acquire all the shares in Twig Ltd at a price of £2.50 per share, to be satisfied by the allotment of five shares in Bough Ltd for every four shares in Twig Ltd.

By the expiry date of the offer, which was 1 January 19X2, shareholders owning 75% of the shares in Twig Ltd had accepted, and the acquisition was effective from the date.

The accounting date of Twig Ltd was 31 March in each year, but, to conform with Bough Ltd accounts were prepared to 30 June 19X2, covering the 15 months to that date.

The draft summarised accounts of the companies on 30 June 19X2, which do not include any entries regarding the acquisition of shares in Twig Ltd, were as follows:

Balance sheets on 30 June 19X2

	Bough Ltd £	Bough Ltd £	Twig Ltd £	Twig Ltd £
Freehold property, at cost		200,000		38,000
Plant and machinery at cost	50,000		12,000	
Less: depreciation	18,000		3,000	
		32,000		9,000
		232,000		47,000
Quoted investments, at cost		7,000		—
Stock, at cost		32,000		21,000
Debtors		41,000		17,000
Balance at bank		15,000		8,000
		327,000		93,000
Share capital: ordinary shares of £1 each:				
Authorised		330,000		75,000
Issued and fully paid		150,000		60,000
Reserves:				
General reserve		55,000		
Profit and loss account		62,000		20,000
		267,000		80,000
Current liabilities		27,000		7,000
Corporation tax		33,000		6,000
		327,000		93,000

Profit and loss account

	Bough Ltd Year £	Twig Ltd 15 months £
Period ended 30 June 19X2		
Balance brought forward	14,000	12,000
Profit for period	80,000	18,000
	94,000	30,000
Taxation for period	32,000	6,000
Interim dividend paid 30 November 19X1	—	4,000
Balance carried forward	62,000	20,000
	94,000	30,000

The directors of Bough Ltd had recommended the payment of a final dividend of 20% to all shareholders on the register on 30 June 19X2. The directors of Twig Ltd had proposed a final dividend of 12½% payable on 30 September 19X2.

You are required to prepare a consolidated balance sheet of Bough Ltd as at 30 June 19X2. (Ignore ACT.)

12 PQ Ltd acquired 80% of the ordinary share capital of JK Ltd on 1 January 19X6 for £153,000.

From the information given below you are required to prepare the consolidated balance sheet of PQ Ltd at 31 December 19X6.

All workings must be shown.

The draft balance sheets of the two companies as at 31 December 19X6 are set out below.

	PQ Ltd £	JK Ltd £
Freehold property, at cost	104,000	
Plant and machinery at cost	228,000	104,000
Investment in JK Ltd	153,000	
Trade investments	48,000	
Stocks	210,000	101,000
Debtors	152,200	71,200
Bank balance: bank A		7,600
Cash	1,100	800
Current account: JK Ltd	12,700	
	909,000	284,600
Issued share capital: ordinary shares		
of £1 each:	300,000	100,000
Share premium account	15,000	
Profit and loss account, 1 January 19X6	137,000	19,400
Retained profits for 19X6	17,000	3,000
Taxation	78,000	27,000
Creditors, trade	162,000	71,400
Bank overdraft: bank B	74,000	
Depreciation:		
Freehold property	9,000	
Plant and machinery	87,000	39,000
Dividend	30,000	15,000
Current account: PQ Ltd		9,800
	909,000	284,600

Notes

1   No interim dividends were paid in 19X6.

2   A remittance of £1,700 from JK Ltd in December 19X6 was not received by PQ Ltd until January 19X7.

3   An invoice for £1,200 for stock material (including £240 profit) had been included in the 19X6 sales by PQ Ltd, but had not been received by JK Ltd.

4   In JK Ltd's stock at 31 December 19X6 were goods to the value of £8,000 ex PQ Ltd on which a profit of £1,600 had been taken by PQ.

5   Consolidated balance sheet 4: acquisition of subsidiary during its accounting period

13   Fairy Ltd acquired its shareholding in Queen Ltd on 30 November 19X5. The following summarised balance sheets have been prepared at 31 March 19X6:

	Fairy Ltd		Queen Ltd	
	£	£	£	£
Shares in Queen Ltd:				
10,000 preference shares	12,000			
36,000 ordinary shares	130,000			
		142,000		
Sundry assets		418,000		500,000
		560,000		500,000
Creditors	150,000		192,000	
Proposed dividends:				
Preference			3,000	
Ordinary	10,000		5,000	
		160,000		200,000
		400,000		300,000
Financed by:				
Share capital:				
12% preference shares of £1 each		—		50,000
Ordinary shares of £1 each		100,000		60,000
Profit and loss account		300,000		190,000
		400,000		300,000

The profit and loss account of Queen Ltd is made up as follows:

	£	£
Balance at 1 April 19X5		169,000
Profit for the year, after taxation		36,000
		205,000
Less:		
Preference dividends:		
Paid (1 October 19X5)	3,000	
Proposed	3,000	
Ordinary dividends:		
Interim, paid (1 November 19X5)	4,000	
Final, proposed	5,000	
		15,000
		190,000

Fairy Ltd has not yet taken account of the dividends receivable from Queen Ltd.

You are required to prepare a consolidated balance sheet as at 31 March 19X6.

6   Consolidated balance sheet 5: piecemeal acquisitions

14   Delta Ltd has progressively built up its interest in Nile Ltd until it held 90% of the company's ordinary shares on 31 December 19X7. Details of acquisitions are as follows.

Date	Number of shares	Cost £000	Reserves of Nile Ltd £000
31 Dec 19X3	100,000	130	100
31 Dec 19X5	100,000	160	200
31 Dec 19X7	250,000	520	300

The balance sheets of the two companies at 31 December 19X8 were as follows:

	Delta Ltd £000	Nile Ltd £000
Fixed assets	680	640
Investment: shares in Nile Ltd	810	
Net current assets	260	310
	1,750	950
Called-up share capital	1,000	500
Reserves	750	450
	1,750	950

You are required:

(a) To prepare a consolidated balance sheet for Delta Ltd and its subsidiary at 31 December 19X8, calculating pre-acquisition reserves by reference to the balance on reserves at the time when control was first gained.

(b) To make revised calculations using the reserve balances at the date of each acquisition and to show how, if at all, the consolidated balance sheet would be affected.

7 Consolidated balance sheet 6: more complex group structures

15 The following are the summarised balance sheets of Ashton Ltd, Batley Ltd and Corby Ltd at 31 December 19X5:

	Ashton Ltd £	Batley Ltd £	Corby Ltd £
80,000 shares in Batley Ltd at cost	60,000	—	—
90,000 shares in Corby Ltd at cost	150,000	—	—
Sundry assets	290,000	200,000	350,000
	500,000	200,000	350,000
Issued share capital (£1 shares)	200,000	100,000	150,000
Profit and loss account:			
Credit (debit) balance at 31 December 19X3	99,000	(10,800)	64,300
Net profit (loss): 19X4	26,000	(3,200)	28,000
Net profit (loss): 19X5	14,400	5,000	(6,000)
Sundry liabilities	160,600	109,000	113,700
	500,000	200,000	350,000

Ashton Ltd acquired the shares in its subsidiaries as follows:

| 31 December 19X3 | 80,000 shares in Batley Ltd |
| 31 December 19X4 | 90,000 shares in Corby Ltd |

No dividends were paid or proposed by any of the companies in the relevant years.

You are required to prepare the consolidated balance sheet for the group at 31 December 19X5. (Ignore taxation.)

(Chartered Institute of Bankers)

16   Tents Ltd, Pegs Ltd and Ropes Ltd are engaged in manufacturing camping equipment. Their balance sheets as on 31 December 19X2 are summarised below:

	Tents Ltd		Pegs Ltd		Ropes Ltd	
	£	£	£	£	£	£
Capital employed:						
Share capital: authorised and issued:						
Ordinary shares of £1 each fully paid		150,000		50,000		20,000
10% preference shares of £1 each fully paid				30,000		
General reserve		60,000		30,000		10,000
Profit and loss account		25,000		(8,000)		4,000
		————		————		————
		235,000		102,000		34,000
Employment of capital:						
Fixed assets at cost less depreciation		140,000		63,000		17,000
Shares in subsidiaries		50,000		19,000		—
		————		————		————
		190,000		82,000		17,000
Current assets						
Stock	20,000		12,000		16,000	
Debtors	48,000		20,000		8,000	
Cash	27,000		14,000		11,000	
	————		————		————	
	95,000		46,000		35,000	
Current liabilities:						
trade creditors	50,000		26,000		18,000	
	————	45,000	————	20,000	————	17,000
		————		————		————
		235,000		102,000		34,000

The following information is relevant:

(a)   Tents Ltd purchased 30,000 ordinary shares in Pegs Ltd on 1 January 19X1 for £34,000 and 5,000 preference shares on 1 January 19X2 for £6,000.

(b)   On 1 January 19X2 Tents Ltd purchased 5,000 ordinary shares in Ropes Ltd for £10,000 and Pegs Ltd purchased 11,000 ordinary shares in Ropes Ltd for £19,000.

(c)   Balances on profit and loss account were as follows:

Pegs Ltd	1 January 19X1	£5,000 (Dr)
	1 January 19X2	£6,000 (Dr)
Ropes Ltd	1 January 19X2	£3,000

(d)   Balances on general reserve were:

Pegs Ltd	1 January 19X1	£10,000
	1 January 19X2	£20,000
Ropes Ltd	1 January 19X2	Nil

(e)   Inter-company balances are included in debtors and trade creditors:

Debtors:	Tents Ltd:	£6,000 due from Ropes Ltd
	Pegs Ltd:	£3,000 due from Tents Ltd
		£2,000 due from Ropes Ltd

(f)   Ropes Ltd sent a £2,000 remittance to Tents Ltd which did not receive it until 3 January 19X3. The cash was sent on 30 December 19X2. Apart from this all inter-company balances agree.

(g)   Preference shareholders are not entitled to participate in profits.

(h)   Tents Ltd sold goods to Pegs Ltd for £8,000 which cost them £6,000 originally. Pegs Ltd still had £2,000 worth at invoiced price in stock on 31 December 19X2.

You are required to prepare a consolidated balance sheet for Tents Ltd and its subsidiaries, Pegs Ltd and Ropes Ltd, as on 31 December 19X2.

17   The following is a summary of the balances in the books of Gross Ltd, Pot Ltd and Bulge Ltd, as on 31 December 19X5:

	Gross Ltd £	Pot Ltd £	Bulge Ltd £
Credits			
Authorised and issued share capital:			
Ordinary shares of £1 each, fully paid	140,000	60,000	20,000
6% cumulative preference shares of			
£1 each, fully paid		15,000	
Profit and loss accounts	52,300	31,600	5,250
5% debentures		8,000	
Provision for depreciation of fixed assets	48,000	27,000	8,000
Debenture interest accrued		400	
Proposed dividends	16,800	6,900	
Creditors	45,700	19,800	12,750
	302,800	168,700	46,000

	£	£	£
Debits			
Fixed assets, at cost	134,000	97,200	30,600
45,000 ordinary shares in Pot Ltd, at cost	81,000		
18,000 ordinary shares in Bulge Ltd, at cost		25,600	
£5,000 5% debentures of Pot Ltd	5,000		
Current assets	82,800	45,900	15,400
	302,800	168,700	46,000

Gross Ltd acquired the shares of Pot Ltd, cum dividend, on 31 December 19X4 and Pot Ltd acquired the shares in Bulge Ltd on 31 December 19X3.

The balances on the profit and loss accounts of Pot Ltd and Bulge Ltd are made up as follows:

	Pot Ltd	Bulge Ltd
Balances on 31 December 19X3	22,600	2,450
Net profits 19X4	9,600	2,000
	32,200	4,450
Less: provision for proposed dividends (19X4)	5,700	
Balances on 31 December 19X4	26,500	4,450
Net profits 19X5	12,000	800
	38,500	5,250
Less: provision for proposed dividends (19X5)	6,900	
	31,600	5,250

The provision for dividends (£5,700) in the profit and loss account of Pot Ltd for the year 19X4 represents the dividends on the preference shares (£900) and the proposed ordinary dividend (£4,800), both of which were subsequently paid; the dividend received by Gross Ltd from Pot Ltd has been credited to the profit and loss account of Gross Ltd. No entries have been made in the books of Gross Ltd in respect of debenture interest due from Pot Ltd, or for the holding company's share of the proposed dividends of Pot Ltd for 19X5.

You are required to prepare the consolidated balance sheet of Gross Ltd and its subsidiary companies as at 31 December 19X5.

Revision questions: chapters 2 to 7

18   The summarised balance sheets of Trunk Ltd and Bough Ltd as on 31 December 19X2 were as follows:

	Trunk Ltd £	Bough Ltd £
Plant, at cost less depreciation	72,000	45,000
Fixtures, at cost, less depreciation	13,000	5,700
Stock, at cost	43,000	19,500
Debtors	62,700	21,100
Investments at cost	—	2,500
Balance at bank	10,000	3,000
Current account: Trunk Ltd	—	3,200
Shares in Bough Ltd: 48,000 shares, at cost	54,000	
	254,700	100,000
Called-up share capital	120,000	60,000
Share premium account	18,000	—
Capital reserve on 1 January 19X2	8,000	6,000
General reserve on 1 January 19X2	15,000	10,000
Profit and loss account on 1 January 19X2	40,000	8,000
Profit for 19X2	16,000	5,000
Creditors	35,000	11,000
Current account: Bough Ltd	2,700	—
	254,700	100,000

The following information is relevant:

(a)   On 1 January 19X2 Trunk Ltd had allotted shares at a premium of 50p each in exchange for 48,000 shares in Bough Ltd.

(b)   In arriving at the consideration for the shares in Bough Ltd, plant was revalued at £54,000 and fixtures at £5,000 and the trade investment was deemed to be valueless. No adjustment was made in the books in respect of these valuations, and there were no purchases or sales of these assets during 19X2, but the directors wish to give effect to the revaluations in the consolidated accounts.

(c)   The depreciated figures for plant and fixtures at 31 December 19X2 are after providing depreciation for 19X2 on the book values at 1 January 19X2 at the rates of 10% and 5% per annum respectively.

(d)   The stock of Bough Ltd included £4,000 from Trunk Ltd invoiced at cost plus 25%.

(e)   A cheque for £500 from Trunk Ltd to Bough Ltd sent before 31 December 19X2 was not received by the latter company until January 19X3.

You are required to prepare the summarised consolidated balance sheet of Trunk Ltd and its subsidiary Bough Ltd as on 31 December 19X2.

19   The summarised balance sheets as on 31 December 19X6 of England Ltd, Surrey Ltd and Dorking Ltd were:

	England Ltd £	Surrey Ltd £	Dorking Ltd £
Capital authorised, issued and fully paid:			
ordinary shares of £1 each	300,000	200,000	100,000
Profit and loss accounts:			
Balances before taking into account			
proposed dividends	80,000	50,000	31,000
Creditors	10,000	12,000	5,000
	390,000	262,000	136,000
Sundry fixed assets	170,000	110,000	120,000
Investment acquired on 1 January 19X6:			
150,000 shares in Surrey Ltd	160,000	—	—
80,000 shares in Dorking Ltd	—	100,000	—
Stocks	30,000	10,000	5,000
Debtors, cash and bank balances	30,000	42,000	11,000
	390,000	262,000	136,000

You are informed that:

		England Ltd	Surrey Ltd	Dorking Ltd
(a)	On 1 January 19X6, credit balances on profit and loss accounts after taking into account proposed dividends were	£40,000	£24,000	£2,000
(b)	On 31 March 19X6, dividends in respect of the year 19X5 had been distributed by England Ltd and Surrey Ltd of	10%	10%	
(c)	England Ltd had credited the dividend received from Surrey Ltd to profit and loss account.			
(d)	Dividends proposed for 19X6 to be wholly paid out of that year's profits are	10%	5%	6%

You are required to prepare a summarised consolidated balance sheet of the England Ltd group as on 31 December 19X6.

8 Consolidated profit and loss account

20 Set out below are the draft profit and loss accounts of Acquirer plc and its subsidiary company Swallowed Ltd for the year ended 31 December 19X2.

On 31 December 19X0 Acquirer plc purchased, ex div, 75,000 ordinary shares and £10,000 10% debentures in Swallowed Ltd. At that date the profit and loss account of Swallowed Ltd showed a credit balance of £3,000.

The issued share capital of Swallowed Ltd is 200,000 £1 ordinary shares, and it had £30,000 10% debentures outstanding on 31 December 19X2. Swallowed Ltd pays its debenture interest on 31 December each year.

	Acquirer plc £	Swallowed Ltd £
Turnover	600,000	300,000
Cost of sales	(427,000)	(232,000)
Gross profit	173,000	68,000
Distribution costs	(41,000)	(14,000)
Administrative expenses	(52,000)	(31,000)
Income from shares in group companies	7,500	—
Income from other fixed asset investments (dividends from UK listed companies: amounts received)	3,000	1,000
Other interest receivable from group companies	1,000	—
Interest payable	—	(3,000)
Profit on ordinary activities before taxation (Note 1)	91,500	21,000
Tax on profit on ordinary activities	(38,500)	(8,000)
Profit on ordinary activities after taxation	53,000	13,000
Dividends (proposed)	(30,000)	(10,000)
Transfer to general reserve	(13,000)	(1,000)
Retained profit for the year	10,000	2,000
Retained profits brought forward	30,000	12,000
Retained profits carried forward	40,000	14,000

Note 1

Profit before taxation has been arrived at after charging:		
Depreciation	20,000	6,000
Auditors' remuneration and expenses	5,000	2,000
Directors' emoluments	10,000	4,000

The following additional information is relevant:

(a) During the year Acquirer plc sold goods to Swallowed Ltd for £20,000, making a profit of £5,000. These goods were all sold by Swallowed Ltd before the end of the year.

(b) Included in the directors' emoluments of £4,000 in Swallowed Ltd's accounts is £1,000 paid to a director of Acquirer plc.

You are required to prepare for presentation to members the consolidated profit and loss account for the year ended 31 December 19X2. Acquirer plc does not propose to publish its own profit and loss account. Assume basic rate income tax to be 27%.

21 The following are the draft profit and loss accounts of Cash Ltd and Carry Ltd for the year ended 31 December 19X4:

	Cash Ltd £	Carry Ltd £
Turnover	3,000,000	900,000
Cost of sales	(1,700,000)	(600,000)
Gross profit	1,300,000	300,000
Distribution costs	(300,000)	(100,000)
Administrative expenses	(600,500)	(96,600)
Income received from shares in group companies	1,000	—
Income from other fixed asset investments (dividends from UK listed companies)	7,500	1,800
Other interest receivable from group companies	1,600	
Interest payable	—	(3,200)
Profit on ordinary activities before taxation	409,600	102,000
Tax on profit on ordinary activities	(159,600)	(40,000)
Profit on ordinary activities after taxation	250,000	62,000
Dividends:		
Ordinary, proposed	(20,000)	(4,000)
Preference, paid	—	(3,000)
Transfers to general reserve	(50,000)	(5,000)
Retained profit for the year	180,000	50,000
Retained profits brought forward	100,000	25,000
Retained profits carried forward	280,000	75,000

You are informed:

(a)   The profit on ordinary activities before taxation is after charging the following:

	£	£
Depreciation	27,000	15,000
Auditors' remuneration and expenses	5,000	1,500
Directors' emoluments	42,000	10,000

(b)   The issued share capital of the two companies is:

Cash Ltd   £100,000 in £1 ordinary shares
Carry Ltd   £20,000 in £1 ordinary shares
                  £30,000 in £1 10% preference shares

(c)   Both companies have proposed ordinary dividends of 20% for 19X4.

(d)   Cash Ltd bought an interest in Carry Ltd on 1 January 19X2, as follows:

(i)   12,000 ordinary shares
(ii)   10,000 preference shares
(iii)   £20,000 (out of £40,000) 8% debentures at par

These purchases were made after all dividends and interest had been paid for 19X1. On 1 January 19X2 the balance on Carry Ltd's profit and loss account was £12,000.

(e)   None of the directors of Carry Ltd are directors of Cash Ltd.

(f)   During 19X4, sales by Carry Ltd to Cash Ltd amounted to £100,000, including £10,000 worth which were still held in the stock of Cash Ltd at 31 December 19X4, and on which Carry Ltd had taken a profit of £2,000.

You are required to prepare, for presentation to members, the consolidated profit and loss account of Cash Ltd and its subsidiary Carry Ltd for the year ended 31 December 19X4.

Assume basic-rate income tax at 25%.

22 The following figures for the year to 30 April 19X6 have been extracted from the books and records of three companies which form a group:

	Old plc £	Field Ltd £	Lodge Ltd £
Revenue reserves at 1 May 19X5	30,000	40,000	50,000
Stocks at 1 May 19X5	90,000	150,000	80,000
Sales	1,250,000	875,000	650,000
Purchases	780,000	555,000	475,000
Distribution expenses	125,000	85,000	60,000
Administrative expenses	28,000	40,000	72,000
Interim dividends:			
Paid 31 July 19X5, ordinary	45,000	35,000	15,000
Paid 31 October 19X5, preference		4,000	
Share capital: fully paid:			
Ordinary shares of £1 each	450,000	350,000	200,000
8% preference shares of £1 each		100,000	
Stocks at 30 April 19X6	110,000	135,000	85,000

Profits are deemed to accrue evenly throughout the year.

Other information:

(a)   Corporation tax of the following amounts is to be provided on the profits of the year:

      Old plc   £125,000
      Field Ltd   £75,000
      Lodge Ltd   £20,000

(b)   Final dividends proposed are:

      Old plc   15p per share
      Field Ltd   12.5p per share on the ordinary shares and a half year's dividend on the preference shares
      Lodge Ltd   7.5p per share

(c)   Field Ltd sells goods for resale to both Old plc and Lodge Ltd. At 30 April 19X6, stocks of goods purchased from Field Ltd are:

      in Old plc   £40,000
      in Lodge Ltd   £28,000

The net profit percentage for Field Ltd on sales of these goods is 25%. Old plc had £36,000 of these goods in stock at 1 May 19X5. Total sales in the year by Field Ltd to Old plc were £150,000 and to Lodge Ltd £120,000.

(d)   Old plc acquired the whole of the ordinary shares in Field Ltd many years ago. 50,000 of the preference shares were acquired on 1 August 19X5. Old plc acquired 120,000 shares in Lodge Ltd on 1 August 19X5.

Required:

A consolidated profit and loss account for Old plc and its subsidiaries for the year ended 30 April 19X6, together with any relevant notes.

(ACCA Advanced Accounting Practice)

9 Associated companies

23 Anglo Ltd is a well-established private company which, over a number of years, built up a large balance of liquid resources surplus to operating requirements. The decision was taken, late in 19X2, to use these resources to diversify the company's activities, and substantial shareholdings were subsequently acquired in Bangle Ltd and Carmen plc. The latter acquisition caused Anglo to arrange for a bank overdraft secured on its freehold property.

The following information is provided in respect of the three companies:

(a) Summary of balances at 31 December 19X3:

	Anglo £000	Bangle £000	Carmen £000
Assets:			
Goodwill at cost	—	—	104
Freehold property at cost less depreciation	200	180	700
Plant and equipment at cost less depreciation	756	107	1,113
Investments:			
Bangle Ltd (180,000 shares)	440	—	—
Carmen plc (500,000 shares)	760	—	—
Current assets	521	351	976
	2,677	638	2,893
Share capital, reserves and liabilities:			
Issued share capital (£1 ordinary shares)	1,000	200	2,000
Retained profit at 1 January 19X3	950	210	128
Net profit for 19X3	247	90	236
Bank overdraft	374	—	—
Other current liabilities	106	138	529
	2,677	638	2,893

(b) The shares in Carmen were purchased on 1 January 19X3 and in Bangle on 31 December 19X3

(c) Following the share acquisition, directors were appointed to the boards of both Bangle and Carmen to take an active part in their financial and operating decisions.

(d)   The freehold property of Bangle possessed a fair value of £300,000 on 31 December; there were no other significant differences between the fair values and book values of the assets of Bangle and Carmen at the acquisition dates.

(e)   Anglo's freehold property was recently valued at £230,000. This valuation is *not* to be written into the books.

Required:

A consolidated balance sheet of the group at 31 December 19X3, not necessarily in a form for publication but complying, so far as the information permits, with the requirements of SSAPs 1 and 14. (Ignore taxation.)

(Chartered Institute of Bankers)

24   The draft balance sheets as at 31 December 19X9 of three companies are set out below:

	Lanchester Ltd £000	Norman Ltd £000	Thorne Ltd £000
Fixed assets	300	100	160
Investment at cost:			
18,000 shares in Norman	75	—	—
18,000 shares in Thorne	30	—	—
Net current assets	345	160	80
	750	260	240
Ordinary shares of £1 each	250	30	60
Profit and loss account	400	180	100
Loans	100	50	80
	750	260	240

The reserves of Norman Ltd and Thorne Ltd when the investments were acquired were £70,000 and £30,000 respectively.

You are required to prepare the consolidated balance sheet as at 31 December 19X9, complying with SSAP 1.

25 The draft profit and loss accounts for the year ended 30 September 19X9 of Paine Ltd, Webber Ltd and Hill Ltd are set out below:

	Paine Ltd £000	Webber Ltd £000	Hill Ltd £000
Turnover	2,000	1,200	600
Cost of sales	800	450	200
Gross profit	1,200	750	400
Distribution costs	150	180	130
Administrative expenses	250	210	150
Profit on ordinary activities	800	360	120
Tax on profit on ordinary activities	400	180	60
Profit on ordinary activities after taxation	400	180	60
Extraordinary income	—	70	20
Profit for the financial year	400	250	80
Dividends proposed	100	120	30
Retained profit for the year	300	130	50

Paine Ltd has not yet recognised its share of dividends receivable from Webber Ltd and Hill Ltd.

Paine Ltd acquired 80% of the issued ordinary share capital of Webber Ltd on 1 February 19X9. You may assume that operating profit accrues evenly but that the extraordinary item relates entirely to the period after acquisition.

Paine Ltd has owned 25% of the issued ordinary share capital of Hill Ltd for a number of years.

You are required to prepare the consolidated profit and loss account for the year ended 30 September 19X9.

26 The profit and loss account for the year ended 31 March 19X2 of Boustead Ltd and its subsidiary, Kidder Ltd are set out below:

	Boustead Ltd	Kidder Ltd
	£000	£000
Turnover	1,500	1,600
Cost of sales	600	600
Gross profit	900	1,000
Distribution costs	120	200
Administrative expenses	180	300
Profit on ordinary activities	600	500
Tax on profit on ordinary activities	300	250
Profit for the financial year	300	250
Proposed dividends	100	80
Retained profit for the year	200	170

Several years ago Boustead Ltd acquired 30% of the issued ordinary share capital of Kidder Ltd; it has consistently treated Kidder Ltd as an associated company. On 1 July 19X1 Boustead Ltd increased its holding to 90%. Boustead Ltd has not accounted for its share of the dividend receivable from Kidder Ltd. You may assume that profits accrue evenly over the period.

You are required to prepare the consolidated profit and loss account for the year ended 31 March 19X2, using the method of including the appropriate proportions of the turnover and expenses of Kidder Ltd.

27 Velos Ltd owned 65% of Dawn Ltd and 40% of Rubber Ltd. Their draft balance sheets at 31 March 19X9 were as follows:

	Velos Ltd		Dawn Ltd		Rubber Ltd	
	£	£	£	£	£	£
Fixed assets:						
Intangible assets: goodwill				5,000		7,500
Tangible assets		182,500		77,000		61,250
Investment in Dawn Ltd and						
Rubber Ltd		75,000				
Loan to Rubber Ltd		10,000				
		267,500		82,000		68,750
Current assets:						
Stocks	4,250		3,000		5,900	
Debtors	6,000		1,460		20	
Cash	100		485		7,990	
	10,350		4,945		13,910	

Creditors: amounts falling due within one year						
Trade creditors	4,675		2,035		4,100	
Taxation	—		190		1,020	
	4,675		2,225		5,120	
		5,675		2,720		8,790
		273,175		84,720		77,540
Creditors: amounts falling due after more than one year		—		—		10,000
		273,175		84,720		67,540
Share capital: £1 ordinary shares		50,000		25,000		25,000
Reserves: profit and loss account		223,175		59,720		42,540
		273,175		84,720		67,540

Velos Ltd acquired its investments as follows:

Company	Date	Shares acquired	Cost £	Reserves £
Dawn Ltd	1 January 19X1	12,000	37,500	45,000
	30 June 19X2	4,250	12,000	43,000
Rubber Ltd	28 March 19X5	10,000	27,000	38,040

You ascertain the following:

(a) During the year, Velos Ltd sold to Dawn Ltd goods for £4,000, making a mark-up of 25%. Half had been sold, the rest remained in stock and the directors of Dawn wished to make a 15% provision against them. Rubber Ltd sold to Velos Ltd goods costing £1,000 for £1,300, all of which were in stock at 31 March 19X9.

(b) Although Dawn Ltd had never paid a dividend, Rubber Ltd invariably did so, and wished to provide a 10% final dividend in respect of the year. Rubber Ltd had paid a dividend in respect of the year ended 31 March 19X5, and Velos Ltd had credited the appropriate part to its cost of investment account.

(c) The goodwill of Dawn Ltd and any goodwill arising on consolidation are to be written off.

You are required to prepare the consolidated balance sheet of Velos Ltd as at 31 March 19X9.

Revision questions: chapters 2 to 9

28 On 1 April 19X1 Machinery Ltd bought 80% of the ordinary share capital of Components Ltd and on 1 April 19X3 Machinery Ltd was itself taken over by Sales Ltd who purchased 75% of the ordinary shares in Machinery Ltd.

The balance sheets of the three companies at 31 October 19X5 prepared for internal use showed the following position:

	Sales Ltd £	Sales Ltd £	Machinery Ltd £	Machinery Ltd £	Components Ltd £	Components Ltd £
Fixed assets:						
Freehold land at cost		89,000		30,000		65,000
Buildings at cost	100,000		120,000		40,000	
Less: Accumulated depreciation	36,000		40,000		16,400	
		64,000		80,000		23,600
Plant and equipment at cost	102,900		170,000		92,000	
Less: Accumulated depreciation	69,900		86,000		48,200	
		33,000		84,000		43,800
		186,000		194,000		132,400
Investments:						
Shares in Machinery at cost		135,000				
Shares in Components at cost				96,000		
Current assets:						
Stocks	108,500		75,500		68,400	
Debtors	196,700		124,800		83,500	
Cash at bank	25,200		—		25,400	
		330,400		200,300		177,300
		651,400		490,300		309,700
Current liabilities:						
Creditors	160,000		152,700		59,200	
Bank overdraft	—		37,400		—	
Corporation tax	57,400		47,200		24,500	
Proposed dividends	80,000		48,000		12,000	
		279,400		285,300		95,700
		354,000		205,000		214,000
Ordinary shares		200,000		120,000		100,000
10% preference shares		—		—		40,000
Revenue reserves		154,000		85,000		74,000
		354,000		205,000		214,000

Additional information:

(a) All ordinary shares are £1 each, fully paid.

(b) Preference shares in Components Ltd are 50p each fully paid.

(c) Proposed dividends in Components Ltd are:

On ordinary shares   £10,000
On preference shares   £2,000

(d) Proposed dividends receivable by Sales Ltd and Machinery Ltd are included in debtors.

(e) All creditors are payable within one year.

(f) Items purchased by Machinery Ltd from Components Ltd and remaining in stock at 31 October 19X5 amounted to £25,000. The profit element is 20% of selling price for Components Ltd.

(g) Depreciation policy of the group is to provide for:

(i)   buildings at the rate of 2% of cost each year;

(ii) plant and equipment at the rate of 10% of cost each year including full provision in the year of acquisition.

These policies are applied by all members of the group.

Included in the plant and equipment of Components Ltd is a machine purchased from the manufacturers, Machinery Ltd, on 1 January 19X4 for £10,000. Machinery Ltd recorded a profit of £2,000 on the sale of the machine.

(h) Intra-group balances are included in debtors and creditors respectively and are as follows:

			£
Sales Ltd	Creditors	Machinery Ltd	45,600
		Components Ltd	28,900
Machinery Ltd	Debtors	Sales Ltd	56,900
Components Ltd	Debtors	Sales Ltd	28,900

(i) A cheque drawn by Sales Ltd for £11,300 on 28 October 19X5 was received by Machinery Ltd on 3 November 19X5.

(j) At 1 April 19X1, reserves in Machinery Ltd were £28,000 and in Components Ltd £20,000. At 1 April 19X3 the figures were £40,000 and £60,000 respectively.

Required:

Prepare a group balance sheet at 31 October 19X5 for Sales Ltd and its subsidiaries complying, so far as the information will allow, with the accounting requirements of the Companies Act 1985.

(ACCA Advanced Accounting Practice)

29   X Ltd holds shares in other companies as follows:

A Ltd   150,000 ordinary shares of £1 each, acquired 1 July 19X1.
B Ltd   80,000 ordinary shares of £1 each, acquired 1 April 19X2.
C Ltd   30,000 ordinary shares of £1 each, acquired 1 January 19X2.

From the information given below you are required to prepare a consolidated profit and loss account for the year ended 31 December 19X2. This account should show the make-up by company of the retained profit for the year ended 31 December 19X2.

Workings should be shown.

(a)   The profit and loss accounts of the companies for the year ended 31 December 19X2 are set out below:

	X Ltd	A Ltd	B Ltd	C Ltd
Trading profits	126,000	72,000	84,000	40,000
Dividends receivable	58,680	2,400	—	6,000
	184,680	74,400	84,000	46,000
Corporation tax	54,180	30,000	37,200	22,000
	130,500	44,400	46,800	24,000
Dividends proposed	90,000	30,000	36,000	12,000
	40,500	14,400	10,800	12,000
Balance brought forward	252,750	108,000	73,500	27,000
Balance carried forward	293,250	122,400	84,300	39,000

(b)   The issued share capital of the various companies, which has been unchanged since 1 January 19X1, is as follows:

A Ltd   200,000 ordinary shares of £1 each
B Ltd   100,000 ordinary shares of £1 each
C Ltd   120,000 ordinary shares of £1 each

(c)   Trading profits are deemed to accrue evenly throughout the year.

(d)   X Ltd received a dividend of £4,380 from a trade investment during the year.

(e)   In September 19X2 X Ltd sold a machine, which had cost £21,000, to B Ltd for
       £25,000.

(f)   A 'group election' for tax purposes in respect of distributions was in force at all
       relevant times.

(g)   In the year ended 31 December 19X1 A Ltd made a profit of £60,000 of which
       taxation absorbed £27,000 and dividends £16,000.

(h)   Take income tax as 27%.
                    (CIMA Financial Accounting 3 — now Advanced Financial Accounting)

30 You are given the following information relating to the XYZ group:

The profit and loss accounts of XYZ Ltd and its 60% subsidiary ABC Ltd for the year ended 31
December 19X4:

(a)

	XYZ Ltd £000	ABC Ltd £000
Sales	10,876	3,762
Change in stocks of finished goods and work-in-progress	1,213	(490)
	12,089	3,272
Materials consumed	(3,172)	(1,005)
Staff costs	(4,269)	(698)
Depreciation	(2,814)	(484)
Operating profit	1,834	1,085
Income from shares in subsidiary company	150	—
Profit before taxation	1,984	1,085
Taxation	(880)	(515)
Profit after taxation	1,104	570
Extraordinary items	—	(250)
	1,104	320
Dividends paid	(300)	(250)
Retained profit for the year	804	70

(b)   XYZ Ltd acquired its shareholding in ABC Ltd on 1 January 19X4. At this time the
       fair value of the depreciable fixed assets of ABC Ltd exceeded their book value by
       £500,000. These assets had an estimated five-year life at the date of acquisition and
       none of them had been disposed of by ABC Ltd at 31 December 19X4.

(c)   During 19X4, ABC Ltd sold direct materials costing £500,000 to XYZ Ltd for £800,000. At 31 December 19X4 half of these materials had been sold as part of finished goods by XYZ Ltd, one quarter were contained in XYZ Ltd's work-in-progress and the remainder were held as materials stock.

(d)   Group accounting policies:

      (i)   taxation on intra-group profits in stocks is not deferred;

      (ii)   the elimination of intra-group profits in stocks is borne by both the majority and minority interests where these profits were earned by the subsidiary company.

You are required to prepare a consolidated profit and loss account for the year ended 31 December 19X4 for the XYZ group in a form suitable for presentation to shareholders.
         (CIMA Financial Accounting 3, now Advanced Financial Accounting)

10   Requirements of the Companies Act 1985, SSAP 14 and the EEC Seventh Directive

31   In large and complex groups of companies, there are often difficulties in deciding how to treat certain companies when preparing the consolidated financial statements for the year.

Required:

(a)   State the treatments, required by legislation and by UK and Irish accounting standards, of subsidiaries which are unsuitable for inclusion in the consolidated accounts.

(b)   Comment on the validity of each of the treatments so required.
         (ACCA Advanced Financial Accounting)

32 (a)   Explain the term 'equity method of accounting' as defined in SSAP 14 'Group accounts' and indicate two examples of where this is generally used.

      (b)   What are the advantages and disadvantages of preparing financial statements using this method?
         (ACCA Regulatory Framework of Accounting)

33   How will the introduction of the EEC Seventh Directive affect UK practice in the preparation of consolidated accounts?

11   Disposal of shares in subsidiaries

34   The summarised balance sheets as on 30 September 19X6 of Tom Ltd, of its subsidiaries and of the consolidated group are given below, together with an extract of the individual companies' profit and loss accounts for the year ended 30 September 19X7.

Summarised balance sheets on 30 September 19X6

	Tom Ltd £000	Cat Ltd £000	Jerry Ltd £000	Tom Ltd Consolidated £000
Ordinary shares of £1 (fully paid)	1,500	500	600	1,500
Retained profits	3,500			4,240
On acquisition		200	250	
Post-acquisition		300	500	
Minority interests				200
	5,000	1,000	1,350	5,940
Net assets	2,950	1,000	1,350	5,300
Investments in subsidiaries at cost:				
600,000 shares in Jerry Ltd	1,250			
400,000 shares in Cat Ltd	800			
Goodwill on consolidation				640
	5,000	1,000	1,350	5,940

Extract from the profit and loss account for the year ended 30 September 19X7

	Tom Ltd £000	Cat Ltd £000	Jerry Ltd £000
Operating profit after tax	500	80	150

Notes

1 On 31 March 19X7, Tom Ltd sold its entire holding in Jerry Ltd to Mouse Ltd for £1,600,000 in cash.

2 The profits of each company have been earned evenly over the year.

3 There have been no changes in the capital structure of the group during the year.

You are required:

(a) To show by means of journal entries how the sale of shares in Jerry Ltd is to be entered in the books of Tom Ltd and explain how this transaction is to be reflected in the accounts of Tom Ltd.

(b) To illustrate and fully explain the method of dealing with the sale of the shares in Jerry Ltd in the consolidated accounts of the group as on 30 September 19X7.

(c) To prepare the consolidated balance sheet for the group as at 30 September 19X7.

35 The following information relates to the draft accounts of Biggar Ltd, Mike Ltd and Suzi Ltd.

Summarised balance sheets as at 31 December 19X6

	Biggar Ltd	Mike Ltd	Suzi Ltd
	£000	£000	£000
Fixed assets:			
Tangible assets	1,780	700	460
Investments:			
Shares in group companies: Mike Ltd	800		
Shares in related companies: Suzi Ltd	120	—	—
Net current assets	2,000	460	290
Total assets less current liabilities	4,700	1,160	750
Creditors: amounts falling due after more than			
one year: 12% loan stock	1,500	—	—
Provisions for liabilities and charges:			
deferred taxation	200	100	100
	3,000	1,060	650
Capital and reserves:			
Called-up share capital	1,000	400	300
Profit and loss account	2,000	660	350
	3,000	1,060	650

Summarised profit and loss accounts for the year ended 31 December 19X6

	Biggar Ltd	Mike Ltd	Suzi Ltd
	£000	£000	£000
Turnover	1,500	400	200
Cost of sales	520	150	40
Gross profit	980	250	160
Distribution and administrative expenses	300	100	60
Interest payable	180	—	—
Profit on ordinary activities	500	150	100
Tax on profit on ordinary activities	260	78	52
Profit for the financial year	240	72	48
Proposed dividends	80	20	16
Retained profit	160	52	32

The following information is relevant:

(a)   Biggar Ltd acquired 80% of the issued ordinary share capital of Mike Ltd on 1 July
       19X6.

(b)   On 1 April 19X6 Biggar Ltd sold two thirds of its holding in Suzi Ltd for £4 per share.
       Biggar Ltd originally acquired 75% of the ordinary share capital of Suzi Ltd for
       £360,000 when the reserves of the latter company stood at £100,000. The share
       capital has remained unchanged since that date. None of the premium on acquisition
       had been written off at the date of sale.

(c)   In its draft accounts Biggar Ltd has adjusted its reserves for the profit or loss on
       disposal of its holding in Suzi Ltd. Under the sale agreement Biggar Ltd still has the
       power to appoint a director to the board of Suzi Ltd.

(d)   Profits can be assumed to have been earned evenly throughout the period.

(e)   Biggar Ltd does not account for dividends until they are received.

You are required (ignoring taxation):

(a)   To prepare the consolidated balance sheet as at 31 December 19X6.

(b)   To prepare the consolidated profit and loss account for the year ended 31 December
       19X6.

(c)   To state, according to SSAP 14:

       (i)   what is the effective date for dealing with the acquisition and disposal of
              subsidiaries; and

       (ii)   what information should be disclosed about the effects of acquisitions and
              disposals.

12   Consolidation by the merger method

36   Using the information in appendices 1-4 (following): prepare for consolidation as at 31
December 19X6 by preparing a consolidated balance sheet for Watersports Ltd, Roadsports Ltd
and Propulsion Ltd.

N.B. The consolidation is to be carried out (i) using the merger method for Roadsports Ltd and
(ii) treating Propulsion Ltd as an associate.

(ACCA Advanced Accounting Practice)

Appendix 1   General introduction to Watersports Ltd

Watersports Ltd carries on business as a wholesaler of sports equipment. The company has
decided to pursue a policy of growth by acquisition and made the following investments:

Date of purchase	Shares acquired	Consideration provided by Watersports Ltd	Carrying value of the investment in the balance sheet £
31.12.X6	945,000 ordinary shares in Roadsports Ltd	700,000 ordinary shares in Watersports Ltd	350,000
1. 1.X6	441,000 ordinary shares in Propulsion Ltd	Cash	332,500
1. 1.X6	1,050,000 ordinary shares in Speedsports Ltd, a wholesaler operating in Germany	Cash	400,000

It is the group policy to write off goodwill at the rate of 20% per annum commencing in the year of acquisition.

A recent valuation of the ordinary shares of Watersports Ltd carried out by the company's auditors places a value of 75p on each ordinary share.

The issued share capital of Speedsports Ltd is 1,400,000 shares.

Appendix 2:   Draft balance sheet and profit and loss account of Watersports Ltd for the year ended 31 December 19X6

Balance sheet as at 31 December 19X6

	£	£
Fixed assets: tangible assets (net book value)		550,000
Investments		1,082,500
Current assets:		
Stock	259,000	
Debtors	238,000	
Cash	7,000	
	504,000	
Creditors (due within one year):		
Trade and other creditors	246,200	
Bank overdraft	227,000	
Proposed dividends	21,000	
	494,200	
Net current assets		9,800
Total assets less current liabilities		1,642,300

Creditors (due after one year):
9% debentures	245,000	
Deferred tax	52,500	
	———	297,500

Net assets		1,344,800

Capital and reserves:
Ordinary shares of 50p each (fully paid up)	700,000	
Share premium account	320,000	
Revaluation reserve	225,000	
Other reserves	30,000	
Profit and loss account	69,800	
	———	1,344,800
		1,344,800

Profit and loss account of Watersports Ltd for the year ended 31 December 19X6

	£	£
Sales		605,850
Cost of sales		245,000
		360,850
Gross profit		360,850
Administration expenses	160,200	
Selling expenses	96,350	
	———	256,550
Trading profit		104,300
Interest payable		25,200
		79,100
Taxation		27,000
		52,100
Dividends		28,000
Retained		24,100
Reserve movement		
Profit brought forward		45,700
Profit retained		24,100
Profit carried forward		69,800

Dividends receivable for 19X6 have not been taken into account in the profit and loss account.

Appendix 3: Draft balance sheet and profit and loss account of Roadsports Ltd for the year ended 31 December 19X6

Balance sheet as at 31 December 19X6

	£	£
Fixed assets: tangible assets (net book value)		1,100,000
Current assets:		
Stock	175,250	
Debtors	132,500	
Cash	74,750	
	382,500	
Creditors (due within one year):		
Trade and other creditors	236,000	
Bank overdraft	283,300	
Proposed dividends	14,000	
	533,300	
Net current assets		(150,800)
Total assets less current liabilities		949,200
Creditors (due after one year):		
10% debentures	106,750	
Deferred tax	23,450	
		130,200
Net assets		819,000
Capital and reserves:		
Ordinary shares of 50p each (fully paid up)	525,000	
Reserves	140,000	
Profit and loss account	154,000	
		819,000
		819,000

Profit and loss account of Roadsports Ltd for the year ended 31 December 19X6

	£	£
Sales		565,000
Cost of sales		232,500
		332,500
Administration expenses	110,300	
Selling expenses	130,400	
		240,700
Trading profit		91,800
Interest payable		20,950
		70,850
Taxation		24,000
		46,850
Dividends		14,000
Retained profit		32,850
Reserve movement		
Profit brought forward		121,150
Profit retained		32,850
Profit carried forward		154,000

During 19X6 Watersports Ltd had sold goods to Roadsports Ltd to an invoiced value of £80,500.

At 31 December 19X6 Roadsports Ltd still held in stock such goods with an invoiced value of £21,500.

Watersports Ltd invoiced goods to Roadsports Ltd at 25% on cost.

The fair value of the tangible fixed assets in Roadsports Ltd was £1,250,000.

Appendix 4: Draft balance sheet and profit and loss account of Propulsion Ltd for the year ended 31 December 19X6

Balance sheet as at 31 December 19X6

	£	£
Fixed assets: tangible assets		2,090,000
Current assets:		
Stock	300,250	
Debtors	160,200	
Cash	11,000	
	471,450	
Creditors (due within one year):		
Trade and other creditors	491,130	
Bank overdraft	68,950	
	560,080	
Net current assets		(88,630)
Total assets less current liabilities		2,001,370
Creditors (due after one year):		
10% debentures	350,000	
Deferred tax	103,250	
		453,250
Net assets		1,548,120
Capital and reserves:		
Ordinary shares of 50p each	1,050,000	
Share premium account	70,000	
Revaluation reserve	300,000	
Profit and loss account	128,120	
		1,548,120
		1,548,120

Profit and loss account of Propulsion Ltd for the year ended 31 December 19X6

	£	£
Sales		524,790
Cost of sales		215,130
		309,660
Administration expenses	138,400	
Selling expenses	78,720	
		217,120
Trading profit		92,540
Interest payable		36,000
		56,540
Taxation		35,000
Retained		21,540

Propulsion Ltd revalued its assets on 31 December 19X5 and created a revaluation reserve of £250,000 in order to show its assets at fair value at that date.

During 19X6 Propulsion Ltd increased the revaluation reserve by £50,000 which represented an increase in asset valuation that occurred during 19X6.

37 The summarised balance sheets of Glia Ltd and its subsidiary Zygon Inc. as on 30 September 19X6 are as follows:

	Glia Ltd		Zygon Inc.	
			thousand	thousand
Fixed assets:	£000	£000	eurons	eurons
Tangible assets		4,820		2,000
Investments: shares in group company		515		
Current assets:				
Stocks	1,320		580	
Trade debtors	2,640		1,250	
Cash at bank and in hand	720		20	
	4,680		1,850	
Creditors: amounts falling due within one year:				
Trade creditors	2,840		960	
Taxation	915		550	
Proposed dividend	500		300	
	4,255		1,810	
Net current assets		425		40
Total assets less current liabilities		5,760		2,040
Creditors: amounts falling due after more than one year: loan stock		1,000		1,000
		4,760		1,040
Capital and reserves:				
Called-up share capital		2,000		500
Reserves		2,760		540
		4,760		1,040

Summarised profit and loss accounts for the year ended 30 September 19X6:

	£000	thousand eurons
Turnover	24,115	16,100
Cost of sales	17,225	12,075
Gross profit	6,890	4,025
Distribution costs	2,750	1,875
Administrative expenses	2,250	1,250
Profit on ordinary activities	1,890	900
Tax on profit on ordinary activities	915	550
Profit after tax on ordinary activities	975	350
Dividend	500	300
Retained profit	475	50

The following information is relevant:

(a) Glia Ltd acquired a 60% interest in Zygon Inc. three years ago when the reserves of Zygon Inc. were 300,000 eurons and 1 euron = £1.

(b) The following exchange rates applied:

	Eurons per £1 sterling
30 September 19X5	1.2
30 September 19X6	1.5
Average for year ended 30 September 19X6	1.25

(c) Glia Ltd does not account for dividends until they are received.

(d) The balance on the exchange difference reserve in the consolidated financial statements at 30 September 19X5 was £275,000 (credit).

You are required:

(a) To produce the consolidated balance sheet at 30 September 19X6 and the consolidated profit and loss account for the year ended on that date.

(b) To produce a statement showing the movement on consolidated reserves for the year ended 30 September 19X6.

Your answer should use the closing rate method as detailed in SSAP 20.

38 Hatch plc operates in the UK, and its subsidiary Match Ltd operates in the country of Utopia, whose currency is the ducat. Their profit and loss accounts and balance sheets (simplified) are given below. Translation of ducats (D) to pounds sterling (£) is effected by the closing rate/net investment method, with use of the average rate for the year in the case of profit and loss account items.

Required

Prepare a consolidated profit and loss account and consolidated balance sheet from the accounts given below and the notes which follow them. No analysis of consolidated retained earnings, or earnings per share figure, is required.

(ACCA Advanced Financial Accounting)

Profit and loss accounts for the year ended 31 December 19X5

	Hatch plc		Match Ltd	
			thousand	thousand
	£000	£000	ducats	ducats
Turnover		7,000		22,000
Cost of sales		(5,600)		(16,500)
Gross profit		1,400		5,500
Distribution costs	(200)		(600)	
Administrative expenses	(600)		(2,000)	
	—	(800)	—	(2,600)
		600		2,900
Income from shares in group company	68		—	
Income from shares in related company	30		—	
	—	98	—	—
		698		2,900
Interest payable		(150)		—
Profit on ordinary activities before taxation		548		2,900
Tax on profit on ordinary activities		(240)		(1,000)
Profit on ordinary activities after taxation		308		1,900
Extraordinary profit (loss)	100		(250)	
Tax on extraordinary loss (profit)	(45)		75	
	—	55	—	(175)
Profit for the financial year		363		1,725
Dividends		(250)		(1,000)
Retained profit for the financial year		113		725

Balance sheets as at 31 December 19X5

	Hatch plc £000	Hatch plc £000	Match Ltd thousand ducats	Match Ltd thousand ducats
Fixed assets:				
Tangible (net)		1,700		4,000
Investments:				
Shares in group company (cost)	900		—	
Shares in related company (cost)	300		—	
		1,200		—
		2,900		4,000
Current assets:				
Stocks	1,500		5,000	
Debtors				
Trade debtors	900		4,000	
Amount owed by group company	—		1,000	
	900		5,000	
Cash at bank and in hand	214		425	
	2,614		10,425	
Creditors: amounts falling due within one year:				
Trade creditors	(600)		(2,000)	
Amount owed to group company	(100)		—	
Other creditors including taxation and social security	(100)		(925)	
Proposed dividend	(150)		(500)	
ACT on proposed dividend	(64)		—	
	(1,014)		(3,425)	
Net current assets		1,600		7,000
Total assets less current liabilities		4,500		11,000

Financed by:
Creditors: amounts falling due after
  more than one year:

Debenture loans		1,000		—
Provisions for liabilities and charges:				
Taxation, including deferred taxation		136		—
Capital and reserves:				
Called-up share capital: ordinary				
shares	2,000		8,000	
Revaluation reserve	500		—	
Profit and loss account	864		3,000	
		3,364		11,000
		4,500		11,000

Notes

(a)   Rates of exchange (ducats to the pound sterling):

31 December 19X4	10.00
Average for year 19X5	11.00
31 December 19X5	12.00

(b)   Hatch plc acquired 600,000 of the 10 ducats ordinary shares of Match Ltd (no more have been issued since) at a time when Match's profit and loss account showed a credit balance of 1,000,000 ducats. At that time the exchange rate was 9.00 ducats to the £.

(c)   'Shares in related company' consist of 200,000 £1 ordinary shares in Despatch plc (i.e., 40% of its issued equity capital), acquired when Despatch's reserves were £125,000. Hatch has a seat on Despatch's board of directors. During the year ended 31 December 19X5, Despatch had pre-tax profits of £200,000, taxation thereon £80,000, and no extraordinary items. As at 31 December 19X5, Despatch's reserves were £300,000.

(d)   The dividends from Despatch plc have been grossed up on the basis of the income tax basic rate of 30%. The dividends from Match Ltd (an overseas company) have not been grossed up; they have been converted to sterling at the average rate of exchange for the year. The proposed dividend of Match Ltd as at 31 December 19X5 has not been taken into Hatch plc's accounts.

(e)   Goods invoiced in sterling at £500,000 have been sold by Hatch plc to Match Ltd over the year. Of these goods, £100,000 were in Match Ltd's hands at 31 December 19X5; they had cost Hatch £80,000. At 31 December 19X4 the corresponding amounts were £80,000, and £64,000, respectively. (Ignore deferred taxation in respect of these items.)

(f)   Hatch plc's policy is to write off all purchased goodwill (positive or negative) to reserves in the consolidated accounts.

14.4   Answers

1   **Park Ltd and its subsidiary**
Consolidated balance sheet as at 31 December 19X4

	£	£
Freehold property		99,000
Other fixed assets		217,300
		316,300
Current assets	130,100	
Current liabilities	79,700	
		50,400
		366,700
Unsecured loan		30,000
		336,700
Share capital		200,000
Profit and loss account		78,300
		278,300
Minority interest		58,400
		336,700

Workings

Cost of control

	£		£
Shares in Gate	72,000	60% share capital	48,000
		60% pre-acquisition reserves	22,500
		Balance: goodwill written off	1,500
	72,000		72,000

Minority interest

	£		£
Balance to CBS	58,400	40% share capital	32,000
		40% profit and loss account	26,400
	58,400		58,400

Profit and loss account

	£		£
Minority interest: 40% × £66,000	26,400	Park	62,700
Cost of control: 60% × £37,500	22,500	Gate	66,000
Cost of control: goodwill written off	1,500		
Balance to CBS	78,300		
	128,700		128,700

2   **Redan Ltd and its subsidiary**
Consolidated balance sheet as at 30 June 19X8

	£	£
Fixed assets:		
Tangible assets		390,000
Current assets	456,000	
Creditors: amount falling due within one year	362,000	
Net current assets		94,000
		484,000
Capital and reserves:		
Called-up share capital		200,000
Share premium account		25,000
Profit and loss account		155,400
		380,400
Minority interests		103,600
		484,000

Workings

Cost of control account

	£		£
Shares in Pyrton Ltd:		Share capital:	
Ordinary	95,000	Ordinary (60%)	54,000
Preference	15,000	Preference (20%)	8,000
		Profit and loss account	30,000
		Share premium account	5,400
		Profit and loss account — goodwill	
		written off	12,600
	110,000		110,000

Minority interest account

	£			£
Consolidated balance sheet	103,600	Share capital:		
		Ordinary (40%)		36,000
		Preference (80%)		32,000
		Profit and loss account		32,000
		Share premium account		3,600
	103,600			103,600

Consolidated profit and loss account

	£		£
Cost of control account:		R	150,000
(60% × £50,000 pre-acquisition)	30,000	P	80,000
Minority interest account:			
(40% × £80,000)	32,000		
Cost of control: goodwill written off	12,600		
Balance to CBS	155,400		
	230,000		230,000

Consolidated share premium account

	£		£
Cost of control account:		R	25,000
(60% × £9,000 pre-acquisition)	5,400	P	9,000
Minority interest account:			
(40% × £9,000)	3,600		
Balance to CBS	25,000		
	34,000		34,000

3   **Pig Ltd and its subsidiary**
                          Consolidated balance sheet as at 31 December 19X6

			£
Sundry net assets			230,000
			230,000

Financed by:
Capital and reserves:

		£
Preference shares of £1 each		100,000
Ordinary shares of £1 each		20,000
Profit and loss account		86,000
		206,000
Minority interests		24,000
		230,000

Cost of control account

	£		£
Shares in Whistle Ltd:		Whistle Ltd share capital:	
Preference	5,000	Preference (30%)	6,000
Ordinary	35,000	Ordinary (80%)	8,000
		Whistle Ltd profit and loss account	20,000
		Profit and loss account: goodwill	
		written off	6,000
	40,000		40,000

Minority interest account

	£		£
Balance to CBS	24,000	Whistle Ltd share capital:	
		Preference (70%)	14,000
		Ordinary (20%)	2,000
		Whistle Ltd profit and loss account	8,000
	24,000		24,000

Consolidated profit and loss account

	£			£
Cost of control account:		P		80,000
(80% × £25,000)	20,000	W		40,000
Minority interest account:				
(20% × £40,000)	8,000			
Cost of control account: goodwill	6,000			
Balance to CBS	86,000			
	· 120,000			120,000

4 (a) In the books of S Ltd a profit on sale will have been credited to the profit and loss account of £15,000 − £12,000 = £3,000. In the books of H Ltd the depreciation provision made for the year will have been 20% × £15,000 = £3,000.

Had the 'cost to the group' and accumulated depreciation been transferred, the asset would stand in the books at cost (£20,000), less accumulated depreciation to the date of transfer (£8,000), less the provision for the year (20% × £20,000 = £4,000).

Therefore, to create such a situation the following adjustments must be made:

		£	£
DR	Asset account	5,000	
DR	Consolidated profit and loss account:		
	Additional depreciation	1,000	
	Elimination of profit	3,000	
CR	Provision for depreciation		9,000

(b)

		£	£
DR	Consolidated profit and loss account:		
	elimination of profit	4,000	
CR	Fixed assets		4,000
DR	Provision for depreciation account	800	
CR	Consolidated profit and loss account: decrease in		
	depreciation charge for the year: (20% × £4,000)		800

5   **Parent Ltd and its subsidiary**
                        Consolidated balance sheet as at 31 December 19X1

	£	£
Fixed assets (£381,000 − £14,000)		367,000
Current assets:		
Stock (£40,000 − 20/120 × £4,800)	39,200	
Bills receivable	1,300	
Debtors and bank	37,000	
	77,500	
Creditors: amounts falling due within one year:		
Creditors	52,500	
Bills payable (Working 1)	2,800	
	55,300	
Net current assets		22,200
		389,200
Called-up share capital: ordinary shares of 50p each		300,000
Reserves: revenue reserve		10,000
Profit and loss account		49,200
		359,200
Minority interest		30,000
		389,200

Note

There is a contingent liability in respect of bills receivable discounted of £900.

Cost of control

	£		£
Cost of shares in Subsidiary Ltd	100,000	Share capital S: 75%	75,000
		Profit and loss account S:	
		75% × pre-acquisition	7,500
		Revenue reserve S:	
		75% × pre-acquisition	7,500
		Revenue reserves: goodwill	
		written off	10,000
	100,000		100,000

Minority interest

	£		£
Balance to CBS	30,000	Share capital S: 25%	25,000
		P & L account S: 25%	2,500
		Revenue reserves S: 25%	2,500
	30,000		30,000

Profit and loss account

	£		£
Stock account: unrealised profit	800	P Ltd	50,000
Cost of control:		S Ltd	10,000
75% × pre-acquisition £10,000	7,500		
Minority interest 25%	2,500		
Balance to CBS	49,200		
	60,000		60,000

Revenue reserve

	£		£
Cost of control:		P Ltd	20,000
75% × pre-acquisition £10,000	7,500	S Ltd	10,000
Minority interest 25%	2,500		
Cost of control: goodwill			
written off	10,000		
Balance to CBS	10,000		
	30,000		30,000

Workings

1 Bills payable. The bills payable of Subsidiary Ltd are £3,500. This includes £1,000 due to Parent Ltd. As the Parent Ltd balance sheet includes only £700 due from Subsidiary Ltd, Parent Ltd must have discounted bills totalling £300 due from Subsidiary.

The calculation is therefore:

	£
Bills payable per Subsidiary Ltd balance sheet	3,500
Less: due to Parent Ltd	1,000
	2,500
Add: bill discounted by Parent	300
	2,800

As we are recognising the £300 bill as a liability in the consolidated balance sheet, the note regarding the contingent liability needs to refer to £900 only.

Note that the net balance of bills payable and bills receivable is the same in the individual balance sheets and in the consolidated balance sheet:

	Individual balance sheets £	Consolidated balance sheet £
Bills payable	3,500	2,800
Bills receivable	2,000	1,300
	1,500	1,500

6   (a)   Cost of control

	£		£
Cost of shares	161,000	80% share capital	200,000
Balance to CBS: capital reserve	57,400	80% general reserve pre-acquisition	16,800
		80% profit and loss pre-acquisition	1,600
	218,400		218,400

Minority interest

	£		£
Balance to CBS	56,600	20% share capital	50,000
		20% general reserve	5,000
		20% profit and loss	1,600

General reserve

	£		£
Cost of control:		A	60,000
80% × pre-acquisition £21,000	16,800	B	25,000
Minority interest: 20% × £25,000	5,000		
Balance to CBS	63,200		
	85,000		85,000

Profit and loss account

	£		£
Unrealised profit on stock	8,000	A	27,000
Cost of control:		B	8,000
80% × pre-acquisition £2,000	1,600		
Minority interest: 20% × £8,000	1,600		
Balance to CBS	23,800		
	35,000		35,000

Able plc and its subsidiary
Consolidated balance sheet as at 30 June 19X2

	£	£
Fixed assets		1,595,390
Current assets:		
Stock (£253,700 − £8,000)	245,700	
Debtors	111,862	
Bank	23,265	
	380,827	
Less: creditors: amounts due within one year	225,217	
		155,610
		1,751,000
Less: creditors: amounts due after more than one year:		
12% debentures		50,000
		1,701,000
Share capital: 1.5 million ordinary shares of £1 each		1,500,000
Reserves:		
Capital reserve arising on consolidation		57,400
General reserve		63,200
Profit and loss account		23,800
		1,644,400
Minority interest		56,600
		1,701,000

(b)   The profit on intra-group sales, so far as it is not realised by sale outside the group, has to be eliminated from the group profit. In (a) above the whole unrealised profit of £8,000 (25% of £32,000 cost) has been excluded.

An alternative would be to exclude only the group's share of that profit on the basis that as far as the minority interest was concerned, the profit had been realised. That would mean excluding 80% of £8,000 or £6,400. The effect on the group balance sheet would be:

	£
Profit and loss account balance would be increased by £1,600 to	25,400
Stock would be increased by £1,600 to	247,300

7   **Cat Ltd and its subsidiary**
                        Consolidated balance sheet as at 31 December 19X4

	£000	£000
Fixed assets:		
Cost		130
Accumulated depreciation		50
		80
Current assets:		
Stock	40	
Debtors	35	
Bills receivable	4	
Cash at bank (including cash in transit £4,000)	16	
	95	
Less: liabilities:		
Trade creditors	(42)	
Bills payable	(2)	
	—	51
		131
Issued share capital: ordinary shares of £1 each		50
Reserves		70.2
		120.2
Minority interest		10.8
		131.0

Workings

Cost of control

	£		£
Shares in Mouse	20	60% share capital	12
		60% pre-acquisition reserves	4.8
		Balance: goodwill written off	3.2
	20		20.0

Minority interest

	£		£
Balance to CBS	10.8	40% share capital	8
		40% reserves	2.8

Reserves

	£		£
Minority interest: 40% × £7,000	2.8	Cat	74
Cost of control: 60% × £8,000	4.8	Mouse	7
Cost of control: goodwill written off	3.2		
Balance to CBS	70.2		
	81.0		81.0

Tutorial notes

(a)   Inter-company accounts. The £14,000 asset in Cat's balance sheet has been offset against the £10,000 liability in Mouse. The difference of £4,000 is cash in transit and is added as part of the cash balance in the consolidated balance sheet.

(b)   Bills of exchange. Cat clearly has £4,000 of bills receivable from sources other than Mouse. This appears as an asset in the consolidated balance sheet. Mouse has bills payable of £10,000. £8,000 of this figure cancels with Cat, leaving £2,000 of bills payable. £1,000 is due to the bank with which Cat has discounted a bill, and the remaining £1,000 is due to an outsider. Note that the net bill position in the consolidated balance sheet (£4,000 minus £2,000 = net asset £2,000) is the same as the net position in the individual balance sheets (£12,000 minus £10,000 = net asset £2,000).

8   **Dog Ltd and its subsidiary**
Consolidated balance sheet as at 30 June 19X6

	£000	£000
Fixed assets		
Cost		138
Less: aggregate depreciation		(55.5)
		82.5
Current assets:		
Stock (£40,000 + £25,000 − £1,000)	64	
Debtors	48	
Cash at bank	15	
	127	
Less: creditors	(80)	
		47
		129.5
Issued share capital: ordinary shares of £1 each		50
Reserves:		
Capital reserve arising on consolidation	1	
Profit and loss account	62.9	63.9
		113.9
Minority interest		15.6
		129.5

Workings

Cost of control

	£000		£000
Cost of shares in Duck	20	70% share capital	14
Capital reserve to CBS	1	70% pre-acquisition reserves	7
	21		21

Minority interest

	£000		£000
Balance to CBS	15.6	30% share capital	6
		30% reserves	9.6
	15.6		15.6

Reserves

	£000		£000
Dog's profit on sale of asset	2	Dog	50
Stock adjustment for URP	1	Duck	32
Minority interest: 30% × £32,000	9.6	Adjustment to depreciation	0.5
Cost of control: 70% × £10,000	7		
Balance to CBS	62.9		
	82.5		82.5

Adjustment to fixed assets	£	
Cost — to be reduced by	2,000	
Aggregate depreciation — to be reduced by	(500)	(25% × £2,000)
	1,500	

Profit to be reduced by:	
Dog's profit on sale	2,000
Reduction in depreciation	(500)
	1,500

We therefore have:	£000
Cost (£100,000 + £40,000 − £2,000)	138
Depreciation (£40,000 + £16,000 − £500)	55.5
	82.5

Debit to profit and loss account	1.5

9   **Close Ltd**
Consolidated balance sheet as at 31 December 19X2

	£	£
Fixed assets: tangible assets (Note 1)		168,200
Current assets:		
Stocks	29,200	
Debtors: trade debtors	83,800	
Investments	2,500	
Cash at bank and in hand	13,500	
	129,000	
Creditors: amounts falling due within one year	46,000	
Net current assets		83,000
		251,200

Capital and reserves:
Called-up share capital: £1 ordinary shares, fully paid	120,000
Share premium account	18,000
Other reserves (Note 2)	38,200
Profit and loss account	57,200
	233,400
Minority interests	17,800
	251,200

Notes

1

Tangible fixed assets	Plant & machinery £	Fixtures, fittings & equipment £	Total £
Net book value at 31 December 19X2	142,000	26,200	168,200

2 Other reserves

	£
Capital reserve	8,000
Capital reserve on consolidation	15,200
General reserve	15,000
	38,200

Workings

Cost of control account

	£		£
Shares in Steele	54,000	Share capital 80%	48,000
Pre-acquisition dividend	(2,000)	Capital reserve 80%	4,800
		General reserve 80%	8,000
	52,000	Profit and loss account 80%	6,400
Balance to CBS: capital reserve	15,200		
	67,200		67,200

Minority interest account

	£		£
Balance to CBS	17,800	Share capital 20%	12,000
		Capital reserve 20%	1,200
		General reserve 20%	2,000
		Profit and loss account 20%	2,600
	17,800		17,800

Consolidated capital reserves

	£		£
Cost of control account		C	8,000
(80% × £6,000) *	4,800	S	6,000
Minority interest account			
(20% × £6,000)	1,200		
Balance to CBS	8,000		
	14,000		14,000

Consolidated general reserve

	£		£
Cost of control account		C	15,000
(80% × £10,000)	8,000	S	10,000
Minority interest account			
(20% × £10,000)	2,000		
Balance to CBS	15,000		
	25,000		25,000

Consolidated profit and loss account

	£		£
Provision for unrealised profit		C	56,000
on stock	800	S	13,000
Cost of control: pre-acquisition			
dividend	2,000		
Cost of control account			
(80% × £8,000)	6,400		
Minority interest account			
(20% × £13,000)	2,600		
Balance to CBS	57,200		
	69,000		69,000

10   **Black Ltd and its subsidiary**
                         Consolidated balance sheet as at 31 March 19X2

	£	£	£
Fixed assets at cost less depreciation			380,000
Current assets (£288,900 less £3,200)		285,700	
Less: creditors: amounts falling due within one year			
Sundry	119,200		
Debenture interest (£1,200 − £300)	900		
Proposed dividend:			
Black	30,000		
Minority	3,900	154,000	131,700
			511,700
Less: creditors: amounts falling due after			
more than one year: 6% debentures			15,000
			496,700
Share capital: £1 ordinary shares			300,000
General reserve			18,950
Profit and loss account			111,650
			430,600
Minority interest			66,100
			496,700

Cost of control

	£		£
Cost of shares in Bird:		Share capital Bird:	
Ordinary	165,000	Ordinary 75%	90,000
P & L: pre-acquisition dividend	(3,750)	Preference 75%	60,000
Preference	60,000	General reserve	15,000
P & L: pre-acquisition dividend	(4,200)	Profit and loss account	21,000
		General reserve: goodwill	
		written off	31,050
	217,050		217,050

Minority interest

	£		£
Balance to CBS	66,100	Share capital:	
		Ordinary 25%	30,000
		Preference 25%	20,000
		General reserve 25%	5,000
		Profit and loss account 25%	11,100
	66,100		66,100

Profit and loss account

	£			£
Stock: unrealised profit	3,200	Black		98,500
Cost of control: pre-acquisition		Dividends from Bird	4,200	
dividends			7,500	11,700
Ordinary	3,750			
Preference	4,200	Debenture interest from Bird		300
		Bird		44,400
Cost of control: pre-acquisition				
75% × £28,000	21,000			
Minority interest: 25% × £44,400	11,100			
Balance to CBS	111,650			
	154,900			154,900

General reserve

	£		£
Cost of control: pre-acquisition		Black	50,000
75% × £20,000	15,000	Bird	40,000
Share capital: bonus issue	20,000		
Minority interest: 25% × £20,000	5,000		
Cost of control: goodwill			
written off	31,050		
Balance to CBS	18,950		
	90,000		90,000

11   **Bough Ltd and its subsidiary**
                   Consolidated balance sheet as at 30 June 19X2

	£	£
Fixed assets		
Freehold property at cost less depreciation		238,000
Plant and machinery at cost less depreciation		41,000
		279,000
Current assets:		
Stock	53,000	
Debtors	58,000	
Investments (all quoted) at cost	7,000	
Balance at bank	23,000	
	141,000	
Less: creditors: amounts due within one year:		
Current liabilities	34,000	
Corporation tax	39,000	
Proposed dividend		
Bough	41,250	
Minority interest	1,875	
	116,125	
Net current assets		24,875
		303,875
Share capital: £1 ordinary shares		206,250
Share premium account		56,250
Profit and loss account		23,250
		285,750
Minority interest		18,125
		303,875

Cost of control

	£		£
Cost of shares	112,500	Share capital 75%	45,000
		P & L account 75%	11,400
		General reserves: goodwill	
		written off	56,100
	112,500		112,500

Minority interest

	£		£
Balance to CBS	18,125	Share capital 75%	15,000
		Profit and loss account 25%	3,125
	18,125		18,125

Profit and loss account

	£		£
Proposed dividend: Bough	41,250	Bough	62,000
Cost of control: pre-acquisition		Dividends from Twig	5,625
75% × £15,200		Twig	20,000
(Working 1)	11,400		
Proposed dividend: T	7,500		
Minority interest: 25% × £12,500	3,125		
Transfer general reserve	1,100		
Balance to CBS	23,250		
	87,625		87,625

General reserves

	£		£
Cost of control: goodwill		Bough	55,000
written off	56,100	P & L account	1,100
	56,100		56,100

Workings

1   Calculation of pre-acquisition profit

	£	£
Balance brought forward		12,000
Profit for fifteen months	18,000	
Less: tax	6,000	
	12,000	
9/15ths thereof	7,200	
Less: interim dividend	4,000	
		3,200
Profit at date of acquisition		15,200

12   **PQ Ltd and its subsidiary**
                          Consolidated balance sheet as at 31 December 19X6

	Cost £	Depreciation £	Net book value £
Fixed assets:			
Freehold property	104,000	9,000	95,000
Plant and machinery	332,000	126,000	206,000
	436,000	135,000	301,000
Trade investments			48,000
			349,000
Current assets:			
Stocks (£210,000 + £101,000 − £1,840 + £1,200		310,360	
Debtors		223,400	
Cash at bank		7,600	
Cash in hand		1,900	
		543,260	
Less: creditors: amounts due within one year:			
Trade creditors	233,400		
Taxation	105,000		
Bank overdraft (£74,000 − £1,700)	72,300		
Proposed dividends:			
PQ	30,000		
Minority	3,000	443,700	
			99,560
			448,560
Capital and reserves:			
Issued share capital: ordinary shares of £1 each			300,000
Share premium account			15,000
Profit and loss account			109,080
			424,080
Minority interest			24,480
			448,560

Workings

Cost of control

	£		£
Shares in JK	153,000	80% share capital	80,000
		80% pre-acquisition reserves	15,520
		Balance: goodwill written off	
		to profit and loss account	57,480
	153,000		153,000

Minority interest

	£		£
Balance to CBS	24,480	20% share capital	20,000
		20% profit and loss	4,480

Profit and loss

	£		£
Unrealised profit on stock		PQ	154,000
(£1,600 + £240)	1,840	Dividend receivable from JK	12,000
Minority interest (20% × £22,400)	4,480	JK	22,400
Cost of control (80% × £19,400)	15,520		
Cost of control: goodwill written off	57,480		
Balance to CBS	109,080		
	188,400		188,400

13   **Fairy Ltd and its subsidiary**
              Consolidated balance shet as at 31 March 19X6

	£	£	£
Sundry assets			918,000
Creditors		342,000	
Proposed dividends:			
Holding company	10,000		
Due to minority (W3)	4,400		
		14,400	
			356,400
			561,600

	£
Share capital, ordinary shares of £1 each	100,000
Capital reserve, arising on consolidation	15,200
Profit and loss account	306,400
	421,600
Minority interest	140,000
	561,600

Cost of control account

	£		£
Shares in Queen Ltd:		Share capital:	
Preference £12,000 − £200 (W2)	11,800	Preference	10,000
Ordinary £130,000 − £1,200 (W2)	128,800	Ordinary	36,000
Capital reserve to CBS	15,200	Profit and loss account	109,800
	155,800		155,800

Minority interest account

			£
Balance to CBS	140,000	Share capital:	
		Prefrence	40,000
		Ordinary	24,000
		Profit and loss account	76,000
	140,000		140,000

Consolidated profit and loss account

	£		£
Cost of control account (W1)	109,800	F	300,000
Minority interest account		Dividends receivable from	
(40% × £190,000)	76,000	Queen Ltd:	
Balance to CBS	306,400	Preference (20% × 4/12 × £6,000)	400
		Ordinary (60% × 4/12 × £9,000)	1,800
		Q	190,000
	492,200		492,200

Workings

1   Pre-acquisition profits

	£	£	£
Balance at 1 April 19X5		169,000	
Add: profits to date of acquisition			
(8/12 × £36,000)		24,000	
		193,000	
Less: pre-acquisition dividends:			
Preference (8/12 × £6,000)	4,000		
Ordinary (8/12 × £9,000)	6,000		
		10,000	
Pre-acquisition retained profits		183,000	(60%) 109,800

2   Treatment of final dividends receivable

	Ordinary £	Preference £
Dividends receivable		
(60% × £5,000)/(20% × £3,000)	3,000	600
Less: post-acquisition:		
(4/12 × £9,000) × 60%	1,800	
(4/12 × £6,000) × 20%		400
Paid out of pre-acquisition profits	1,200	200

3   Proposed dividends due to minority shareholders

	£
Preference (80% × £3,000)	2,400
Ordinary (40% × £5,000)	2,000
	4,400

14 (a)

Delta Ltd and its subsidiary
Consolidated balance sheet as at 31 December 19X8

	£
Fixed assets	1,320
Net current assets	570
	1,890
Called-up share capital	1,000
Reserves	795
	1,795
Minority interest	95
	1,890

Cost of control

	£000		£000
Cost of shares in N	810	Share capital 90%	450
		Reserves	
		20% × £100,000	20
		20% × £200,000	40
		50% × £300,000	150
		Reserves: goodwill written off	150
	810		810

Minority interest

	£000		£000
Balance to CBS	95	Share capital 10%	50
		Reserves 10%	45
	95		95

Reserves

	£000			£000
Cost of control: pre-acquisition		D		750
20% × £100,000	20	N		450
20% × £200,000	40			
50% × £300,000	150			
Minority interest 10%	45			
Cost of control: goodwill written off	150			
Balance to CBS	795			
	───			───
	1,200			1,200
	───			───

(b)   The consolidated balance sheet will be unchanged. The pre-acquisition profit
transferred out of reserves is different (see working below) but when goodwill is
written off to the profit and loss account the result is exactly as in (a).

Note. This will not always be the case. If a reserve on consolidation exists, or if the goodwill is
written off against reserves other than the profit and loss account, the balance sheets will not be
identical.

Workings

Cost of control

	£		£
Cost of shares in N	810	Share capital 80%	450
		Reserves 90% × £300,000	270
		Reserves: goodwill written off	90
	───		───
	810		810
	───		───

Reserves

	£000			£000
Cost of control: pre-acquisition		D		750
90% × £300,000	270	N		450
Minority interest 10%	45			
Cost of control : goodwill written off	90			
Balance to CBS	795			
	───			───
	1,200			1,200
	───			───

15
Ashton Ltd and its subsidiary
Consolidated balance sheet as at 31 December 19X5

	£
Sundry assets	840,000
Less: sundry liabilities	383,300
	456,700
Called-up share capital	200,000
Reserve arising on consolidation	6,740
Profit and loss account	137,240
	343,980
Minority interest	112,720
	456,700

Cost of control

	£		£
Cost of shares:		Share capital:	
Batley	60,000	Batley 80%	80,000
Corby	150,000	Corby 60%	90,000
Profit and loss account: Batley	8,640	Profit and loss account: Corby 60%	55,380
Balance to CBS	6,740		
	225,380		225,380

Minority interest

	£		£
Profit and loss account: Batley 20%	1,800	Share capital:	
Balance to CBS	112,720	Batley 20%	20,000
		Corby 40%	60,000
		Profit and loss account: Corby 40%	34,520
	114,520		114,520

Profit and loss account

	£		£
Batley	9,000	Ashton	139,400
Cost of control:		Cost of control:	
Corby 60% × £92,300	55,380	Batley: 80% × £10,800 (loss)	8,640
Minority interest: Corby 40%	34,520	Minority interest: Batley 20%	1,800
Balance to CBS	137,240	Corby	86,300
	236,140		236,140

16   **Tents Ltd**
Consolidated balance sheet as at 31 December 19X9

	£	£
Fixed assets: tangible assets		220,000
Current assets:		
Stocks	47,500	
Debtors	65,000	
Cash at bank and in hand	54,000	
	166,500	
Creditors: amounts falling due within one year	85,000	
Net current assets		81,500
		301,500

	£
Capital and reserves:	
Called-up share capital: £1 ordinary shares, fully paid	150,000
Reserves: general reserve	77,800
Profit and loss account	13,220
	241,020
Minority interests	60,480
	301,500

Workings

Group structure		Pegs Ltd				Ropes Ltd
		Ordinary	Preference			
		%			%	
Tents Ltd:	direct	60	1/6		25	
	indirect			(60% × 55%) =	33	58%
					___	
Minority:	direct	40	5/6		20	
	indirect			(40% × 55%) =	22	42%
		___	___		___	___
		100	1		100	100

Cost of control account

	£		£
Cost of shares in Pegs Ltd:		Pegs Ltd share capital:	
Ordinary	34,000	Ordinary 60%	30,000
Preference	6,000	Preference 1/6th	5,000
Cost of shares in Ropes Ltd:		Ropes Ltd share capital: 58%	11,600
Owned by Tents Ltd	10,000	Pegs Ltd, general reserve 60%	
Owned by Pegs Ltd (60%)	11,400	pre-acquisition	6,000
Pegs Ltd, profit and loss account	3,000	Ropes Ltd, profit and loss account	
		(58%)	1,740
		Profit and loss account: goodwill	
		written off	10,060
	_____		_____
	64,400		64,400
	_____		_____

Minority interest account

	£		£
Cost of shares in Rope Ltd (40%)	7,600	Pegs Ltd share capital:	
Pegs Ltd profit and loss account	3,200	Ordinary 40%	20,000
Balance to CBS	60,480	Preference 5/6ths	25,000
		Ropes Ltd, share capital (42%)	8,400
		Pegs Ltd, general reserve	12,000
		Ropes Ltd, general reserve	4,200
		Ropes Ltd, profit and loss account	1,680
	_____		_____
	71,280		71,280
	_____		_____

Consolidated general reserves

	£		£
Tents Ltd		Brought forward	60,000
Pegs Ltd:		Brought forward	30,000
Cost of control account			
(60% × £10,000)	6,000		
Minority interest account			
(40% × £30,000)	12,000		
Ropes Ltd:		Brought forward	10,000
Minority interest account			
(42% × £10,000)	4,200		
Consolidated balance sheet	77,800		
	100,000		100,000

Consolidated profit and loss account

		£		£
P: Debit balance		8,000	T	25,000
Stock provision			Cost of control account	
$\dfrac{2,000}{8,000} \times £2,000$		500	(60% × £5,000)	3,000
			Minority interest account	
Cost of control account:			(40% × £8,000)	3,200
(25% × £3,000)	750		R	4,000
(33% × £3,000)	990			
		1,740		
Minority interest account				
(42% × £4,000)		1,680		
Cost of control: goodwill written off		10,060		
Balance to CBS		13,220		
		35,200		35,200

17   **Gross Ltd and its subsidiaries**
Consolidated balance sheet as at 31 December 19X5

	£	£	£
Fixed assets: tangible assets			
Cost		261,800	
Accumulated depreciation		83,000	
			178,800
Current assets		144,100	
Creditors: amounts falling due within one year:			
Sundry creditors	78,250		
Debenture interest	150		
Dividend due to minority shareholders	2,400		
Proposed dividend	16,800		
		97,600	
Net current assets			46,500
Total assets less current liabilities			225,300
Creditors: amounts falling due after more			
than one year: 5% debentures			3,000
			222,300
Capital and reserves:			
Called-up share capital: £1 ordinary shares			140,000
Profit and loss account			42,594
			182,594
Minority interests			39,706
			222,300

Workings

		Pot Ltd		Bulge Ltd	
Gross Ltd	Direct	75%		—	
	Indirect		75% × 90% =		67½%
Minority	Direct	25%		10%	
	Indirect		25% × 90% =	22½%	32½%
		100%			100%

Cost of control account

	£		£
Investment in Pot Ltd		Pot Ltd:	
(£81,000 − £3,600)	77,400	75% Share capital: ordinary	45,000
Investment in Bulge Ltd		Profit and loss account	
(75% × £25,600)	19,200	75% pre-acquisition profit	19,875
		Bulge Ltd:	
		67½% share capital	13,500
		67½% profit and loss account	3,004
		Profit and loss account:	
		goodwill written off	15,221
	96,600		96,600

Minority interest account

	£		£
Investment in Bulge Ltd		Pot Ltd: share cpaital:	
(25% × 25,600)	6,400	75% ordinary	15,000
Balance to CBS	39,706	100% preference	15,000
		25% profit and loss account	7,900
		Bulge Ltd:	
		32½% share capital	6,500
		32½% profit and loss account	1,706
	46,106		46,106

Consolidated profit and loss account

	£		£
Gross Ltd: shares in Pot Ltd		Brought forward	52,300
(pre-acquisition dividend)		Debenture interest receivable	
(75% × £4,800)	3,600	(5% × £5,000)	250
Pot Ltd:		Dividend receivable (75% × £6,000)	4,500
Cost of control account		Brought forward	31,600
(75% × £26,500)	19,875		
Minority interest account			
(25% × £31,600)	7,900		
Bulge Ltd:			
Cost of control account		Brought forward	5,250
(67½% × £4,450)	3,004		
Minority interest account			
(32½% × £5,150)	1,706		
Cost of control account			
goodwill written off	15,221		
Balance to CBS	42,594		
	93,900		93,900

Tutorial notes

Having effected the adjustment in the books of Gross Ltd for the dividend and interest receivable from Pot Ltd, the inter-company balances may be cancelled, leaving only the amounts due to the minority to be included in the consolidated balance sheet:

		£
Debenture interest (5% × £3,000)		150
Proposed dividends:		
Preference	900	
Ordinary (25% × £6,000)	1,500	
	———	2,400

The following diagrammatic analysis of the Bulge Ltd profit and loss account in the consolidated accounts prepared by Gross Ltd may help you:

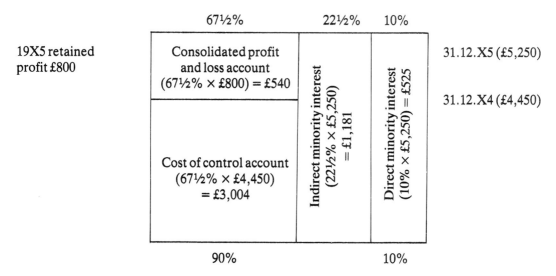

18 *Discussion*

Before attacking the question in detail, some preliminary work is necessary. First of all, we must reflect the revaluation of the assets of Bough, and adjust the depreciation charge accordingly.

Note that the use of the word 'had' in note (a) in the question confirms that the share issue on the acquisition of the shares in Bough Ltd is already reflected in Trunk's balance sheet.

Trunk Ltd and its subsidiary
Consolidated balance sheet as at 31 December 19X2

	£	£
Fixed assets:		
Plant as revalued, less depreciation (Working 1)		120,600
Fixtures as revalued, less depreciation (Working 1)		17,750
		138,350
Current assets:		
Stock at cost (£62,500 − £800)	61,700	
Debtors	83,800	
Cash at bank (13,000 + 500)	13,500	
	159,000	
Creditors: amounts due within one year	46,000	
Net current assets		113,000
		251,350
Called-up share capital		120,000
Reserves:		
Share premium account	18,000	
Capital reserve	8,000	
Reserve arising on consolidation	13,600	
General reserve	15,000	
		54,600
Profit and loss account		58,920
		233,520
Minority interest		17,830
		251,350

Cost of control

	£		£
Cost of shares in Bough	54,000	Share capital B: 80%	48,000
Balance to CBS	13,600	Capital reserve B:	
		80% pre-acquisition	4,800
		General reserve B:	
		80% pre-acquisition	8,000
		Profit and loss B:	
		80% pre-acquisition	6,400
		Revaluation reserve B: 80%	400
	67,600		67,600

Minority interest

	£		£
Balance to CBS	17,830	Share capital B: 20%	12,000
		Capital reserve B: 20%	1,200
		General reserve B: 20%	2,000
		Profit and loss B: 20%	2,530
		Revaluation reserve B: 20%	100
	17,830		17,830

Capital reserve

	£		£
Cost of control 80% ×		T	8,000
pre-acquisition £6,000	4,800	B	6,000
Minority interest 20%	1,200		
Balance to CBS	8,000		
	14,000		14,000

General reserve

	£		£
Cost of control: 80% ×		T	15,000
pre-acquisition £10,000	8,000	B	10,000
Minority interest 20%	2,000		
Balance to CBS	15,000		
	25,000		25,000

Profit and loss account

	£		£
Cost of control: 80% ×		T	56,000
pre-acquisition £8,000	6,400	B	13,000
Depreciation: plant	400	Depreciation: fixtures	50
Stock: unrealised profit	800		
Minority interest: 20% × £12,650	2,530		
Balance to CBS	58,920		
	69,050		69,050

Revaluation reserve

	£		£
Fixtures	1,000	Plant	4,000
Investments	2,500		
Balance c/d	500		
	4,000		4,000
Cost of control	400	Balance b/d	500
Minority interest	100		
	500		500

Workings

1   Plant and fixtures

	Plant £	Fixtures £
Per balance sheet:		
Trunk	72,000	13,000
Bough	45,000	5,700
Revaluation:		
£54,000 − (£45,000 + £5,000)	4,000	
£5,000 − (£5,700 + £300)		(1,000)
	121,000	17,700
Depreciation adjustment		
10% × £4,000 increase	(400)	
5% × £1,000 decrease		50
	120,600	17,750

19   **England group**
                        Consolidated balance sheet as at 31 December 19X6

	£	£
Fixed assets: tangible assets		400,000
Current assets		
Stocks	45,000	
Debtors and cash and bank balances	83,000	
	128,000	
Creditors: amounts falling due within one year (see note)	60,700	
Net current assets		67,300
		467,300
Capital and reserves:		
Called-up share capital: £1 ordinary shares, fully paid		300,000
Reserves: capital reserve on consolidation		9,200
Profit and loss account		71,900
		381,100
Minority interests		86,200
		467,300

Note

Creditors: amounts falling due within one year:	
Creditors	27,000
Other creditors: proposed dividend to minority	3,700
Proposed dividend	30,000
	60,700

Workings

Group structure		Surrey Ltd %		Dorking Ltd %
England	Direct	75		
	Indirect		75% × 80% =	60
Minority	Direct	25	20	
	Indirect		25% × 80% = 20	40
		100%		100%

Cost of control account

	£		£
Cost of shares in Surrey Ltd		Share capital:	
(£160,000 − £15,000)	145,000	Surrey Ltd 75%	150,000
Cost of shares in Dorking Ltd 75%	75,000	Dorking Ltd 60%	60,000
Balance to CBS: capital reserve	9,200	Surrey Ltd, profit and loss account:	
		75% pre-acquisition	18,000
		Dorking Ltd, profit and loss	
		account: 60% pre-acquisition	1,200
	229,200		229,200

Minority interest account

	£		£
Cost of shares in Dorking Ltd 25%	25,000	Surrey Ltd, share capital 25%	50,000
Consolidated balance sheet	86,200	Dorking Ltd, share capital 40%	40,000
		Surrey Ltd, profit and loss	
		account 25%	11,200
		Dorking Ltd, profit and loss	
		account 40%	10,000
	111,200		111,200

Profit and loss account

	£		£
England Ltd: shares in Surrey Ltd:		E:	
(Pre-acquisition dividend)	15,000	Balance	80,000
Proposed dividend	30,000	Dividend receivable from	
		Surrey Ltd	7,500
Surrey Ltd		S:	
Proposed dividend	10,000	Balance	50,000
Cost of control account		Dividend receivable from	
(75% × £24,000)	18,000	Dorking Ltd	4,800
Minority interest account			
(25% × (£54,800 − £10,000))	11,200		
Dorking Ltd			
Proposed dividend	6,000	D: Balance	31,000
Cost of control account			
(60% × £2,000)	1,200		
Minority interest account			
(40% (£31,000 − £6,000))	10,000		
Balance to CBS	71,900		
	173,300		173,300

Tutorial notes

This is a very important question. If you are happy with your ability to answer it you have nothing to fear as regards dividends in examination questions.

Notice how the proposed dividend adjustments are made in the profit and loss account working:

(a)   England's dividend. This is simply a provision for the holding company's dividend — debit profit and loss account and include in creditors in the consolidated balance sheet.

(b)   Surrey's dividend. The entries are:

    (i)   Debit profit and loss account with Surrey's total dividend.
    (ii)   Credit profit and loss account with the 75% receivable by England.
    (iii) Show the remaining 25% (£2,500) as a liability in the consolidated balance sheet (part of dividend due to minority).

(c)   Dorking's dividend. Particular care is needed with this one. We again debit profit and loss account with the total dividend. Next we credit profit and loss account with the *80%* actually receivable by Surrey, and the remaining 20% is added to the minority interest in Surrey's dividend to give the total of £3,700.

Note too that the minority interests are calculated on the profit and loss account balances after dealing with all aspects of the proposed dividend, because the minority interest is in the final balance after all adjustments.

20   *Workings and discussion*

1   Turnover. The total turnover is £900,000 but the inter-company sale must be eliminated, leaving £880,000.

2   Cost of sales. Similarly, total cost of sales is £659,000 but eliminating the inter-company amount will leave £639,000.

The adjustment for the inter-company sale has thus been:

	£	£
DR Sales	20,000	
CR Cost of sales		20,000

There is no profit to be eliminated since the items were all sold on to third parties outside the group by the end of the year.

3   Distribution costs and administrative expenses. These are simply crosscast and in the example there are no eliminations necessary.

4   Investment income and interest payable. Income from shares in group companies which represents the dividend receivable from the subsidiary must be excluded from the consolidated profit and loss account.

Similarly, the interest receivable from group companies must be cancelled against the interest payable in Swallowed Ltd's profit and loss account to leave the net interest payable to people outside the group of £2,000.

This leaves income from other fixed asset investments which is identified as dividend income from UK companies. Casting your mind to the requirements of SSAP 8, you will recall that franked investment income should be shown inclusive of the attributable tax credit. Thus the other investment income should be shown as £4,000 × 100/73 or £5,479.

5   Taxation on profit on ordinary activities. This will comprise:

	£
Aggregate charge of both companies	46,500
Tax credit on franked investment income	1,479
	47,979

6   Minority interests. Since there is no preference entitlement the minority interest is simply 25% × £13,000 = £3,250.

7   Dividends. Acquirer plc's dividend only, £30,000.

8   Transfers to general reserve. Remember that, when minority interests have been taken out, every item thereafter is dealt with in terms of the holding company's share only. Therefore, the transfer to reserve will be:

	£
Acquirer plc	13,000
Swallowed Ltd: group share (75% × £1,000)	750
	13,750

9   Retained profits brought forward. Remember we only include the holding company's share of the *post-acquisition* profits of a subsidiary:

	£
Acquirer plc	30,000
Swallowed Ltd (75% × (£12,000 − £3,000))	6,750
	36,750

10   Retained profits carried forward. As a double check on the accuracy of the consolidated profit and loss account, we can prove retained profits carried forward in a similar manner:

	£
Acquirer plc	40,000
Swallowed Ltd (75% × (£14,000 − £3,000))	8,250
	48,250

11 Disclosure of directors emoluments. Emoluments paid to directors of Acquirer plc only which are £10,000 + £1,000 = £11,000.

12 Profits dealt with in the accounts of Acquirer plc. In this case the figure is easy to calculate since there are no adjustments to be made to the accounts of Acquirer plc. The figure is therefore £53,000.

Answer

Acquirer plc
Consolidated profit and loss account for the year ended 31 December 19X2

	£
Turnover	880,000
Cost of sales	(639,000)
Gross profit	241,000
Distribution costs	(55,000)
Administrative expenses	(83,000)
Income from other fixed asset investments	5,479
Interest payable	(2,000)
Profit on ordinary activities before taxation (Note 1)	106,479
Tax on profit on ordinary activities (Note 2)	(47,979)
Profit on ordinary activities after taxation	58,500
Minority interests	(3,250)
Profit for the financial year attributable to the group (Note 3)	55,250
Dividends proposed	(30,000)
Transfer to general reserve	(13,750)
Retained profit for the year	11,500
Retained profits brought forward	36,750
Retained profits carried forward	48,250

Notes to the accounts

1   Profit before taxation has been arrived at after charging:

	£
Depreciation	26,000
Auditors' remuneration and expenses	7,000
Directors' emoluments to the directors of Acquirer plc	11,000

2   Tax on profit on ordinary activities comprises:

	£
Corporation tax on income	46,500
Tax credit on UK dividends received	1,479
	47,979

21   Cash Ltd and subsidiary
Consolidated profit and loss account for the year 31 December 19X4

	£
Turnover (W1)	3,800,000
Cost of sales (W1)	2,202,000
Gross profit (W1)	1,598,000
Distribution costs	(400,000)
Administrative expenses	(697,100)
Income from other fixed asset investments	12,400
Interest payable (W2)	(1,600)
Profit on ordinary activities before taxation (Note 1)	511,700
Tax on profit on ordinary activities (Note 2)	(202,700)
Profit on ordinary activities after taxation	309,000
Minority interests (W3)	25,600
Profit for the financial year attributable to the group (Note 3)	283,400
Dividends (proposed)	(20,000)
Transfers to general reserve (W5)	(53,000)
Retained profit for the year	210,400
Retained profits brought forward (W6)	107,800
Retained profits carried forward	318,200

Notes to the accounts

1 Profit before taxation has been arrived at after charging:

	£
Depreciation	42,000
Auditors' remuneration and expenses	6,500
Directors' emoluments	42,000

2 Tax on profit on ordinary activities comprises:

	£
Corporation tax on income at X%	199,600
Tax credit on UK dividends received	3,100
	202,700

3 Of the profit for the financial year attributable to the group, £252,400 (W4) has been dealt with in the accounts of Cash Ltd.

Workings

1 Turnover, cost of sales and gross profit. Turnover and cost of sales must *both* be reduced by £100,000 to reflect the inter-company transactions. Note that the full figure must be deducted from cost of sales, as that is the figure actually included in Cash Ltd's purchases. We then have to eliminate the unrealised profit of £2,000. This reduces the value of Carry Ltd stock and thus increases cost of sales.

The trading account must therefore be:

	£
Turnover (£3,000,000 + £900,000 − £100,000)	3,800,000
Cost of sales (£1,700,000 + £600,000 − £100,000 + £2,000)	2,202,000
Gross profit	1,598,000

2 Interest payable

	£
Carry Ltd: interest payable	3,200
Less: Cash Ltd: interest receivable (intra-group)	1,600
Interest payable outside group	1,600

3 Minority interests

	£	£
Profit on ordinary activities after taxation	62,000	
Less: preference dividend	3,000 (⅔)	2,000
	59,000 (40%)	23,600
		25,600

4   Profit dealt with in the accounts of Cash Ltd

	£
Per draft accounts	250,000
Add: dividend receivable from Carry Ltd (60% × £4,000)	2,400
	252,400

5   Transfers to general reserve

	£
Cash Ltd	50,000
Carry Ltd (60% × £5,000)	3,000
	53,000

6   Retained profits brought forward

	£
Cash Ltd	100,000
Carry Ltd (60% × (£25,000 − £12,000))	7,800
	107,800

22   *Discussion*

As a preliminary, it is necessary to establish the make-up of the group. Old owns:

100% of Field's ordinary shares.
50%   of Field's preference shares (acquired three months into the current year).
60%   of Lodge ordinary shares (acquired three months into the current year).

The question may be answered by including the whole of turnover and expenses and then deducting the pre-acquisition proportion or by deducting the pre-acquisition portion from each figure in the consolidated profit and loss account. The answer which follows adopts the second of these methods. Whichever method you adopted, work the question again at a revision stage using the alternative method.

A worthwhile amount of time is saved in answering questions in which the figures are a round thousand pounds by working in thousands of pounds. If hundreds etc. appear in the course of the answer, resort to decimals as shown.

Old plc and its subsidiaries
Consolidated profit and loss account for the year ended 30 April 19X6

	Reference to workings	£000	£000
Turnover	1		2,372.5
Cost of sales	2		1,450.5
Gross profit			922.0
Distribution expenses	3		(255.0)
Administrative expenses	4		(122.0)
Operating profit before taxation			545.0
Taxation	5		(215.0)
			330.0
Minority interest in profit	6		(12.4)
			317.6
Pre-acquisition dividend	7		(1.0)
Group profit after tax (Note 1)			316.6
Dividends proposed			
Interim paid		45	
Final proposed		67.5	(112.5)
Retained profit for year			204.1
Retained profit brought forward	8		61.0
Retained profit carried forward			265.1

Note 1

The group profit after tax is dealt with as follows:			
In the accounts of Old plc	9		294.75
In the accounts of subsidiaries			21.85
			316.6

Workings

			£000	£000
1	Turnover			
	O		1,250	
	F		875	
	L 9/12 × £650,000		487.5	
			———	
			2,612.5	
	Less: inter-company			
	F to O		(150)	
	F to L 9/12 × £120,000		(90)	
			———	2,372.5
				———

		£000	£000	£000
2	Cost of sales			
	O (£780,000 + £90,000 − £110,000)		760	
	F (£555,000 + £150,000 − £135,000)		570	
	L (£475,000 + £80,000 − £85,000) × 9/12		352.5	
			———	
			1,682.5	
	Less: inter-company as above		240	
			———	
			1,442.5	
	Add: unrealised profit in closing stock:			
	O (£40,000 − £36,000)	4		
	L	28		
		—		
		32		
		—		
	25% thereon		8	
			———	1,450.5
				———

		£000	£000
3	Distribution expenses		
	O	125	
	F	85	
	L 9/12 × £60,000	45	
		——	255
			——
4	Administrative expenses		
	O	28	
	F	40	
	L 9/12 × £72,000	54	
		—	122
			——

5	Taxation	£000	£000
	O	125	
	F	75	
	L 9/12 × £20,000	15	
		——	215

6   Minority interest

Note. If, as in this question, no profit and loss accounts are provided for the companies in the group, it is necessary to work out the post-tax profit to enable the minority interest to be calculated.

Figures can be picked up fairly quickly from workings 1 to 5 above.

Lodge profit and loss account

	£000
Turnover	487.5
Cost of sales	352.5
	135.0
Distribution expenses	(45.0)
Administrative expenses	(54.0)
	36.0
Taxation	15.0
Profit after tax	21.0

Minority interest is:	
Lodge: 40% × £21,000	8.4
Field: 50% × preference dividend £8,000	4.0
	12.4

7   Dividends receivable by Old

	£000
From Field:	
Ordinary:	
Paid	35
Proposed	43.75
Preference	
Paid	2*
Proposed	2
From Lodge: ordinary proposed	9
	91.75

*Half of this dividend must be deducted as pre-acquisition.

8   Retained profit brought forward

	£000
O	30
F	40
L	nil (not in group)
	—
	70
Less: unrealised profit on stock	9
	—
	61
	—

9   Profit dealt with in the accounts of Old plc

	£000
Per Old profit and loss account as below	204
Dividends from subsidiaries (per working 7)	90.75
	————
	294.75
	————

Old profit and loss account

	£000
Turnover	1,250
Cost of sales	760
	————
	490
Distribution expenses	(125)
Administrative expenses	(28)
	————
	337
Less: tax	(125)
	————
	212
	————

23   *Discussion*

Our first step is to establish the group structure:

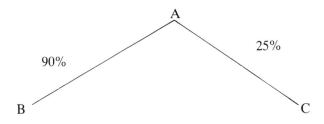

We have to prepare a consolidated balance sheet in the normal way, and introduce Carmen as an associate. The shares in Bangle were acquired at the balance sheet date — thus all the profits are pre-acquisition, divided 90 : 10 between cost of control and minority interest. The shares in

Carmen were acquired at the beginning of the year, so the closing balance sheet value is cost plus the group's share of Carmen's retained profits for the year. Taxation is to be ignored, so the entry is simply:

	£	
Debit Investment in associated company	59,000	
Credit Profit and loss account		59,000

Before proceeding with the consolidation of Anglo and Bangle, it is necessary to give effect to the revaluation of Bangle's freehold property, and to divide the resultant revaluation reserve between cost of control and minority interest.

The calculation of the analysis of the £819,000 balance sheet value of the investment in Carmen requires us first to arrive at the group's share of the tangible net assets of Carmen, then to find the goodwill value. This is the goodwill already in Carmen's balance sheet (25% of £104,000) plus the premium on acquisition. The calculation of the premium on acquisition requires us to deduct from cost 25% of the net assets at acquisition. We obtain this figure by looking at the share capital plus reserves at acquisition: 25% × (£2,000,000 + £128,000).

Answer

Anglo Ltd and its subsidiary
Consolidated balance sheet as at 31 December 19X3

	£000	£000	£000
Freehold property at cost less depreciation or valuation			500
Plant and machinery at cost less depreciation			863
			1,363
Investment in associated company (Note 1)			819
			2,182
Current assets		872	
Less: creditors:			
Bank overdraft	374		
Other	244	618	
	—	—	254
			2,436
Issued share capital (£1 ordinary shares)			1,000
Capital reserve			118
Profit and loss account			1,256
			2,374
Minority interest			62
			2,436

Note 1

	£000	£000
Investment in associated company		
Share of tangible net assets (25% × (£2,364,000 − £104,000))		565
Share of goodwill (25% × £104,000)	26	
Premium on acquisition (see working)	228	
	——	254
		——
		819
		——

Workings

Cost of control

	£000		£000
Shares in Bangle	440	90% share capital: Bangle	180
Balance: capital reserve to CBS	118	90% pre-acquisition profit	270
		90% revaluation reserve	108
	——		——
	558		558
	——		——

Minority interest

	£000		£000
Balance to CBS	62	10% share capital: Bangle	20
		10% profit and loss account	30
		10% revaluation reserve	12
	—		—
	62		62
	—		—

Profit and loss account

	£000		£000
Minority interest (10% × £300,000)	30	Anglo	1,197
Cost of control (90% × £300,000)	270	Bangle	300
Balance to CBS	1,256	Share of profit: Carmen	
		(25% × £236,000)	59
	——		——
	1,556		1,556
	——		——

Revaluation reserve

Minority interest (10% × £120,000)	12	Freehold property: Bangle	120
Cost of control (90% × £120,000)	108		
	120		120

Working for premium on acquisition of Carmen

	£000
Cost of shares	760
Group's share of net assets at acquisition (25% × £2,128,000)	532
Premium on acquisition	228

Tutorial note

The £819,000 valuation of the shares in Carmen as at 31 December 19X3 on the equity basis may be arrived at by simply adding the group's share of the profits since acquisition (£59,000) to the cost (£760,000). It is then necessary to calculate the information shown in note 1 to comply with the disclosure requirements of SSAP 1.

24 **Lanchester Ltd**
Consolidated balance sheet as at 31 December 19X9

	£000
Fixed assets:	
Tangible assets	400
Investments: shares in associated company (Note 1)	51
	451
Net current assets	505
Total assets less current liabilities	956
Creditors: amounts falling due in more than one year	150
	806
Capital and reserves:	
Called-up share capital	250
Profit and loss account	472
	722
Minority interest	84
	806

Cost of control

	£000		£000
Shares in N	75	60% share capital N	18
		60% profit and loss	
		N pre-acquisition	42
		Profit and loss account:	
		goodwill written off	15
	75		75

Minority interest

	£000		£000
Balance to CBS	84	40% share capital N	12
		40% profit and loss N	72
	84		84

Profit and loss account

	£000		£000
Cost of control: 60%		L	400
pre-acquisition profit	42	N	180
Minority interest 40%	72	T 30% post-acquisition	
Cost of control: goodwill		profit (30% × (£100,000	
written off	15	− £30,000))	21
Balance to CBS	472		
	601		601

Shares in associated company

	£000		£000
Cost of shares	30	Balance to CBS	51
Profit and loss account (working)	21		
	51		51

Note 1

The shares in associated company are valued at:

	£000	£000
Share of net assets 31 December 19X9		48
Premium on acquisition:		
Cost	30	
Share of net assets at acquisition (30% × £90,000)	27	
	—	3
		51

25 *Note*

The answer which follows shows two methods of presenting the consolidated profit and loss account. The inset columns headed 'Method 1' includes the group's proportion of the subsidiary's post-acquisition turnover and expenses, while the columns headed 'Method 2' show the techniques advocated in chapter 8 as generally quicker — the inclusion of *total* turnover and expenses and subtraction of the pre-acquisition portion of the group's share of profit after tax.

Paine Ltd
Consolidated profit and loss account for the year ended 30 September 19X9

	Method 1		Method 2	
	£000	£000	£000	£000
Turnover (£2,000,000 + 8/12 × £1,200,000		2,800		3,200
Cost of sales (£800,000 + 8/12 × £450,000)		1,100		1,250
Gross profit		1,700		1,950
Distribution cost (£150,000 + 8/12 × £180,000)		270		330
Administrative expenses (£250,000 + 8/12 × £210,000)		390		460
		1,040		1,160
Income from shares in related company (25% × £120,000)		30		30
Profit on ordinary activities		1,070		1,190
Tax on profit on ordinary activities:				
Group (£400,000 + 8/12 × £180,000)	520		580	
Related company (25% × £60,000)	15		15	
	—	535	—	595
Profit on ordinary activities after taxation		535		595
Minority interest (20% × 8/12 × £180,000)		24		36
		511		559
Pre-acquisition profit (80% × 4/12 × £180,000)				48
				511
Extraordinary income (80% × £70,000)	56		56	
(25% × £20,000)	5		5	
	—	61	—	61
Profit for the financial year attributable to shareholders		572		572
Proposed dividend		100		100
		472*		472*

*	Retained by	£
	Parent company	371,500
	Subsidiary	88,000
	Related company	12,500
		472,000

26   **Boustead Ltd**
Consolidated profit and loss account for the year ended 31 March 19X2

	£	£
Turnover (£1,500,000 + 9/12 × £1,600,000)		2,700,000
Cost of sales (£600,000 + 9/12 × £600,000)		1,050,000
		1,650,000
Distribution costs (£120,000 + 9/12 × £200,000)		(270,000)
Administrative expenses (£180,000 + 9/12 × £300,000)		(405,000)
		975,000
Income from shares in associated company (30% × 3/12 × £500,000)		37,500
Profit on ordinary activities		1,012,500
Tax on profit on ordinary activities:		
Group (£300,000 + 9/12 × £250,000)	487,500	
Related company (30% × 3/12 × £250,000)	18,750	
		(506,250)
Profit on ordinary activities after taxation		506,250
Minority interest (10% × 9/12 × £250,000)		(18,750)
Profit for the financial year attributable to shareholders		487,500
Proposed dividend		(100,000)
		387,500*

* Retained by:	£
Parent company	260,000
Associated company	127,500
	387,500

27   **Velos Ltd**
Consolidated balance sheet as at 31 March 19X9

	£	£
Fixed assets:		
Tangible assets		259,500
Investment in associated company (Note 1) (W6)		36,180
		295,680
Current assets:		
Stocks	6,850	
Debtors:		
Trade debtors	7,460	
Dividend receivable	1,000	
Cash	585	
	15,895	
Creditors: amounts falling due within one year:		
Trade creditors	6,710	
Taxation	190	
	6,900	8,995
		304,675
Share capital: £1 ordinary shares		50,000
Reserves: profit and loss account (W1) (Note 2)		226,878
		276,878
Minority interest (W1)		27,797
		304,675

Notes

1   Investment in associated company (W6)

	£
Share of net assets	22,896
Goodwill	3,284
Investing group's interest	26,180
Loan to associated company	10,000
	36,180

There are no related companies other than those described as associated.

2   Of the accumulated reserves, £680 is retained in the associated company.

Workings

Adjustment account

	£		£
Cost of Dawn Ltd	49,500	Dawn Ltd:	
		Shares	16,250
		Profit and loss	25,660
		Profit and loss account: goodwill	
		written off	7,590
	49,500		49,500

Minority interest

	£		£
Balance to CBS	27,797	Dawn Ltd:	
		Shares	8,750
		Profit and loss	19,047
	27,797		27,797

Profit and loss

	£		£
Stocks, unrealised profit (W2)	100	Velos Ltd	223,175
Stocks, write-down (W2)	300	Dividend receivable	1,000
Goodwill, write-off	5,000	Dawn Ltd	59,720
Minority interest (W3)	19,047	Rubber Ltd (W5)	680
Pre-acquisition profit (W4)	25,660		
Cost of control: goodwill			
written off	7,590		
Balance to CBS	226,878		
	284,575		284,575

2   Stock

(a)   Adjustment to be made in Dawn Ltd books in respect of stock write-down

£4,000 × ½ × 15% = £300

	£	£
DR Dawn Ltd, profit and loss	300	
CR Dawn Ltd, stock		300

(b)   Adjustment to be made on consolidation in respect of unrealised stock profit:

	£
Adjusted stock figure (£2,000 − £300)	1,700
Less: group cost (£2,000 × 100/125)	1,600
Unrealised stock profit	100

	£	£
DR Group reserves	100	
CR Group stocks		100

3   Minority interest:

(£59,720 − £5,000 − £300) × 35% = £19,047

4   Pre-acquisition reserves:

		£
1 January 19X1	(£45,000 − £5,000) × 48% =	19,200
30 June 19X2	(£43,000 − £5,000) × 17% =	6,460
		25,660

5   Share of post-acquisition retained profits in Rubber Ltd:

	£	£
Profit and loss per draft balance sheet		42,540
Less:		
Dividends	2,500	
Stock adjustment	300	
		2,800
Adjusted profit and loss at 31 March 19X9		39,740
Less: profit and loss on acquisition		38,040
		1,700
Velos Ltd's share (£1,700 × 40%)		680

6 Investing group's interest in Rubber Ltd:

	£	£	£
Share of net assets other than goodwill			
(£67,540 − £7,500 − £2,500 − £300) × 40%			22,896
Share of goodwill (£7,500 × 40%)		3,000	
Premium on acquisition:			
Cost	25,500		
Net assets acquired	25,216	284	3,284
			26,180
Loan to Rubber Ltd			10,000
			36,180

Tutorial notes

This is by no means an easy question. The following notes may help you to understand points of difficulty.

(a) Cost of investment in Dawn Ltd and Rubber Ltd. The investments appear in the balance sheet of Velos Ltd at £75,000, yet the cost details in the question add up to £76,500. The difference of £1,500 must be the dividend paid by Rubber Ltd for the year ended 31 March 19X5, which we are told had been credited by Velos Ltd against the cost of the investment. That explains why the cost of the shares is taken in working 6 to be £25,500.

(b) Minority interest in profits of Dawn Ltd. This is calculated on the profit as reduced by the goodwill write-off and the stock provision set up by Dawn Ltd.

(c) Pre-acquisition reserves. The piecemeal acquisition of the shares in Dawn Ltd is calculated by reference to the reserves at the date of each acquisition. This is normally the basis to be adopted in examination questions but it would be equally correct to take the reserves at 30 June 19X2 for the whole 65%, to give £24,700. The £5,000 goodwill written off is taken to be out of the pre-acquisition balance.

28

Sales Ltd and its subsidiaries
Balance sheet as at 31 October 19X5

	Reference to workings	Cost £	Aggregate depreciation £	Net book value £
Fixed assets:				
Freehold land		184,000		184,000
Buildings		260,000	92,400	167,600
Plant and equipment	2	362,900	203,700	159,200
		806,900	296,100	510,800
Current assets:				
Stock (less £5,000 URP)			247,400	
Debtors	3		275,200	
Cash	3		50,600	
			573,200	
Less: creditors: amounts due within one year:				
Bank overdraft	3	26,100		
Creditors	3	297,400		
Corporation tax		129,100		
Dividends		80,000		
Dividends to minority	4	16,000		
			548,600	
				24,600
				535,400
Share capital: ordinary shares of £1 each				200,000
Reserve: capital reserve arising on consolidation				9,000
Profit and loss account				189,550
				398,550
Minority interest				136,850
				535,400

Cost of control

	£		£
Shares in M	135,000	75% share capital M	90,000
Shares in C	72,000	60% share capital C	60,000
Balance to CBS: capital reserve	9,000	75% pre-acquisition profits M	30,000
		60% pre-acquisition profits C	36,000
	216,000		216,000

Minority interest

	£		£
Shares in C 25%	24,000	25% share capital M	30,000
Balance to CBS	136,850	40% share capital C	40,000
		100% preference share capital C	40,000
		25% profit and loss M	21,250
		40% profit and loss C	29,600
	160,850		160,850

Profit and loss account

	£		£
Plant: profit (W2)	2,000	S	154,000
Stock: unrealised profit	5,000	M	85,000
Cost of control: pre-acquisition		C	74,000
profit M (75% × £40,000)	30,000	Plant: depreciation (W2)	400
Minority interest M			
(25% × £85,000)	21,250		
Cost of control: pre-acquisition			
profit C (60% × £60,000)	36,000		
Minority interest C			
(40% × £74,000)	29,600		
Balance to CBS	189,550		
	313,400		313,400

Workings

1   Group structure

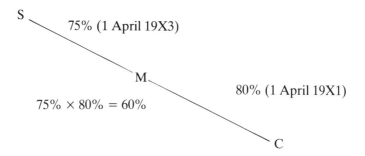

M became a subsidiary on 1 April 19X3. Therefore, C became a subsidiary on 1 April 19X3.

2   Plant and equipment

Adjustment for profit and depreciation on items bought by Components Ltd from Manufacturers Ltd

	Dr £	Cr £
Profit and loss account: profit	2,000	
Plant cost		2,000
Plant depreciation $(2 \times 10\% \times £2,000)$	400	
Profit and loss account		400
	2,400	2,400

Plant is therefore:

	£
Cost	362,900
Aggregate depreciation	203,700
Net book value	159,200

3   Debtors, creditors, cash at bank and overdraft

	Debtors £	Cash at bank £	Creditors £	Overdraft £
Per balance sheets	405,000	50,600	371,900	37,400
Sales/Machinery	(56,900)		(45,600)	(11,300)
Sales/Components	(28,900)		(28,900)	
	319,200	50,600	297,400	26,100
Less: proposed dividends:				
S from M (75% × £48,000)	(36,000)			
M from C (80% × £10,000)	(8,000)			
	275,200			

4   Dividends to minority

	£
M: 25% × £48,000	12,000
C: 20% × £10,000	2,000
Preference dividend	2,000
	16,000

29   **X Ltd and its subsidiaries**
Consolidated profit and loss account for the year ended 31 December 19X2

	Reference to workings	£	£
Operating profit	2		278,000
Dividends receivable	3		8,400
Share of profit of associated company			11,500
			297,900
Taxation:			
Group	4	123,000	
Associate		5,500	128,500
			169,400
Minority interest	5	20,460	
Pre-acquisition profit	6	9,360	29,820
Profit attributable to members of X Ltd (Note 1)			139,580
Proposed dividends			90,000
Retained profit for year			49,580
Retained profit brought forward	7		259,125
Retained profit carried forward			308,705

Note 1

The profit attributable to members of X Ltd includes £119,300 dealt with in the accounts of X Ltd (Working 8).

The retained profit for the year ended 31 December 19X2 is made up as follows:

	£
X Ltd (£119,300 – dividend £90,000)	29,300
A Ltd (75% × £14,400)	10,800
B Ltd (80% × 3/4 × £10,800)	6,480
C Ltd	3,000
	49,580

Workings

1   Group structure:

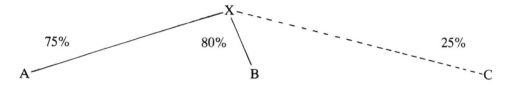

75%	80%	25%
A	B	C

Subsidiaries   Associate

The holding in B was acquired three months into the year under review.

2   Operating profit:

	£
Trading profits:	
X	126,000
A	72,000
B	84,000
	282,000
Less: profit on machine	4,000
	278,000

3   Dividends receivable:

	£	£
X	4,380	
Tax credit	1,620	
	———	6,000
A		2,400
		———
		8,400

4   Taxation: group

	£	£
X	54,180	
Tax credit on dividends received	1,620	
	———	55,800
A		30,000
B		37,200
		———
		123,000

5   Minority interest

	£
X	252,750
A (75% × 6/12 × £17,000)	6,375
B (acquired during year)	nil
C (acquired at beginning of year)	nil
	———
	259,125

8   Profit dealt with in accounts of X Ltd

	£
X Ltd profit and loss account	130,500
Less: profit on plant	4,000
	———
	126,500
Less: pre-acquisition dividend	7,200
	———
	119,300

Tutorial note

The dividends receivable in X's profit and loss account may be reconciled as follows:

	£
Trade investment	4,380
A Ltd (75% × £30,000)	22,500
B Ltd (80% × £36,000)	28,800
C Ltd (25% × £12,000)	3,000
	58,680

It is clear from this analysis that the income from the trade investment has been included without adding the £1,620 tax credit. This is corrected in the consolidated profit and loss account as shown in working 3.

It is also necessary to note that the pre-acquisition portion of the dividend from B Ltd should not have been credited to X's profit and loss account but credited against the cost of the investment. This error has no effect on the consolidated profit and loss account because all dividends from subsidiaries are omitted from it. It does, however, affect the calculation of the profit dealt with in the accounts of the holding company, as shown in working 8 and in the note to the consolidated profit and loss account.

Proof (not essential for answer)

Profit and loss account

	£000		£000
Profit on plant	4,000	X	293,250
Pre-acquisition dividend 3/12	7,200	A	122,400
Cost of control A (75% × £99,500)	74,625	B	84,300
Minority interest A		C (25% × £12,000)	3,000
(25% × £122,400)	30,600		
Cost of control B			
(80% × (£73,500 + £2,700))	60,960		
Minority interest B (20% × £84,300)	16,860		
Balance to CBS	308,705		
	502,950		502,950

30   **XYZ group**
Consolidated profit and loss account for the year ended 31 December 19X4

	Workings	£000	£000
Turnover (£14,638 − £800)			13,838
Change in stocks of finished goods and work in progress	1		648
			14,486
Materials consumed	1		(3,452)
Staff costs			(4,967)
Depreciation (£3,298,000 + £100,000)			(3,398)
Profit on ordinary activities before taxation			2,669
Taxation on profit on ordinary activities			(1,395)
			1,274
Minority interest	2		128
			1,146
Extraordinary items (60% × £250,000)			150
Profit for the year attributable to the shareholders of XYZ Ltd (Note)			996
Dividends paid			(300)
Retained profit for year			696

Note

The profit for the financial year attributable to the group has been dealt with as follows:

	£000
In the accounts of XYZ Ltd (per question)	1,104
In the accounts of ABC Ltd	(108)
	996

Workings

1   Change in stocks etc. and materials consumed. Care is needed for this calculation. Clearly there is £150,000 of unrealised profit, but half must be adjusted on stock movement and half on materials consumed:

	Change in stock etc. £000	Materials consumed £000
Per question	723	(4,177)
Unrealised profit	(75)	(75)
Materials ex ABC		800
	648	(3,452)

2 Minority interest	£000
Profit of ABC per question	570
Depreciation adjustment	(100)
Unrealised profit	(150)
	320
40% × £320,000	128

31 (a)   The Companies Act 1985, s. 229, lays down the statutory grounds on which subsidiaries may be excluded from consolidation. These grounds are that, in the opinion of the directors:

(i)   Inclusion of the subsidiary would be impracticable, or would be of no real value to the members, in view of the insignificant amounts involved.

(ii)   Inclusion of the subsidiary would be expensive or cause delay out of proportion to the value to members.

(iii)   Inclusion of the subsidiary would be misleading.

(iv)   Inclusion of the subsidiary would be harmful to the interest of the company or any of its subsidiaries.

(v)   It would be unreasonable to treat the holding company and the subsidiary as one undertaking because the businesses carried on are so different.

The consent of the Department of Trade and Industry is necessary if exclusion is to be on grounds (iv) or (v).

The Companies Act 1985, sch. 4, para. 69, specifies the disclosure to be made if a subsidiary is excluded from consolidation, but does not specify different treatments for the various cases leading to exclusion. For that we must consider the provisions of SSAP 14 detailed later.

The disclosure requirements of para. 69 for excluded subsidiaries are that these must be shown:

(i)   Reason for non-consolidation.

(ii)   Details of audit qualifications on the accounts which would be material from the point of view of the members of the holding company.

(iii)   Aggregate total investment of the group in the shares of the excluded subsidiary, using the equity method of valuation.

In addition, sch. 5, para. 16, requires the disclosure of the aggregate amount of the excluded subsidiary's capital and reserves and its profit or loss for the year.

Finally, sch. 4, para. 67, requires the disclosure of dealings with or interests in other group companies.

SSAP 14 goes into greater detail in four situations in which subsidiaries may be excluded from consolidation:

     (i)   Activities are dissimilar.
     (ii)   Lack of effective control.
     (iii)   Severe restrictions on control.
     (iv)   Temporary control.

Items (ii), (iii) and (iv) may be regarded as examples of the 'misleading' category in the exclusion grounds of the Companies Act 1985, s. 229.

The treatments specified in SSAP 14 for these four cases are:

     (i)   Activities dissimilar. Include the value on the equity basis of accounting, and include the separate accounts of the subsidiary as an element in the group accounts.

     (ii)   Lack of effective control. In this situation the subsidiary satisfies the legal definition of a subsidiary but real control is lacking, perhaps because of restricted voting rights attaching to the shares held. If the control is sufficient to satisfy the definition of an associated company the equity basis of accounting should be used, otherwise it should be treated as a simple investment valued at cost or valuation.

     (iii)   Severe restrictions on control. In this case SSAP 14 requries the company to be valued on the equity basis of accounting as at the date the restrictions came into force, with provision for any loss in value since that time.

     (iv)   Temporary control. If control is temporary, the investment should be included as a current asset valued at the lower of cost and net realisable value.

In all cases, SSAP 14 stipulates disclosure of the reason for exclusion, the names of principal subsidiaries excluded, the premium or discount on acquisition and any additional information required by the Companies Act 1985.

    (b)   We may separate the treatments for excluded subsidiaries required by the Companies Act 1985 and SSAP 14 into three main types:

     (i)   Provision of separate accounts (when activities are dissimilar).

     (ii)   Inclusion of the subsidiary on the equity basis of accounting (e.g., when real control is lacking).

     (iii)   Inclusion as a current asset at cost or valuation (when control is temporary).

It is difficult to see how any other solution than the provision of separate accounts or group accounts could deal with the problem of dissimilar activities. It is important to the members that the back-up information called for under the Companies Act 1985 and SSAP 14 is also provided, so that the best possible idea of the value of the group as a whole is obtained. The equity basis of accounting is basically a sound method of dealing with subsidiaries or indeed associated companies.

The consolidated accounts could become misleading if the effect was to include profit or value which was not accessible to the group. For example, a company could be excluded from consolidation on the grounds of harm to the group's interests because its country of incorporation was at war with that of the holding company. In such a case it could be misleading to value the subsidiary on the equity basis of accounting, and SSAP 14 recognises that when there are restrictions on control the equity basis of accounting needs modifying as indicated above.

If control is temporary, it would appear to be reasonable to value the investment on the basis that it is a current asset, since that is in fact what it is.

In conclusion, therefore, it would appear that the treatments required by the Companies Act 1985 and SSAP 14 are satisfactory, though it is increasingly being recognised that the definitions of 'subsidiary', even as amended by the Seventh Directive, are not as satisfactory.

32 (a) The equity method of accounting is a way of introducing the real value of investments in associated companies or excluded subsidiaries into group accounts. It means that the investment is valued in the consolidated balance sheet at cost plus the investing company's share of the post-acquisition profits of the other company, less any necessary provisions. In the consolidated profit and loss account the group's share of the company's pre-tax profit is included instead of the dividends receivable. The group's share of the company's tax charge, extraordinary items and retained profit are also included. Two examples of cases in which the equity method of accounting are used are:

   (i)   for associated companies as defined in SSAP 1;

   (ii) for subsidiaries excluded from consolidation because of lack of effective control (assuming that the degree of control fulfils the level specified in SSAP 1 for associated companies).

   (b) The advantages of the equity method are:

   (i)   The method shows more accurately the real value and profit attributable to a substantial investment in an associated company.

   (ii) For non-consolidated subsidiaries it provides a useful alternative to full consolidation.

   (iii) The earnings per share may be more accurately calculated.

(iv)   The method recognises the substance of the relation between the investing company and the other company rather than the legal form.

The disadvantages of the equity method are:

(i)   The use of the method could create a misleading impression in some cases by implying that value and profit were available to the group when in fact they were not.

(ii)   Cost.

(iii)   The legal form of the relation with the other company may not be fully disclosed.

33   The answer to this question is contained in 10.4 in the main text of this book.

34   (a)   Tom Ltd journal entries

	Dr £000	Cr £000
Cash	1,600	
Shares in Jerry Ltd		1,600
Receipt of cash on sale of shares		
Shares in Jerry Ltd	350	
Profit and loss account		350
Transfer of profit on disposal to profit and loss account		

(b)   In the consolidated profit and loss account for the year ended 30 September 19X7 the profit must be disclosed as required by SSAP 14: the profit on sale will be:

	£000	£000
Proceeds of sale		1,600
Net assets at date of disposal		
(100% × (£1,350,000 + 6/12 × £150,000))	1,425	
Goodwill on acquisition (£1,250,000 − (£600,000 + £250,000))	400	
		1,825
Loss on disposal (disclosed as an extraordinary item)		225

The consolidated reserves may be analysed thus:

	Tom Ltd £000	Cat Ltd £000	Total £000
As at 30 September 19X6	3,500	240	
Profit for year	500	64	
Profit on sale of Jerry	350		
	4,350	304	4,654

SSAP 14 requires disclosure of the loss of £225,000. This implies that the reserves of Jerry Ltd to the date of sale must be included:

	Tom Ltd £000	Cat Ltd £000	Jerry Ltd £000	Total £000
As at 30 September 19X6	3,500	240	500	
Profit for year (6 months for Jerry)	500	64	75	
	4,000	304	575	4,879
Less: loss on sale of Jerry				225
				4,654

The important point to appreciate is that SSAP 6 and SSAP 14 require the consolidated accounts to include:

(i)   The profit of Jerry to 31 March 19X7 as part of the profit on ordinary activities.

(ii)   The loss (in this case) on the disposal calculated as specified in SSAP 14 as an extraordinary item.

Both methods of arriving at the consolidated reserves give the same answer.

(c)   **Tom Ltd and its subsidiary**
                 Consolidated balance sheet as at 31 September 19X7

	£000
Goodwill on consolidation	240
Net tangible assets (W1)	6,130
	6,370
Share capital	1,500
Retained profits (per (b))	4,654
	6,154
Minority interest (20% × £1,080,000)	216
	6,370

Workings

1   Net tangible assets

	Tom Ltd £000	Cat Ltd £000	Total £000
As at 30 September 19X6	2,950	1,000	
Profit for year	500	80	
Proceeds of sale of Jerry	1,600		
	5,050	1,080	6,130

35 (a)   **Biggar Ltd**
Consolidated balance sheet as at 31 December 19X6

	£	£
Fixed assets:		
Tangible assets		2,480,000
Investments: shares in related company (Note)		182,500
Net current assets (W2)		2,480,000
Total assets less current liabilities		5,142,500
Creditors: amounts falling due after more than one year:		
12% loan stock		(1,500,000)
Provisions for liabilities and charges: deferred taxation		(300,000)
		3,342,500
Capital and reserves:		
Called-up share capital		1,000,000
Capital reserve on consolidation (W1)		35,200
Profit and loss account (see (b))		2,095,300
		3,130,500
Minority interest (20% × £1,060,000)		212,000
		3,342,500

Note

	£	£
Shares in related company		
Share of net assets (25% × £650,000)		162,500
Premium on acquisition:		
Cost (⅓ × £360,000)	120,000	
Net assets acquired (25% × £400,000)	100,000	
		20,000
		182,500

(b)   **Consolidated profit and loss account for year ended 31 December 19X6**

Preliminary calculations

	Biggar Ltd	Mike Ltd	Suzi Ltd		Consolidated	
	£	£	£	£	£	£
Turnover	1,500,000	200,000		50,000		1,750,000
Cost of sales	520,000	75,000		10,000		605,000
Gross profit	980,000	125,000		40,000		1,145,000
Distribution and						
administrative expenses	300,000	50,000		15,000		365,000
	680,000	75,000		25,000		780,000
Income from shares in						
related company	—	—		18,750		18,750
	680,000	75,000		43,750		798,750
Interest payable	180,000	—		—		180,000
Profit on ordinary activities	500,000	75,000		43,750		618,750
Tax on profit on ordinary activities:						
Group	260,000	39,000	13,000		312,000	
Related company (25% × £39,000)			9,750		9,750	
				22,750		321,750
Profit on ordinary activities after taxation	240,000	36,000		21,000		297,000
Minority interest:						
(20% × £36,000)		7,200				
(25% × £12,000)				3,000		10,200
	240,000	28,800		18,000		286,800
Extraordinary profit on disposal of investment (W4)	360,000	—		(115,000)		245,000
Profit for financial year	600,000	28,800		(97,000)		531,800
Dividend	80,000					80,000
	520,000	28,800		(97,000)		451,800
Retained profit brought forward	1,480,000			163,500		1,643,500
	2,000,000	28,800		66,500		2,095,300

Note

Mike Ltd is consolidated for six months and Suzi Ltd for three months. 9/12 × 25% of Suzi Ltd figures are then included on an associated company basis.

(c) (i)   According to SSAP 14 the effective date of accounting for both acquisition and disposal of a subsidiary should be the earlier of:

   (1)   the date on which consideration passes; or
   (2)   the date on which an offer becomes or is declared unconditional.

   This applies even if the acquiring company has the right under the agreement to share in the profits of the acquired business from an earlier date.

(ii)   SSAP 14 does not state precisely what information must be disclosed about the effects of acquisitions and disposals but merely requires that the consolidated financial statements should contain sufficient information about the results of the subsidiaries acquired or sold to enable shareholders to appreciate the effect on the results.

Workings

		£	£
1	Capital reserve arising on consolidation		
	Mike Ltd: purchase consideration		800,000
	Less: book value of net tangible assets acquired:		
	Share capital	400,000	
	Reserves at: 1 January 19X6 (£660,000 − £52,000)	608,000	
	Profit 1 January 19X6 to 30 June 19X6 (6/12 × £72,000)	36,000	
		1,044,000	
	Group share: 80% ×		835,200
	Capital reserve arising on consolidation		35,200

		£	£
2	Net current assets		
	Biggar Ltd: per accounts		2,000,000
	Add: dividends receivable:		
	Mike Ltd (80% × £20,000)	16,000	
	Suzi Ltd (25% × £16,000)	4,000	
			20,000
			2,020,000
	Mike Ltd		460,000
			2,480,000

3	Profit on sale of investment	£	£
	Sale proceeds		600,000
	Less: cost		240,000
			360,000

4	Profit for disclosure per SSAP 14		
	Sale proceeds		600,000
	Net assets at date of sale 50% × (£618,000 + £12,000*)	315,000	
	Premium on acquisition (see W5)	40,000	355,000
			245,000

*£12,000 is 3/12 of profit for year £48,000.

5	Premium on acquisition of shares in Suzi Ltd	
		£
	Cost	360,000
	Less: 75% × (share capital + reserves at acquisition):	
	75% × (£300,000 + £100,000)	300,000
		60,000
	Of which 50/75 relates to shares sold	40,000

6   Reserves at 1 January 19X6 and 31 December 19X6

[Tutorial note. We are told in the question that Biggar Ltd has already included the £360,000 profit on the sale of the shares in Suzi Ltd in reserves.]

The reserves at 31 December 19X6 may be built up as follows:

	£
Reserves 1 January 19X6	
Biggar (£2,000,000 − (£360,000 + £160,000))	1,480,000
Suzi (75% × (£318,000 − £100,000))	163,500
	1,643,500
Consolidated retained profit for year	451,800
	2,095,300

36   **The Watersports group**
Consolidated balance sheet as at 31 December 19X6

	£	£	£
Fixed assets:			
Tangible assets (net book value)			1,650,000
Investments:			
Subsidiary not consolidated		400,000	
Associated company		343,039	
			743,039
Current assets:			
Stock		429,950	
Debtors		370,500	
Cash		81,750	
		882,200	
Less: creditors due within one year:			
Trade and other creditors	482,200		
Bank overdraft	510,300		
Proposed dividends	21,000		
Dividend to minority	1,400		
		1,014,900	
			(132,700)
			2,260,339
Creditors due after more than one year:			
9% debentures		245,000	
10% debentures		106,750	
Deferred tax		75,950	
			(427,700)
			1,832,639
Called-up share capital			700,000
Share premium account		320,000	
Revaluation reserve		235,500	
Other reserves		156,000	
Reserve arising on consolidation		122,500	
			834,000
Profit and loss account			216,739
			1,750,739
Minority interest			81,900
			1,832,639

Adjustment account

	£		£
Nominal value of shares issued	350,000	Share capital R 90%	472,500
Balance to CBS: reserve arising on consolidation	122,500		
	472,500		472,500

Minority interest

	£		£
Balance to CBS	81,900	Share capital R 10%	52,500
		Reserves R 10%	14,000
		Profit and loss account R 10%	15,400
	81,900		81,900

Reserves

	£		£
Minority interest 10%	14,000	R	140,000
Balance to CBS	126,000		
	140,000		140,000

Profit and loss account

	£		£
Minority interest 10%	15,400	W	69,800
Stock adjustment	4,300	Dividend from R 90%	12,600
Goodwill of P written off		R	154,000
(20% × £22,418)	4,484	Share of profits of P	
Balance to CBS	216,739	21% × £21,540	4,523
	240,923		240,923

Workings

1   Value of associated company

	£
21% × net assets 31 December 19X6	325,105
Goodwill (Working 2)	17,934
	343,039

2   Calculation of goodwill, Propulsion Ltd

	£
Consideration for purchase	332,500
Less: 21% × net assets 31 December 19X6:	
21% × (£1,548,120 − (£21,540 + £50,000))	310,082
	———
Premium on acquisition	22,418
Less: written off 1986: 20%	4,484
	———
	17,934
	———

Tutorial notes

1   Merger basis workings. These workings on the merger basis are obviously less familiar than those for the acquisition method. There are in fact just three differences:

(a)   Cost of control account is renamed adjustment account. This is a small but necessary change to reflect the fact that the concept in merger accounting is not 'control' but pooling of interests.

(b)   Adjustment account is debited with the nominal value of the shares issued, not their fair value.

(c)   No adjustment is made for pre-acquisition profit.

Calculations for the minority interest and for the inclusion of the associate are exactly as in acquisition accounting.

2   Inclusion of associated company. No great problem arises here, but notice that the £50,000 increase in the revaluation reserve must not be included in the cosolidated profit and loss account heading. It has been added to the revaluation reserve.

37   **Glia Ltd and its subsidiary**
Consolidated profit and loss account for the year ended 30 September 19X6

	£000
Turnover (£24,115,000 + 16,100,000 eurons ÷ 1.5 eurons/£)	34,848
Cost of sales (£17,225,000 + 12,075,000 eurons ÷ 1.5 eurons/£)	25,275
Gross profit	9,573
Distribution costs (£2,750,000 + 1,875,000 eurons ÷ 1.5 eurons/£)	(4,000)
Administrative expenses (£2,250,000 + 1,250,000 eurons ÷ 1.5 eurons/£)	(3,083)
Profit on ordinary activities	2,490
Tax on profit on ordinary activities (£915,000 + 550,000 eurons ÷ 1.5 eurons/£	1,282
	1,208
Minority interest (40% × 350,000 eurons ÷ 1.5 eurons/£)	93
Profit for the year attributable to the group	1,115
(of which £1,095,000 has been dealt with in the accounts of Glia Ltd)	
Dividend	500
Retained profit for year	615

Glia Ltd and its subsidiary
Consolidated balance sheet as at 30 September 19X6

	£000	£000
Fixed assets: tangible assets		
(£4,820,000 + 2,000,000 eurons ÷ 1.5 eurons/£)		6,153
Current assets:		
Stocks (£1,320,000 + 580,000 eurons ÷ 1.5 eurons/£)	1,707	
Debtors (£2,640,000 + 1,250,000 ÷ 1.5 eurons/£)	3,473	
Cash (£720,000 + 20,000 eurons ÷ 1.5 eurons/£)	733	
	5,913	
Creditors: amounts falling due within one year:		
Trade creditors (£2,840,000 + 960,000 eurons + 1.5 eurons/£)	3,480	
Taxation (£915,000 + 550,000 eurons + 1.5 eurons/£)	1,281	
Proposed dividend:		
Glia Ltd	500	
Minority	80	
	5,341	
Net current assets		572
		6,725
Creditors: amounts falling due after more than one year:		
Loan stock (£1,000,000 + 1,000,000 eurons ÷ 1.5 eurons/£)		(1,667)
		5,058
Capital and reserves:		
Called-up share capital		2,000
Exchange difference reserve (per (b))		176
Profit and loss account (per (b))		2,605
		4,781
Minority interest (40% × 1,040,000 eurons ÷ 1.5 eurons/£)		277
		5,058

(b)   Movement on consolidated reserves

	Profit and loss £000	Exchange difference reserve £000
As at 30.9.X5		
Glia Ltd	2,010	275
Zygon Ltd: 60% × £25,000 (W1)	15	
	2,025	
Less: goodwill written off	35	
	1,990	
Profit for year	615	
Exchange adjustment		
Opening net assets 990,000 eurons:		
@ 1.5 eurons/£	660	
@ 1.2 eurons/£	825	
Loss	165	
60% thereof		(99)
	2,605	176

Working

1   Reserves of Zygon Inc. as at 30.9.X5

	thousand eurons	Rate	£000
Net assets at 30.9.X5	990	1.2	825
Share capital and reserves at acquisition	800	1.0	800
Post-acquisition reserves	190	(balance)	25

38   **Hatch plc and its subsidiary**
Consolidated profit and loss account for the year ended 31 December 19X5

	Reference to workings	£000	£000
Turnover	1		8,500
Cost of sales	2		(6,604)
Gross profit			1,896
Distribution costs			
(£200,000 + 600,000 ducats ÷ 11 ducats/£			(255)
Administrative expenses			
(£600,000 + 2,000 ÷ 11 ducats/£			(782)
Exchange difference	3		17
Income from shares in related company			
(40% × £200,000)			80
Interest payable			(150)
Profit on ordinary activities before taxation			806
Taxation on profit on ordinary activities	4		363
Profit on ordinary activities after taxation			443
Minority interest	5		(43)
Profit attributable to group			400
(or which £308,000 has been dealt with			
in the accounts of H)			
Extraordinary items:			
Profit		100	
Loss (250,000 ducats ÷ 11 ducats × 75%)		(17)	
		83	
Less: tax ((£45,000 − 75,000 ducats ÷			
11 ducats/£ × 75%)		40	
		—	43
Profit for the financial year			443
Dividends			250
Retained profit for the financial year			193

Hatch Ltd and its subsidiary
Consolidated balance sheet as at 31 December 19X5

	Reference to workings	£000	£000
Fixed assets:			
Tangible assets			
(£1,700,000 + 4,000,000 ducats ÷ 12 ducats/£)			2,033
Investments: shares in associated company	6		320
			2,353
Current assets:			
Stock (£1,500,000 + 5,000,000 ducats ÷ 12 ducats/£ − £20,000)		1,897	
Debtors (£900,000 + 4,000,000 ducats ÷ 12 ducats/£)		1,233	
Cash at bank and in hand			
(£214,000 + 425,000 ducats ÷ 12 ducats/£)		249	
		3,379	
Creditors: amounts falling due within one year:			
Trade creditors (£600,000 + 2,000,000 ducats ÷ 12 ducats/£)		767	
Other creditors including taxation and social security (£100,000 + 925,000 ducats ÷ 12 ducats/£)		177	
Proposed dividend:			
H		150	
Minority (25% × 500,000 ducats ÷ 12 ducats/£)		10	
ACT on proposed dividend		64	
		1,168	
Net current assets			2,211
			4,564
Less: creditors: amounts falling due after more than one year: debenture loans			(1,000)
			3,564
Provision for liabilities and charges: taxation, including deferred taxation			(136)
			3,428

Capital and reserves:
    Called-up share capital: ordinary shares of £1 each   2,000
    Revaluation reserve   500
    Reserves (see tutorial note)   699

                                3,199

Minority interest (25% × 11,000 ducats ÷
    12 ducats/£)   229

                                3,428

Tutorial note

The answer published by ACCA stated that candidates were not expected to compute this figure but to insert it as a balancing figure. The following profit and loss account working shows how it may be arrived at.

Reserves

	£000		£000
Stock: U R P	20	H	864
Pre-acquisition profits: M		Exchange difference on balance	
(75% × 1,000,000 ÷ 9 ducats/£)	83	with M	17
Minority interest M		Dividend from M 75%	31
(25% × 3,000,000 ÷ 12 ducats/£)	63	M: 3,000,000 ducats ÷ 12 ducats/£	250
Exchange difference on		D: 40% × post-acquisition £175,000	70
share capital:			
At acquisition: 6,000,000 ducats			
@ 9 ducats/£	(667)		
At 31.12.X5: 6,000,000 ducats			
@ 12 ducats/£	500		
	167		
Goodwill written off on acquisition			
of M (W7)	150		
Goodwill written off on acquisition			
of D (W8)	50		
Balance per CBS	699		
	1,232		1,232

Workings

1   Turnover

	£000
H	7,000
Less: sales to M	500
	6,500
M 22,000,000 ducats ÷ 11 ducats/£	2,000
	8,500

2   Cost of sales

	£000
H	5,600
M: 16,500,000 ducats ÷ 11 ducats/£	1,500
	7,100
Less: purchases from M	500
	6,600
Add: unrealised profit on stock (£20,000 − £16,000)	4
	6,604

3   Exchange difference on inter-company balance

Debtor in H balance sheet	100
Creditor in M balance sheet 100,000 ducats ÷ 12 ducats/£	83
	17

4   Taxation

H	240
M 1,000,000 ducats ÷ 11 ducats/£	91
D 40% × £80,000	32
	363

5   Minority interest

	£000
25% × 1,900,000 ÷ 11 ducats/£	43

	£000
6 Shares in related company	
40% of net assets at 31 December 19X5:	
40% of share capital	200
40% of reserves	120
	320

	£000
7 Goodwill on acquisition of M	
Cost of shares	900
Net assets acquired (75% × 9,000,000 ducats ÷ 9 ducats/£)	750
	150

	£000
8 Goodwill on acquisition of D	
Cost of shares	300
Net assets acquired: 40% × £625,000	250
	50

Index

.